Seeds of the Kingdom

Seeds of the Kingdom

Utopian Communities in the Americas

ANNA L. PETERSON

OXFORD

UNIVERSITY PRESS

2005

OXFORD
UNIVERSITY PRESS

Oxford University Press, Inc., publishes works that further
Oxford University's objective of excellence
in research, scholarship, and education.

Oxford   New York
Auckland   Cape Town   Dar es Salaam   Hong Kong   Karachi
Kuala Lumpur   Madrid   Melbourne   Mexico City   Nairobi
New Delhi   Shanghai   Taipei   Toronto

With offices in
Argentina   Austria   Brazil   Chile   Czech Republic   France   Greece
Guatemala   Hungary   Italy   Japan   Poland   Portugal   Singapore
South Korea   Switzerland   Thailand   Turkey   Ukraine   Vietnam

Copyright © 2005 by Oxford University Press, Inc.

Published by Oxford University Press, Inc.
198 Madison Avenue, New York, New York 10016

www.oup.com

Oxford is a registered trademark of Oxford University Press

Library of Congress Cataloging-in-Publication Data
Peterson, Anna Lisa, 1963–
Seeds of the kingdom : utopian communities in the Americas / Anna L.
Peterson
p.   cm.
Includes bibliographical references and index.
ISBN-13 978-0-19-518333-7
ISBN 0-19-518333-9
1. Amish Mennonites—United States—History.   2. Christian
sociology—Mennonites—History.   3. Catholic Church—El
Salvador—History.   4. Christian sociology—Catholic Church—History.
I. Title.
BX8129.A5P48   2005
289.7'93—dc22   2005004300

9 8 7 6 5 4 3 2 1

Printed in the United States of America
on acid-free paper

For Manuel

Acknowledgments

It has been a privilege and pleasure to learn about those communities and to talk and visit with the people who inhabit them. In Kansas, I was helped immeasurably by Heidi and David Kreider, John and Reinhild Janzen, their extended families, the members of Zion Elbing Church, and the staff of the Mennonite Library and Archives at Bethel College. In Ohio, David Kline took time to share his knowledge of Amish life, farming, theology, and more. In El Salvador, I benefited, as so often in the past, from the insight, contacts, and comradeship of Ileana Gómez, Miguel Cavada, Norys Ramírez, the people of PRISMA, CORDES, CRIPDES, the Share Foundation, and especially the residents of Guarjila and San Antonio los Ranchos, Chalatenango.

I am grateful to the friends and colleagues who generously shared their own work, read parts of the manuscript, and talked over issues with me: Ariane de Bremond, David Hackett, Toby Hecht, Sarah Lawton, Reed Malcolm, David Matthew, Bill McKibben, Bron Taylor, Les Thiele, Sharon Welch, and Libby Wood. Cynthia Read and Theo Calderara at Oxford University Press have also contributed greatly to this project, as did two careful and insightful anonymous readers for the press. Brandt Peterson has both shared his work and read mine, and conversations with him about El Salvador and utopia, among other things, have been invaluable. I am also grateful to him for bringing into the family my wonderful sister-in-law, Casey Williamson. As usual, Manuel Vásquez is my most patient and incisive reader; he has repeatedly taken time from his own work to help me with mine.

The University of Florida has been an excellent place to conduct interdisciplinary research on sustainable communities and environmental ethics. My work and my work life are better for the presence of colleagues engaged in these questions. I have benefited enormously from the presence of our graduate students studying religion and nature and the Americas, especially from the insights of students in the course I taught in fall 2003, "Ethics, Utopias, and Dystopias." I am most grateful to Anne Newman and Julia Smith for their logistical help. The University of Florida College of Liberal Arts and Sciences supported my research in Ohio in summer 2000 with a Humanities Scholarship Enhancement Grant and a University of Florida Research Professorship funded research in El Salvador in January 2002.

My writing, my thinking, and my sense of hope have benefited enormously from two conferences at Matfield Green, Kansas, organized by the Land Institute. At "Towards a Taxonomy of Boundaries" in June 2002, I presented a paper that first outlined the themes of this book. I thank the participants of that meeting, especially Charles Brown for doing much of the organizing and Clay Arnold for his thoughtful response to my paper. I am also exceedingly grateful to the participants in the June 2004 conference "The Need for an Ignorance-Based Worldview." I am awed by the collective wisdom of Team Ignorance and honored to participate in these conversations. Very special thanks are due to Chairman Wes Jackson, the guiding force behind these and so many other extraordinary happenings. Wes embodies the spirit of this book: a clear-headed utopian who sees and builds the world we need.

Contents

Acronyms

CAFTA Central American Free Trade Agreement. An agreement
       to liberalize trade relations among the United States,
       El Salvador, Nicaragua, Guatemala, Honduras, and
       Costa Rica.

CEB   (Comunidad Eclesial de Base). Grassroots Christian
       community. A small group of neighbors who meet
       regularly to read and discuss biblical texts in relation
       to their own lives and societies; a major pastoral ini-
       tiative of progressive Catholicism in Latin American
       beginning in the late 1960s.

CELAM (Conferencia Episcopal Latinoamericana). Latin Ameri-
       can Episcopal Conference. The administrative body of
       Roman Catholic bishops in Latin America and the
       Caribbean.

CORDES (Fundación para la Cooperación y el Desarrollo Co-
       munal de El Salvador). Foundation for the Commu-
       nal Development of El Salvador. A Salvadoran organi-
       zation that works on rural development, associated
       with CRIPDES.

CRIPDES (Comité Cristiano pro-Desplazados de El Salvador).
       Christian Committee for the Displaced of El Salvador.
       An organization of Salvadoran refugees formed in
       1984 to coordinate the return to places of origin and
       press for refugee rights.

CSA   Community-supported agriculture. A movement in the
United States and elsewhere that links small farmers to
consumers who buy yearly "shares" of produce.

ERP   (Ejercito Revolucionario Popular). Popular Revolutionary
Army. One of the five guerrilla organizations in El Salvador; strongest in Morazán province.

FDR   (Frente Democrático Revolucionario). Democratic Revolutionary Front. The political wing of the FMLN during
the 1980s.

FECCAS   (Federación Cristiana de Campesinos Salvadoreños).
Christian Federation of Salvadoran Peasants. A peasant
organization formed in 1964.

FMLN   (Frente Farabundo Martí para la Liberación Nacional). Farabundo Martí National Liberation Front. The umbrella
organization of five Salvadoran guerrilla groups; named
for a Salvadoran Communist leader killed in 1932.

FPL   (Fuerzas Populares para la Liberación). Popular Liberation
Forces. One of the five guerrilla organizations in El Salvador; strongest in Chalatenango province.

FSLN   (Frente Sandinista para la Liberación Nacional). Sandinista Front for National Liberation. The Nicaraguan
guerrilla organization that defeated the dictator Anasta-
zio Somoza in 1979; named for Nicaraguan nationalist
leader Augusto César Sandino, assassinated in 1934.

FUNPROCOOP   (Fundación para la promoción de Cooperativas). Foundation for the Promotion of Cooperatives. A program established by the Archdiocese of San Salvadoran in the
1960s to promote agricultural cooperatives and other
peasant self-help and education projects.

GECA   (Granja-Escuela de Capacitación Agrícola). Farm-School
for Agricultural Training. A center for rural education
and self-help in the village of Nueva Concepción, Chalatenango, founded by FUNPROCOOP in the late 1960s.

IPLA   (Instituto Pastoral Latinoamericano). Latin American Pastoral Institute. A Roman Catholic theological and pastoral training school in Quito, Ecuador, where progressive pastoral agents from Latin America took classes.

NAFTA   North American Free Trade Agreement. An agreement
among Canada, Mexico, and the United States to liber-
alize trade relations, which took effect on January 1,
1994.

ORDEN   (Organización Nacionalista Democrática). Nationalist
Democratic Organization. Salvadoran peasant organiza-

tion founded in the late 1960s by landowners and security forces to counter progressive rural movements;
closely associated with death squads.

PTT   (Programa de transferencia de tierras). Land transfer program. The land reform and redistribution program that
forms part of the negotiated settlement ending the Salvadoran civil war in 1992.

UCS   (Unión Comunal Salvadoreña). Salvadoran Communal
Union. A Salvadoran peasant organization formed in
1969.

UNHCR   United Nations High Commission on Refugees.

UTC   (Unión de Trabajadores del Campo). Union of Farmwork-
ers. Salvadoran peasant organization formed in 1974.

Research Methods
and Sources

I come to this project as a Latin Americanist with a focus on Central America. I began conducting research on progressive Catholicism in 1986 in Nicaragua, where I worked with Nicaraguans and Salvadoran refugees. Since my first trip to El Salvador in 1988, I have returned ten times. I have visited every region of the country, although my research has been concentrated in Chalatenango and the San Salvador area. I have also worked with Salvadoran refugees in Mexico, Nicaragua, and the United States. I returned to El Salvador most recently in 2002 to conduct final research for this book. My field research includes open-ended interviews, oral histories, focus group discussions, and participant-observation of church services, meetings, and other events. I have also collected primary documents in a variety of sites in El Salvador and Nicaragua; the most important of these were in the archives of the Archdiocese of San Salvador. Finally, I conducted survey research as part of a comparative study of Catholics and Protestants in El Salvador, Peru, and U.S Latino communities between 1996 and 1999.

In the United States I conducted research for this project in two midwestern communities. In June and July 2000, I visited south central Kansas, in and around the towns of Newton and Elbing, to begin exploring Mennonite culture and agriculture. I conducted interviews with a number of Mennonites, mostly but not all farmers, asking about their personal and family histories, their agricultural practices, their ideas about nature and the land, their roles in the church, and their self-understanding as Mennonites. I also attended church services and visited farms. In May and June 2001, I made a similar trip to Holmes County, Ohio, the site of the world's largest Amish population. There I visited several Amish farms, interviewed David Kline, spoke with several other community members, and visited a small archive, maintained by an Amish family, with valuable primary and secondary sources, many out of print or unavailable elsewhere. Also in Holmes County, I spent a day at the Behalt, an Amish-Mennonite information center; visited local Amish markets, stores, and enterprises; and collected a variety of Amish newsletters and local papers. To supplement these firsthand observations of Amish life, I drew on as many primary sources and firsthand accounts as I could find, including the work of David Kline and writings from the Amish magazine *Family Life* published by Brad Igou. In addition to primary sources, I have relied on the excellent scholarship of specialists on Amish culture, history, and thought.

Algo pasa en el mundo, como un soplo que antes
no sentíamos entre las olas de la pólvora.

(Something is happening in the world, like a breath that before
We did not sense among the waves of gunpowder.)

—Pablo Neruda, "Canto al Ejército Rojo a su
llegada puertas de Prusia,"
Residencia en la tierra (1945)

Seeds of the Kingdom

Introduction: Residence on Earth

This book is about utopian dreams and their partial realization on earth. It reflects on the experiences of two kinds of communities, radically different from the norm in both wealthy and poor nations. These communities are among the many groups of people, scattered throughout the world, that embody alternatives at the same time that they challenge, implicitly if not always openly, both the inevitability and the "rightness" of dominant models. Many of these communities have achieved a great deal, despite frequent legal obstacles, lack of resources, even violent repression. Many have faltered in the face of these same challenges. The survivors confront countless problems of both external and internal origin. Still, they embody real possibilities, valuable and even essential if we are to map out better ways of living on the only planet we have.

At the heart of my exploration of these small communities is a question that has driven my work and activism for more than two decades: How can local projects contribute to large-scale social, economic, and environmental change? I started to think seriously about this question when, after graduating from high school in Portland, I began working for Oregon Fair Share. Fair Share was a neighborhood-based social movement organizing poor and working-class people around such issues as affordable housing, neighborhood safety, and health care. It emerged out of Saul Alinsky's approach to social change, grounded in "the belief that organizing people to build power at the grassroots is the only way to win change in the long term, because that is the only way to change the balance of power."[1] My work with Fair Share gave me a twofold conviction: first, that people are most effectively moved to act on the basis of things close to home, and second, that these locally grounded concerns can be connected, by skilled organizers and thoughtful activists, to much larger questions about structures and distributions of power. Since that time I have tried, as an activist and a scholar, to work out the theoretical and practical implications of these basic insights.

In particular, I have studied and reflected on the political roles of religious institutions, communities, practices, and ideas. These all have the capacity to repress and exclude, to bolster an oppressive status quo and to weaken efforts at social change. However, religion also harbors the potential to make uniquely powerful contributions to movements for social change. This potential stems from the fact that for most people in the world, religion remains the primary context for thinking about big questions. Religious stories and practices encourage us to reflect on the moral and transcendent dimensions of our daily lives, the shape of our societies, and the possibilities for a better future. Religion thus remains a primary locus for efforts to transform society. Religion's importance in efforts at social change stems in large part from an ability to make connections. The most effective religious movements effectively link experiences that are local, sometimes literally parochial, to the larger task of building a new kind of society. Many religions contain rich and diverse traditions of thought about how to connect the local and the universal, the real and the utopian, and how to weave these connections into a narrative that unites past, present, and future. Within Western Christianity, the tradition I know best and that has most influenced the North American society in which I live, this coherence is often accomplished through the idea of the reign of God.[2] This concept has various faces: an ideal government, the restoration of the creation's original justice and harmony, the consummation of the work of true believers, the destruction and redemption of the created world.

Since the time of the first disciples, many Christians have understood their community as a microcosm of the reign of God, a step on the way toward it, or perhaps both. This is particularly true for the two groups I study, Anabaptists and progressive Catholics. Emerging out of the radical wing of the Protestant Reformation, Anabaptists have sought to embody the reign of God in the everyday practice and faith of the believing community. "The church is called to be now what the world is called to be ultimately," declares Mennonite theologian John Howard Yoder. Christians ought to be "doing already on behalf of the wider world what the world is destined for in God's creative purpose. The church is . . . called to be a microcosm of the wider society, not only as an idea, but also in her function."[3] Roman Catholic theology also understands the Christian community as a microcosm of a better society, albeit with some important differences from the Anabaptist-Mennonite view. The Catholic natural law tradition has long understood human institutions and practices to be part of a larger divine plan, imperfect reflections and pieces of the perfection of the created world. In Latin America and elsewhere, progressive Catholics call believers not only to act as individuals in accord with God's will but also to try to bring social structures into line with that will. They describe themselves as making a twofold contribution to social change, by both modeling and helping to institute the reign of God.

Within such theological traditions, institutions and practices can bring together the means and the ends of social change. Religious communities and congregations both embody and work toward a better society. One reason they do this so effectively is because their practices and ideals are embedded, and embodied, in religious narratives. Such narratives show how memories and historical experiences, even creation stories and tales of past heroes, relate to contemporary experiences and understandings. Biblical stories about the persecution of the early disciples of Jesus, for example, have helped Anabaptists, progressive Catholics, and other Christians to make sense of and endure their own suffering at the hands of political and religious authorities. And biblical descriptions of ideal societies, from the garden of Eden to the community of the first apostles, have provided blueprints for many believers' own efforts to create a better world.

In this book, I draw on ethics, theology, history, and ethnography to shed light on the narratives and community practices of contemporary Anabaptists and Catholics. How do believers interpret and live out their traditions' stories? How do they enact transcendent values in concrete practices and structures, and how are these values transformed in the process of being interpreted and lived? Just as these Christians strive to embody in their lives the stories they take to be true, in writing about them I aim to embody a model of scholarship that begins with living communities as a proper setting for thinking about ethics. This approach poses questions that academics sometimes ignore or avoid: What big questions do ordinary people ask about morality, justice, and the future? What traditions and resources help them reflect about these issues? How do they weave their ethical concerns into their everyday lives?

These questions have no simple or definitive answers. More generally, there is never a direct, uncomplicated relationship between ideas and social life or, indeed, between what people think and what they do, individually or collectively. This does not mean that ideas have no connection to behavior. Their relationship, however, is complex, varied, and fluid, and it deserves a great deal more explicit reflection than it has so far received. Quite simply, ethicists too often fail to make sense of or appreciate the importance and complexity of the relations between big ideas and real life. This is true even of "applied ethics," the standard academic model for linking ethical ideas and practices. Too often applied ethicists take a top-down approach, which applies an established theoretical model to a practical problem. This misses the mutual shaping of practices and ideas, as well as the ways that historical and social contexts, personal relationships, and a host of other factors enter into ethical decisions and actions. As an alternative approach, I focus on ethics as embedded practices,[4] emerging out of philosophical and religious reflection, cultural traditions, biographical and collective experiences, and much more. I begin not with ethical theories but with real communities and ask how they learn about, understand, and transform moral traditions in the course of both everyday and extraordinary circumstances.

The Communities

In any scholarly work with ethnographic content, the process by which communities are selected is very important. There is perhaps always a degree of arbitrariness, inherent in the fact that among so many communities the researcher has to select one or a few. The selection, of course, cannot be completely arbitrary. Criteria do exist that make certain communities better "objects of study" than others. These criteria depend on the goals of the study, of course, as well as the interests, experience, and training of the researcher. In this project, I had several clear conditions in mind, shaped by my interest in exploring divergent but also comparable communities.

First, and most important, I wanted to find communities that were by some measures more environmentally and socially sustainable than mainstream U.S. culture. This meant identifying places that consumed less nonrenewable energy and other resources, but also those that did so out of clear values and principles, not just because poverty or lack of access prevented them from overconsuming. In particular, I wanted to reflect on the experiences and practices of communities that were working out the possibilities and contradictions of human relationships to nature. All people everywhere, of course, depend on the natural environment for the physical requirements of life, although many of us in urban, industrial societies need reminding of this fact. Equally clearly, no ecosystem in the present world can survive without human foresight and care. This mutual dependence may be most striking, and its vulnerabilities most evident, in rural, primarily agricultural settings. Agriculture has a tremendous environmental impact, and changes in farming practices are vital for the construction of more sustainable societies.[5] Agricultural sustainability does not involve farmers alone, however, but remains the foundation for almost all human life. Even in highly urban, industrialized settings, in which a small minority of people actually engage in food production, "there is no such thing as a 'post-agricultural' society."[6] Despite the continued necessity of agriculture, social and environmental ethicists have paid it remarkably little attention. And the related subfield of political ecology has focused on agricultural and land issues understood largely in technical and economic terms, with little attention to underlying worldviews and values.

The other crucial variable was that these be religious communities. In accord with my long-time interest in lived ethics, I wanted to look at groups of people who are trying to work out the practical moral implications of their theological beliefs. Religious communities are intentional, but when they consist of people who live in the same place, share a common history and traditions, and live in roughly similar ways, they are also "natural." Exploring the coincidence of history and intentionality in these settings, I think, helps shed light on what the term "community" might mean in our globalized, fragmented, and highly mobile world. The notion of community is fluid and in many ways problematic. Place, history, and a host of other factors contribute to making a group of people a community, and both the group itself and its self-understanding change over time. Thus, any study of communities must include some reflection on the term, including its symbolic dimensions: the ways that communities are socially constructed and the ways that community itself is a contested concept.

A final criterion for selection was that the communities be located in the Americas. This hemisphere, with its history of colonization and its biological and cultural diversity, has been the site of intense debate on a number of crucial political and environmental issues, including the preservation of wild areas and species, the status of indigenous people, and the social role of religious ideas and practices. Much environmental philosophy has also developed in North America, with significant contributions from South and Central America as well. The Americas are home to some of the most significant experiments in sustainable development, ecological restoration, and alternative agriculture. With these criteria in mind, I selected two communities, or clusters of communities, in North and Central America.

The Old Order Amish

As Anabaptists, the Old Order Amish are part of a minority group of Christians tracing roots back to early sixteenth-century Europe. The Anabaptists conceived of themselves as a "third way" between Protestant and Catholic Christianity; they were also called the Radical Reformation because they extended certain theological convictions from the mainstream Protestant Reformation. In particular, they rejected infant baptism, believing that baptism entails a serious commitment on the part of the believer, a voluntary covenant with God, which should be entered into only by willing and knowledgeable adults. Anabaptists believed that only by holding fast to their interpretation of Christianity, in the face of opposition from Roman Catholics, Lutherans, and Calvinists, would they gain the kingdom promised to true believers. Remarkably, they succeeded in communicating their faith so powerfully that the movement was not crushed despite the widespread use of torture and painful methods of execution, including strangling, burning, drowning, and beheading. As one German official lamented in 1529, "What shall I do? The more I cause to be executed, the more they increase."[7] By 1535, ten years into the movement, about 50,000 Anabaptists had been killed, probably more than all the Christians killed by Romans in the first three centuries of the common era. Thousands more were killed in the succeeding decades. An early Anabaptist text records the fate of Maeyken Wens, arrested and imprisoned in Antwerp in April 1573:

> When she could by no manner of means, not even by severe tortures, be turned from the steadfastness of her faith, they, on the fifth day of October, 1573, passed sentence upon her . . . the following day, the sixth of October, this pious and God–fearing heroine of Jesus Christ, as also her fellow believers that had been condemned with a like sentence, were brought forth, with their tongues screwed fast, as innocent sheep for the slaughter, and each having been fastened to a stake in the marketplace, deprived, by fierce and terrible flames, of their lives and bodies, so that in a short time they were consumed to ashes; which severe punishment of death they steadfastly endured; hence the Lord shall hereafter change their vile bodies, and fashion them like unto His glorious body (Phil. 3:21).
>
> The oldest son of the afore–mentioned martyress, named Adriaen Wens, aged about fifteen years, could not stay away from the place of execution on the day on which his dear mother was offered up; hence he took his youngest little brother, named Hans (or Jan) Mattheus Wens, who was about three years old, upon his arm and went and stood with him somewhere upon a bench, not far from the stakes erected, to behold his mother's death. But when she was brought forth and placed at the stake, he lost consciousness, fell to the ground, and remained in this condition until his mother and the rest were burnt. Afterwards, when the people had gone away, having regained consciousness, he went to the place where his mother had been burnt, and hunted in the ashes, in which he found the screw with which her tongue had been screwed fast, which he kept in remembrance of her.[8]

It is hard not to stop at the image of Maeyken Wens's son collecting the tongue screw used to prevent her from speaking to the crowd gathered for her execution. By showing how persecution tore families apart, the authors of early martyr stories underlined the force of the Anabaptists' faith: their belief in God's promise of a new world was strong enough to make them give up what was most precious in their lives in this world. This theme emerges in the words of another Anabaptist martyr, Claesken, executed in Friesland in 1559: "Do you think we run on uncertainties? . . . We forsake our dear children, whom I would not forsake for the whole world, and we stake upon it all we have—should we run on uncertainties yet?"[9]

Their certainty endured despite, or even because of, the violence applied against them by both the state and established churches. A Dutch Anabaptist strangled at the stake in 1553 elaborated their confidence of both persecution and salvation: "If the house is truly built upon the cornerstone, it cannot fall. Let everyone take good heed; for the time of trial is at hand, and we know that it will not always stop at mere words; for Christ Himself suffered. If they laid their hands on His blessed body, they will do the same to us. Let us arm ourselves with the Word of God; for the Word of God is the true door. It is the bread of life. The time of weeping is come; hence our deliverance is nigh."[10]

The tight link between weeping and deliverance reverberates in the Anabaptist present, embedded and elaborated in memories of persecution from the sixteenth century as well as in the sacred narratives of the Bible. Many of these tales are recorded in *The Martyrs' Mirror*, first published in Holland in 1660, a massive book documenting the persecution of Anabaptists in sixteenth- and seventeenth-century Europe. More than four centuries after the events it describes, *The Martyrs' Mirror* remains central to contemporary Anabaptist religious and cultural life. An exhibit based on the book traveled to different Mennonite churches and museums in the late 1990s, and the book continues to be a popular wedding gift. In Holmes County, Ohio, seat of the world's largest Amish population, the heart of the Amish-Mennonite information center is the *Behalt* (a German term meaning "to keep or remember"), a cycloramic mural of Anabaptist history that covers nearly 3,000 square feet. The mural's overwhelming theme is martyrdom, beginning with Jesus' crucifixion, passing through the early Anabaptist movement, and finishing with twentieth-century victims, including two Hutterite brothers who were tortured at Alcatraz and then died at Fort Leavenworth in 1917 because they refused to serve in the army.

Keeping alive memories of persecution contributes to a sense of permanent marginalization from both modern Western society and mainstream Christianity, which helps define Anabaptist identity, especially for the Amish and other Old Order Anabaptists. As one Amish man declares, "We are children of martyrs! That phrase sets us apart from other people. . . . If we do not have the spirit of the martyrs, but shrink from hardships—from self-denial, from sacrifice, from a life of discipline and restraint—then the martyrs were not our forbears at all, and we are not their children."[11] Anabaptist culture today continues to cultivate a sense of continuity with this past, which in turn undergirds everyday virtues such as self-denial, discipline, and restraint, along with an awareness that persecution might return at any time.

Persecution led many European Anabaptists to migrate to North America during the nineteenth century. Since that time, most have lived in rural settings, where relations to the land are grounded in close-knit religious and social groups. North American Anabaptists today are divided between more liberal or acculturated denominations, mainly Mennonites, and the Old Orders such as Hutterites, Brethren, Old Order Mennonites, and Amish. The Amish, the largest Old Order group, choose to live without many modern conveniences, including some as basic to mainstream ways of life as electrical utilities, home telephones, and automobiles. These choices are driven by commitments both to the local church community and to a distinctive religious vision, in which growth, profit, and individual preference take a back seat. They seek as much separation and autonomy as possible from the mainstream world and depend on the religious community, or *Gemeinde*, for material as well as moral support and security. The guiding values of the Gemeinde—peaceableness, mutual aid, and separation from the world—are drawn from biblical portraits of the earliest Christian community. Most Amish families live in rural areas, seeking physical as well as cultural separation, even though the percentage living on farms has declined in recent decades.

Many people see the Amish as anachronistic clingers to the past, archaic, backward, at best quaint. While this vision is far from accurate, it is true that history is very much alive in their communities and that they often value tradition over novelty. The Amish define themselves, further, outside mainstream religiosity and culture, as deliberately marginal players in the larger society. Clearly, they provide an alternative to dominant Western culture. The question for anyone wanting to study the Amish in comparative perspective is whether the alternative they pose is so far removed from most people's lives that it has nothing to say to people who are unwilling to wear plain clothes, forgo cars and electricity, and live by strict religious standards. This was my initial impression, which led me to select acculturated Mennonite farmers as the first option for this study. I explained to Mennonites I visited in south central Kansas that I wanted to explore a religious community in the United States with a clear historical and collective identity, residing mostly in rural areas and living and farming in environmentally and socially sustainable ways. Although the Kansas Mennonites fit this description in many respects, they encouraged me to take a closer look at the Old Order groups and especially the Amish. We ought to take the Amish seriously, my Mennonite friends argued, because they are both less archaic and more radical than commonly supposed. The usual quick dismissal of Old Order Anabaptists trivializes their powerful challenge to the values and assumptions, and not just practices, of the North American status quo.

The Amish are among the few historically continuous Christian groups that have both articulated and lived out an alternative vision of religious-social community. They represent the largest, longest-lasting, and most successful counterculture in North America. Looking more closely at the lives of contemporary Amish people opens new ways of seeing and thinking about our relations to each other, to political institutions, and to nature; in short, it helps us think about the possibility of living as if a different world were not only possible but real and in fact necessary.

Repopulated Communities in Chalatenango, El Salvador

The other community discussed in this book is far removed from the Amish, geographically and culturally. I explore the experiences of Catholic peasants in El Salvador who, after decades of different forms of organization and struggle, have returned to former war zones to construct a new kind of community. Their efforts have taken place in a nation that has long been one of the poorest, most violent, and least democratic in the Americas. Their movement challenges a small elite that has ruled since colonial times, backed by government armies and private security forces and employing extreme repression against attempts at protest and reform. The pinnacle of this violence, and a defining moment in Salvadoran history, was the *matanza* (massacre) of January 1932, in which the army killed between 10,000 and 30,000 peasants and indigenous people protesting a military coup that overturned an elected reformist government.[12]

In more recent decades, economic changes have increased the wealth of elites while destabilizing the situation of small farmers, most of whom worked small subsistence holdings supplemented by seasonal wage labor. A growing population coupled with increased production of export commodities such as cotton, sugar, and coffee in the 1950s and 1960s reduced access to land, and by 1975, three-quarters of Salvadoran rural workers owned no land or less than one hectare, often in the least fertile and accessible regions. Tens of thousands of peasants migrated in search of work, and many small farmers fell heavily into debt. In an increasingly untenable situation, efforts began in the late 1960s to form cooperatives, peasant unions, and other movements to improve the immediate situation and, some hoped, ultimately to transform the economic and political landscape of El Salvador.

Their organizations met with harsh repression during the late 1970s and early 1980s, which intensified after the civil war began in earnest in 1981. Nowhere in El Salvador was life harder, before or during the war, than Chalatenango province. On the border with Honduras in northeastern El Salvador, Chalatenango has historically been one of the country's poorest, most isolated, and most repressed regions. It is a sort of Salvadoran Appalachia, overwhelmingly poor and rural, isolated from political and economic hubs, its inhabitants immediately identifiable by their regional accents and widely viewed as the most *campesino* among *campesinos*. After a brief period of relative prosperity during the late 1800s based on the production of indigo for export, Chalatenango has suffered chronic land shortages, poverty, and seasonal and permanent out-migration. In an influential study of the country's history and culture, David Browning describes the region thus: "With its thin deforested soils, undeveloped, exhausted, and eroded; its primitive agriculture, lack of assistance from capital investment or modern supervision, and with its social cohesion weakened by the economic decline, the dispersal of settlements and emigration, [Chalatenango] became, little by little, the forgotten land of the present century."[13] With some of the poorest soils and highest mountains in the country, Chalatenango did not have many large landowners other than occasional cattle ranchers. Most of the land was in small farms, and most farms did not provide enough for the families to live. Thus, many peasants, especially men, traveled in search of seasonal work in sugar, coffee, or cotton harvests. The department had little in the way of educational opportunities, health services, or infrastructure. If El Salvador was an unlikely country for a utopian experiment, Chalatenango seemed the least likely part of the country: the most poor, backward, and miserable region of a poor, backward, and miserable nation.

However, Chalatenango lies at the center of a unique historical experiment. As civil war raged, people who had fled the combat zones by the thousands returned to reinhabit and rebuild their communities. They did so according to a clear vision of what El Salvador could and should be: not like the impoverished, marginalized villages they left, but centers of education, health, solidarity, and material sufficiency. In the struggle to realize these hopes, Chalatenango's activists have encountered not only harsh ecological and economic circumstances but also repression from a government intent on demoralizing and destroying their communities and thus dismantling the utopian dream these embodied.

One such attack occurred on February 11, 1990, in the tiny village of Corral de Piedra (also known as Guancora), when "two rockets fired from a Salvadoran Air Force helicopter hit a house in which 21 civilians had taken refuge, killing five and wounding sixteen. Four of the five killed were children under the age of 10; eleven of the wounded were children between four months and twelve years of age."[14] The civilians killed and wounded in Corral de Piedra had returned to El Salvador from a refugee camp in Honduras barely two months previously. They lacked permanent housing and were living in the shells of houses that had been destroyed by the Salvadoran Air Force in the early 1980s, ruins that provided little protection from rockets, machine guns, or bombs.

I visited Corral de Piedra six weeks after the attack. Dirt paths, some lined with low stone walls, wound among the ruins of prewar houses, most of which had only two or three walls still standing. The repopulators had established temporary quarters in the most complete houses, covering them with plastic or *lámina* (sheet metal) to keep out the rain. Many walls had holes from bullets or shrapnel, some recent and some from a decade earlier. Further evidence of the latest attack lay scattered on the ground: quantities of shrapnel, shells, and even boxes of live bullets. In the shattered house where the man and children had died, blood stains remained on the wall, and a pair of shredded straw hats lay on the floor. A woman nearby told us that when the shelling stopped and she was finally able to go to the house where the victims were, she discovered that a rocket had hit one of her children directly, breaking his body into many pieces. Like the son of the Anabaptist martyr Maeyken Wens, she had fainted in the face of the unbearable.

Our visit to Corral de Piedra fell during Holy Week and one day after the tenth anniversary of the murder of Archbishop Oscar Romero. The timing accentuated the parallels residents saw between their losses and the suffering of other Christians before them. "For sixteen years," one man said, "all the people who read the Bible have been persecuted." He saw the Air Force attack as yet another incident in the ongoing repression of El Salvador's peasant movement. Another resident traced the history back even further, relating the attack to the violence of the first Holy Week: "We see all the suffering [Jesus] had in his life, and now we're experiencing a little of that." These Christians firmly believed that their sacrifices, like those of Jesus and of many others after him, would contribute to a fuller realization of divine purpose. A member of Corral de Piedra's pastoral team explained:

> The gospel says if the grain of wheat doesn't fall, it won't bear fruit. And this is being fulfilled now. For example, the family that was the victim of this tragedy, [the attackers] wanted to see if we would fail. But no, the Holy Spirit gives us strength to continue even if words fail us, and it makes us continue working wherever there's a need to work. Finally God will touch [the enemy's] hearts and the grain of wheat will give fruit. But if it doesn't die, it won't bear fruit. We're being given a test now, to see if we will continue, and God has to give us the means we need to continue forward.[15]

The reference to the fallen yet fruitful grain of wheat captures central themes of the Catholic peasant movement that began in the late 1960s and ultimately gave birth to the repopulations. Christians are called to follow Jesus by building a new society modeled on the reign of God. In the process they will face tests, but their faith demands that they "continue forward" and promises that, in the end, they will see the results of their work and sacrifice; deliverance follows upon weeping. The residents of the repopulations seek to make real a dream that can fairly be called utopian: to create in an impoverished, violent, and despoiled country a reign of justice and solidarity. In the face of overwhelming obstacles, the persistence of this dream, which underlies the characterization of El Salvador as a "promised land" in three different books,[16] may be as surprising, as demanding of explanation as are any effective steps toward its realization. I explore the successes of the repopulations, as well as the challenges they face, to reflect on the possibilities for social reconstruction and ecological restoration in exceedingly difficult circumstances and the endurance of utopian hopes throughout the drama of mass exile and return, war and its aftermath.

Other Worlds?

The two places I have chosen, both rural Christian communities in the Americas, diverge in many important ways, from geography and climate to religious and political history. Exploring their differences and their similarities, their place in the larger society and their visions for the future, helps illuminate some of the broad questions behind this project: How are religious traditions embodied and altered in local histories and practices? What are the relations between social justice and environmental protection? What makes alternative ways of living among people and with nature possible, and what stands in the way of these experiments? What might enable them to expand and have an impact beyond their village borders? Can the New World be, as Christopher Columbus first called it, "another world" (*otro mundo*)? I want to explore these questions not just speculatively, as so many people criticizing the status quo or hoping for something different have done. Speculation has a place, but we ought not to lose sight of real communities and living alternatives. If we permit ourselves to believe that another kind of world is possible only in fantasy, it is an easy step to believing that any real change is impossible. Those of us living in this flawed and failing world are then off the hook, because, as Kant intoned, "ought implies can," and if we *cannot* make another world we have no moral obligation to try.

What "other worlds," though, can survive amid the power and danger of the present one? Of the innumerable efforts to create countercultures or utopian communities, the vast majority have vanished without much impact beyond the contemporary and local. Although these failed experiments can teach us much, dwelling on them tempts us to ignore others that lasted. Of course, we have no sure way to know in advance which are the really significant alternatives, the ones that will outlast others or change the world. The most likely candidates, however, include those rooted in enduring cultural and religious traditions, firmly settled in particular places, and with clear values and visions guiding their everyday practices. This describes both the Amish and the Salvadoran repopulations.

I do not want simply to identify and describe these communities but to suggest real ways that these rural places, geographically and culturally distant from the lives of most people in the industrialized West, are relevant to urgent political and environmental problems facing the United States and other parts of the (over)developed world. I look, further, for some common ways that they are relevant, some shared practices and values that emerge despite their differences. I hope that understanding these commonalities, without forgetting the particularities, can contribute to efforts to construct or strengthen sustainable value systems elsewhere. My aim, at least in part, is to begin developing a comparative framework for understanding communities that are living in more environmentally sustainable and socially just ways. This strikes me as an important step that both complements and moves beyond the many academic and policy-oriented works that present "sustainable" ideas that have never actually been adopted or lived by real people, or at least not by real people living collectively in real circumstances. I want to learn more about how good ideas become embedded practices. Related to this, I want to explore the values that undergird sustainable practices, even when the practitioners may not have systematized the ethical or intellectual grounding for their actions.

I write, then, as a scholar and also as an advocate. I describe and reflect on these communities not only because they are fascinating but also because they shed a critical light on our own status quo. They point, further, to more desirable alternatives, to the possibility of less destructive, and even more satisfying, ways to live. Their hopes are connected to ours. The experiences and values of these small communities, so distant from centers of power, offer vital resources for the necessary struggle to rethink and rebuild our own societies.

I

Farm, Land, Church

Anabaptist Agriculture and Community

Anabaptist History and Belief

The longest lasting utopian experiment in the West was launched in
the early 1500s by members of the Christian group known as the
Anabaptists or Radical Reformation. The movement emerged in
Holland and southern Germany in the wake of the Protestant Reformation, which began in 1517 when Martin Luther, an Augustinian
monk, nailed his 95 *Theses* to the front door of Castle Church in
Wittenberg, Germany. The core of Luther's theological innovation
lay in his rejection of all forms of mediation between the believer
and God. He criticized in particular indulgences, the acceptance by
priests of gifts or donations in return for partial forgiveness of sins,
or, more precisely, for the remission of penalties associated with sin.
For Luther, neither indulgences nor any other work, including rituals and ethical deeds, could influence believers' ultimate fate. Redemption came only "by grace, through faith." Christians did not
need priests or the church to mediate divine grace, because true
faith made possible direct relations between the believer and God.
This was Luther's famous "priesthood of all believers."

The Radical Reformation adopted these Lutheran theological
themes but diverged on an equally central Lutheran claim: the division between the spiritual and secular "kingdoms." Luther taught
that there were two governments, the spiritual and the secular, and
that Christian freedom prevailed only under the first. In all matters
not directly related to faith, he insisted, Christians must obey secular authority ("the sword"), even to the extent of serving as hangmen

or otherwise committing violence.[1] Thus, for orthodox Lutheran theology, as Paul Tillich writes, "There is no relation between the justice of the Kingdom of God and the justice of power structures. The two worlds are separated by an unbridgeable gap."[2]

A number of early Protestants rejected Luther's acquiescence to secular power and his refusal to extend Christian liberty to broader spheres. One of Luther's best-known critics was Thomas Münzer, who from 1524 to 1526 led German peasants in an uprising against the nobles who kept them in serfdom. Münzer had become convinced that the freedom and equality that Luther declared among Christians should prevail more generally. Refusing Luther's sharp dualism between Christianity and the world, Münzer drew on biblical themes to defend "the working people" oppressed by authorities. "The people are hungry," he declared, "they must eat; they intend to eat, as Amos says, and Matthew 5, too."[3] Münzer asked Luther for help, but Luther rejected his theological and political claims and supported the German princes as they crushed the uprising.[4]

The distinctly Anabaptist radicalization of Luther's theology was initiated in Zurich, where Ulrich Zwingli was leading Protestant reforms. Two of Zwingli's followers, Conrad Grebel and Felix Manz, believed Zwingli, like Luther, did not go far enough, although they did not favor Münzer's more radical reforms.[5] Most notably, whereas Zwingli approved infant baptism, Grebel and Manz rejected it, on the grounds that only persons old enough to make a conscious decision to accept Christ should join the church. By 1525, they had split from Zwingli and founded a movement that became known as the Anabaptists, or "rebaptizers." The name came from the fact that all early Anabaptists had to convert from Catholicism. Because they had already been baptized once in the Catholic Church as infants, they had to undergo a second, "believer's" baptism as adults. The Anabaptist movement grew rapidly, with primary strength in Germany, Holland, and northern Italy.

From the beginning, Anabaptists faced severe persecution by both secular and religious powers, Protestant as well as Roman Catholic. The attacks stemmed not just from their religious nonconformity but also from the challenge to state power implicit in their refusal to perform military service, swear oaths, or recognize the ultimate authority of the state. Manz became the first prominent Anabaptist martyr, drowned by order of the Zurich town council in 1527. (Drowning became a common method of execution for Anabaptists, mocking their custom of adult baptism by immersion.) Persecution of leaders and ordinary believers in the Radical Reformation was harshest in the movement's first decades but continued sporadically for two centuries, claiming tens of thousands of lives and permanently marking all aspects of Anabaptist life, from ethics and theology to agricultural practices and technology.

One early result of the repression was the radicalization of some segments of the Anabaptist movement. A number of premillenarian wings emerged, including Jan Matthys's effort to establish the kingdom of God in Münster, Germany. In 1534, Matthys led armed bands of Anabaptists seeking to expel all Roman Catholics and Lutherans who refused rebaptism. Abandoning the established Anabaptist commitment to pacifism, Matthys and his cohorts initiated the bloodshed they believed would precede the imminent second coming of Christ. In response, the local Catholic bishop raised an army that destroyed Matthys's community and killed all its male members. The leaders were tortured to death and their bodies placed in iron cages that still hang from St. Lambert's church. The experience at Münster strengthened the perception of Anabaptists as dangerous revolutionaries, even though most were pacifists and avoided political conflict.

These associations intensified the violence against Anabaptists, prompting many to migrate from their homes in Germany, Holland, and Switzerland into eastern Europe. Others moved away from cities, where members could be easily identified and located, to rural areas, especially in the Vosges Mountains of the Alsace region in southeastern France and the Jura Mountains in northwestern Switzerland. Many Anabaptists worked on large estates, where they were often given marginal lands to farm for themselves, in addition to caring for the owners' livestock and farms. Thus, within a few decades, the movement's base shifted from an urban, intellectual population to a mainly agrarian one, an identity that persists into the present.

Persecution and immigration, along with internal disagreements over theology and practice, spurred the division of the Anabaptist movement into many smaller groups. Three of the early groups still exist today. The largest is the Mennonites, mainly of Dutch and Prussian origin, named for their founder, Menno Simons. In Austria, the Hutterian Brethren, founded by Jacob Huter (who was burned at the stake in 1536), developed a collectivist model of farming and living. The third group was the Swiss Brethren, from whom the Amish split in 1693.[6]

The leader of the Amish faction was Jacob Amman (ca. 1656–1730), whose theology differed from that of the main body of Brethren on several issues. Best known is his insistence on strict enforcement of the ban (*Bann*) and shunning (*Meidung*), disciplinary practices that Swiss Anabaptists were using as early as 1527. (They are described in the Schleitheim Confession from that year.) Applied together, the Bann and Meidung amount to excommunication from the church and community as a result of repeated violations of community norms and rules. Banned members were prohibited not only from participation in religious activities but also from all close contact with members, even their own families.

The ban was important to Amman, as to other early Anabaptists, as a means of maintaining both unity and discipleship. The church ought to be "a disciplined brotherhood . . . made up only of sincere believers who live holy lives."[7] These qualities could be maintained only with collective disciplinary practices that both encouraged obedience and made possible the expulsion of those who refused to follow core values. Some Old Order Anabaptists today question the value of the ban and shunning, but they are still practiced by most Amish and Old Order Mennonite communities. They are employed rarely, however, and only after repeated warnings, and the possibility always remains of repentance and return to the communal fold. As one Amish elder explains, "The *Bann* punishes the evildoer not in the spirit of revenge, but to bring him to repentance."[8]

Amman also worried that persecuted Anabaptists were relying too much on sympathizers, called the *Treuherzige* (true-hearted), who often helped Mennonites avoid problems with authorities. Amman argued that overreliance on the Treuherzige would weaken Anabaptist unity and lead Anabaptists to meld with the mainstream. Again, Amman's principles were aimed at maintaining strict ethical principles and community coherence, which required, he believed, strict separation from the larger society, and even from more liberal Anabaptists. Finally, Amman sought to decentralize church structure and grant more authority to the community of lay believers.[9] He thus laid the foundations for the continuing Amish combination of strict boundaries between the church and the broader society, and broadly democratic and egalitarian relations within the believing community.

Persistent persecution in Europe eventually caused many Mennonite, Hutterite, and Amish families to migrate to North America. The first Anabaptists in the United States settled in the early to mid-1700s in Pennsylvania, where William Penn's religious tolerance enabled Mennonite and Amish communities to thrive alongside Quakers and other nonconformist groups. A second wave of Mennonite and Amish immigrants from Europe arrived in North America in the early 1800s. During the same period, many families and church communities moved westward from Pennsylvania, especially to Ohio and Indiana. Another shift occurred in the 1870s, when groups of Anabaptists also moved west, especially to Kansas and Oklahoma. Other Mennonites, Amish, and especially Hutterites moved to several Canadian provinces. During all these migrations, different Anabaptist groups often settled near each other so that Mennonite, Brethren, and Amish communities were found in the same counties. Few Amish remained in Europe, and those who stayed eventually joined with the more liberal Mennonites, so that today the Old Orders live only in the United States and Canada, apart from several settlements in Latin America founded by migrants from North American communities.

Divisions and the formation of new groups have recurred throughout Anabaptist history. Within the Amish, the most significant division took place after a series of meetings in the mid-1860s between progressive and traditional Amish bishops in Pennsylvania and Ohio. They failed to reach agreement on a number of issues, including technology, clothing, shunning, and the ban. In addition, some of the more liberal Amish favored a formal church structure, while conservatives insisted that each congregation, or church district, must determine and enforce its own communal rules and practices. By 1865 the break was complete between the conservative faction, which became known as the Old Order Amish, and the progressives, who were initially called Amish-Mennonites but eventually dropped the term Amish. Further splits have occurred as Old Order groups have sought to clarify their positions on new technologies and other social changes. A number of church districts in Holmes and Wayne Counties, Ohio, for example, are affiliated with the Swartzentruber and Andy Weaver Amish, which retain stricter rules than other Amish groups regarding both technology and shunning.[10]

Not just the Amish but virtually all Anabaptist communities in North America began as ethnically homogeneous rural enclaves, clustered in a few counties in Pennsylvania, Ohio, Indiana, Kansas, and several Canadian provinces. Mennonites and Amish alike signaled their separation from the mainstream with plain dress, the use of German at home and in church, and a limited range of acceptable occupations, with farming valued above all. The differences between Old Order and liberal or assimilationist groups were significant but not enormous during this time. Especially after World War II, however, technological and social changes sharpened the differences among Anabaptist groups, especially between the majority of "modernizing" Mennonites and smaller populations of Mennonites, Brethren, Hutterites, and Amish who deliberately limited the technological, educational, and occupational changes permitted in their communities.

Today, approximately a million Anabaptists live throughout the world, including growing populations in Latin America, Africa, and Asia, as well as long-established communities in Europe. Most of the 400,000 Anabaptists in North America are Mennonites who have integrated into mainstream Western society in many respects: they frequently reside in urban and suburban areas, dress like their neighbors, speak English at home and in church, send their children to public schools, participate in civil society, use modern technology, and work in a wide range of careers. Their assimilation contrasts sharply with the Old Order Anabaptists' continuing insistence on maintaining a strong and clear boundary between the church and the world.

Anabaptist Theology and Ethics

The Anabaptist movement was called the Radical Reformation because it took Protestant claims about religious freedom, Christian purity, and the requirements of faith into all aspects of life. Against Luther's claim that Christians were citizens of two kingdoms, one worldly and one divine, Anabaptists insisted that true believers belonged only to the reign of God. Their calling on earth was to create a church reflecting the values of this reign: to unite faith and works, as the Letter of James admonished (2:17). This effort demands separation from the inevitable corruption, conflict, and violence of the secular realm.

The Schleitheim Confession (also known as "The Brotherly Union of a number of children of God concerning Seven Articles"), written by Swiss Brethren in 1527, spells out the core themes that still guide Anabaptist theology and practice. It outlines less a systematic theology than a practical ethic, a way to live out Christian beliefs:

> Everything which is not united with our God and Christ cannot be other than an abomination which we should shun and flee from. By this is meant all popish and anti-popish works and church services, meetings and church attendance, drinking houses, civic affairs, the commitments made in unbelief and other things of that kind, which are highly regarded by the world and yet which are carried on in flat contradiction to the command of God, in accordance with all the unrighteousness which is in the world. From all these things we shall be separated and have no part with them for they are nothing but an abomination, and they are the cause of our being hated before our Christ Jesus, who has set us free from the slavery of the flesh and fitted us for the service of God through the Spirit whom He has given us.[11]

The Schleitheim Confession not only rejected infant baptism ("the first and greatest abomination of the pope") but also prohibited military service and the use of violence to resolve conflicts. The Anabaptists agreed with Luther that institutionalized violence, or "the sword," was necessary in the larger world to protect the good and punish the wicked. However, true Christians could not serve this world or use force, including legal coercion or threats, even in self-defense. Anabaptists could not act as magistrates, participate in the legal and political mechanisms of the state, or even swear oaths. In short, their lives and actions were to embody nonviolence, nonresistance, and nonconformity. This constituted true discipleship for Anabaptists, who believed that Christians should not only have faith in Jesus' saving power but also follow his teachings and actions in all aspects of their lives. Christians did not live in two kingdoms, according to Anabaptist cosmology, but in only one, the small, demanding, and infinitely rewarding community of true believers.

Far more than mainstream Protestantism, the Radical Reformation is concerned with correct action (orthopraxy) over correct belief (orthodoxy). "There is no real Amish theology," summarizes David Kline. "We just take the Bible and do what it says."[12] This emphasis on practical ethics and collective religious and social life is shared with Roman Catholicism, although Anabaptists reject the Catholic Church's hierarchical structure and links to secular powers. Because of its distinctions from both Protestantism and Catholicism, Anabaptists often refer to their faith as a "third way." This alternative Christian path is distinguished by the core values of nonviolence and nonresistance, separation from the world, mutual aid, and congregational autonomy. These values remain common to all Anabaptists, despite the diverse ways believers have understood them and tried to live out their faith in particular historical conditions.

Anabaptists' best-known value is pacifism, reflected in their identification, along with Quakers, as "peace churches." Pacifism and antimilitarism are part of a larger Anabaptist value of nonresistance or *Gelassenheit* (sometimes translated as "yieldedness"), summarized by one scholar as "a deep-seated attitude of submission and self-denial."[13] Mennonites and other Anabaptists have often referred to themselves as "the quiet in the land" (*die Stille im Lande*), highlighting their peaceableness and avoidance of conflict. This characteristic includes both a negative rejection of violence and force as a way to resolve problems and also, especially for Mennonites, a positive search for nonviolent routes to personal and social transformation.

Peaceableness must reign within the Christian community, or Gemeinde. Within the community, the only form of discipline allowed is the ban, which Anabaptists trace to Jesus' admonition to wrongdoers "to sin no more." Church members should first warn transgressors and lovingly call them to return to the fold. If these warnings fail to halt the undesired behavior, community leaders enforce the ban to separate true Christians from corrupting influences. The ban also reinforces unity, particularly prior to the Lord's Supper. As the Schleitheim Confession explains, "All those who wish to break one bread in remembrance of the broken body of Christ, and all who wish to drink of one drink in remembrance of the shed blood of Christ, shall be united beforehand by baptism in one body of Christ which is the church of God and whose head is Christ."[14]

Although they reject the use of violence or force to change others, Anabaptists strive to maintain clear boundaries between themselves and the larger world. The Schleitheim Confession calls on believers to separate from the evil and wickedness that the devil has planted in the world: "For as Paul points out we cannot at the same time be partakers of the Lord's table and the table of devils; we cannot at the same time drink the cup of the Lord and the cup of the devil. That is, all those who have fellowship with the dead works of darkness have no part in the light. Therefore all those who follow the devil and the world have no part with those who have been called unto God and out of the world. All who lie in evil have no part in the good." More concisely, "We have no fellowship with them."[15]

Throughout their history, Anabaptists have interpreted the call to separate from the world in a wide variety of ways. Early Anabaptists a refused to take oaths or to consider themselves citizens of the state. For liberal Mennonites today, nonconformity finds expression mainly in pacifism. The Old Orders, notably the Amish, strive for a more extensive nonconformity, including distinctive forms of dress, speech, and transportation, residence in rural communities apart from the center of mainstream culture, and, more generally, a "simple" or "plain" way of living that avoids pride, consumerism, and excessive individualism. This separatism requires a close-knit community of believers to provide material and moral support. Thus, from the start, Anabaptists have insisted on the collective dimensions of faith and of salvation itself and have embodied these values in efforts to create communities as pure, harmonious, egalitarian, and united as the reign of God announced by Jesus and modeled by the early disciples. Early Anabaptists often called each other brother and sister, reflecting the tight bonds among members who supported each other through persecution and exile. The value of mutual aid prevails among Anabaptists today, most obviously in Amish communities, with their barn raisings, and communal provision for sick, old, and needy members. In addition to stressing mutual aid within the believing community, Anabaptists have extended compassion and aid to others, especially those in need. This is embodied in service programs such as Mennonite Disaster Service and the Mennonite Central Committee, which provide assistance to victims of natural and human disasters in the United States and elsewhere.

Although frequently cooperating on such projects, Anabaptists retain a strong principle of congregational autonomy. Unlike both Catholics and mainline Protestants, Anabaptist churches lack bishops and centralized authority structures. Even the Mennonite national conference, the Mennonite Church USA, cannot establish rules or positions for individual congregations, as do the conferences of many mainstream Protestant denominations.[16] Among the Amish, local church districts retain even greater independence. Lacking a denominational conference or organizing body, Amish congregations are kept together by historical and family ties and a common identity. Amish church districts that share common rules may be affiliated or "in fellowship" with each other, but each congregation selects its own minister, deacon, and bishop, arranges its own celebrations, and cares for and disciplines its own members. This autonomy does not stem from excessive individualism or isolation, as the Amish and many other Anabaptists are closely bound by their common history, roots in a shared landscape, and extended family ties. They have a strong collective identity, but it is directed above all toward the local congregation rather than a global whole.

For Anabaptists, the primary mediator of divine grace and redemption is neither the individual believer nor the church as global institution but rather the disciplined, united community of disciples. The identification of the church as the community of believers rather than an institution or place undergirds the Amish tradition of holding Sunday services, weddings, and funerals in members' homes or barns rather than a separate church building. Although Mennonites have church buildings, their *Confession of Faith* asserts that "the church is the new community of disciples sent into the world to proclaim the reign of God and to provide a foretaste of the church's glorious hope. The church is the new society established and sustained by the Holy Spirit."[17] It is a "city on a hill," separate from the corruption and violence of the world that lives by the sword, testifying to and embodying Jesus' teachings. Anabaptist faith is not a millenarian hope for the future realization of the reign of God but an attempt, inevitably partial and flawed, to create it here and now. The fact that this Christian community will always be a minority, even a remnant, makes its obligations no less binding.

The Old Order Amish

The commitment to nonconformity becomes more challenging as the physical and cultural barriers separating most Anabaptists from the rest of the world disintegrate. Liberal Mennonites, who have largely given up external markers such as plain dress and horse-and-buggy transportation, focus more on theological, ethical, and political dimensions of Anabaptist identity. They wrestle with the question of whether it is possible to combine the core Anabaptist values of nonresistance, pacifism, separation, and Gemeinde with full participation in civil society. These acculturated Mennonites, mostly affiliated with the Mennonite Church USA, are divided from Old Order groups such as the Amish, Hutterites, Brethren, and Old Order Mennonites, who believe that separation from the world is necessary to construct and maintain a redemptive community that can pursue the demands of discipleship. Amish people believe that the Mennonite effort to preserve Anabaptist values while reaching out to the larger world has failed. They sometimes say that the Mennonites set out to win the world, but instead the world won the Mennonites.

The Old Orders thus define themselves to some extent against mainstream Mennonites as well as against other religious and cultural groups in the United States and Canada. Although they also differ among themselves, the Old Orders generally share plain dress and uniform hairstyles, rejection of many forms of modern transportation and technology, an insistence on parochial education lasting only through eighth grade, and (except for the Brethren) concentration in small, rural communities. Further, the Amish speak German in church services and Pennsylvania German at home. These differences might suggest that cultural rather than specifically religious heritage is the most important source of Old Order identity. However, the fact that no other Western religious group has produced any significant and enduring parallel movement suggests that the Old Orders take something essential from the Anabaptist tradition, a commitment to nonconformity lacking in other Christian denominations.

The Amish constitute the largest Old Order group by far, with 180,000 baptized adults and children under baptismal age spread over 1,100 church districts. Each district lives according to an *Ordnung* (order), a set of rules, expectations, and common values, usually unwritten. Loose affiliations exist among church districts that share the same Ordnung. Most Amish settlements are in Pennsylvania, Ohio, and Indiana, although church districts also have been established in many other states, as well as in Canada and Latin America. The world's largest Amish population lives in Holmes County, Ohio, followed by Lancaster County, Pennsylvania. The national Amish population has grown rapidly, up from 4,000 a century ago. In Ohio, the Amish population has doubled in the past thirty years. This growth is fueled by birthrates averaging six children per family and retention rates of over 80 percent for most Amish communities.

The Amish have survived many predictions of their demise, especially after World War II brought major changes in transportation, lifestyle, and occupation throughout North America. Although few observers still believe that the Amish will die out or assimilate in the near future, most continue to find them archaic or quaint. Even their neighbors view them as eccentric. (Typical is a local businessman in Holmes County, who warned me to watch for buggies on a road that, he explained, "the Amish use when they come down from their communes in the hills.") The Amish stimulate endless fascination and speculation among scholars, journalists, tourists, and others. They also serve as ideological resources for a variety of groups, who have described them in widely varying ways to support an equally wide range of arguments. Some observers idealize the Amish for emphasizing principles they believe should guide U.S. society, such as local autonomy, "family values," pacifism, and communitarianism. To many of these outsiders, the Amish seem to embody a utopian vision of the way things should be, underlined by a sharp critique of disliked elements of mainstream culture.

The Amish are also utopian from the inside, insofar as they live according to an all-encompassing vision of Christian discipleship as a foretaste of the reign of God. These insider and outsider visions often conflict, and even among the Amish there is no single vision of what their communities are and should be. This points to the need to emphasize, in the face of frequent homogenization and romanticization, the diversity among the Amish and the fact that they are real people with flaws and internal conflicts. The dangers of stereotypes are intensified by the fact that the traditions of separation and Gelassenheit do not encourage Amish people to explain themselves to the larger world. Further, their tendency to avoid conflict means that they rarely correct mistaken assumptions or claims. Thus, the growing discussion about the potential of Amish communities to serve as models or sources of inspiration for more sustainable societies is as risky as it is potentially fruitful.

Amish community life revolves around the church district, a congregation of twenty-five to forty families that meet every other Sunday for worship in the home or barn of a member family. The church district is the site for practicing discipleship not only as individual virtue but also as solidarity and harmony within the community. The concern for consensus and unity shapes, for example, the selection of church leaders, who are chosen by lot. Each church district has two ministers, who preach sermons; a deacon, who coordinates services to needy members and assists the bishop; and the bishop, the spiritual head of the congregation. All these leaders must be married men, and some Ordnungs require that they have children who have joined the church as well. The bishop and ministers make decisions about applying established rules, developing new ones, allowing for exceptions, and disciplining violators. This raises the possibility of abuse of power, a fear or suspicion of many who perceive the Amish (and perhaps all religious) communities as authoritarian and intolerant of differences. However, the authority of Amish leaders is neither absolute nor arbitrary. Preachers and bishops are called by the community and can neither pursue nor refuse leadership posts. Because communities are small and members live near each other, face-to-face contact is frequent, and it is not hard to hold leaders accountable for their decisions. Further, leaders and preachers receive no payment but must make their living through farming or another acceptable occupation. They participate in no regional or national hierarchies or conferences other than occasional meetings between bishops of congregations with the same Ordnung. They do not even control church buildings, as biweekly worship services rotate among members' houses.

Along with the church district, the family is the most important Amish social unit. Generations live and work together, and children are educated at home and then in Amish-run schools attended and staffed by their relatives and neighbors. It is worth noting that the Supreme Court gave the Amish, unique among U.S. religious groups, the right to educate their children in their own schools and to end their education after eighth grade. This is an instance of the way state cooperation has helped make Amish survival possible, a reminder that even these apparently self-sufficient communities are not islands unto themselves.

Their communities are held together by numerous cross-cutting and mutually reinforcing ties. Amish people encounter each other at church, at school, in the fields, and at the local hardware store. There is little chance for anonymity or falling through the cracks. No doubt Amish women, men, and children, like residents of any small community, sometimes wish certain episodes in their lives could pass unnoticed. However, the advantages of living in such close communion outweigh the drawbacks for most Amish people, evidenced both in the high rate of young people who choose to join the church of their parents and in the fact that even those who do not join generally remain in the area, close to family and neighbors (often as members of Mennonite churches).

Shared religious commitments, strong extended families, and locally based economies all help make Amish communities socially and culturally sustainable, meaning they endure over time without losing core values. This capacity results from deliberate decisions intended to keep communities small and separated from the corrupting world outside. One of the most momentous of these decisions was the ban on ownership of motor vehicles instituted in the early 1900s. Donald Kraybill and Carl Bowman explain:

> The car was a symbol of modernity par excellence—automatic mobility, independence, individualism, power, a product of a highly centralized and specialized assembly line. Indeed, the assembly line, with its standardization and efficient productivity, provided a motif for modernity itself. The automobile would obliterate geographical boundaries, expand social horizons, and free individuals from local constraints. For progressives, the automobile was a striking achievement of the forces of modernity. Old Orders thought otherwise. In their minds, the car promised to unravel and fragment their tight-knit ethnic communities. In sum, for Old Orders, modernity was the Great Separator that threatened to pull their corporate life asunder.[18]

The ban on car ownership, one of the major points dividing the Old Orders from other Anabaptists, has contributed to Amish survival by strengthening their social cohesiveness and cultural isolation. Although it originated over concerns about religion and community, the prohibition on motor vehicles has had other far-reaching consequences, including less environmentally damaging ways of living, traveling, and farming. For example, farms stay small because there are limits to what a family can farm with horse and human power. More positively, Amish farmer and writer David Kline asserts that the horse saved the Amish: "If we Amish in northeastern Ohio look at our community and all its small villages that are thriving—Berlin, Mount Hope, Charm, Farmerstown, Fredericksburg, Kidron—in spite of a Wal-Mart ten miles away, we can see it is because of the horse. Seldom do we travel farther than five or six miles to a small town to do our business. Some may go to Wal-Mart, but not on a weekly basis. The standardbred horse helps us, even if we think globally, to act locally."[19] Not only has the dependence on horses "restricted unlimited expansion," Kline adds, "but horses are ideally suited to family life." Keeping farms small means keeping them to a size that one family can maintain. Further, farmers working with horses must stop plowing or threshing to let the teams rest, which gives them time to eat lunch with their family. "And because God didn't create the horse with headlights, we don't work nights."[20]

While reliance on horsepower and other traditional practices provides a certain stability, the Amish have faced significant changes in their conditions of life, especially since World War II. Most communities remain rooted in agriculture, although the percentage of families that earn their living by farming has fallen significantly in recent decades. The decline is due especially to the decreasing availability and increasing cost of farmland. Rising land prices, particularly in Lancaster County, Pennsylvania, have encouraged a few Amish farmers to sell land and begin farming elsewhere, prompting the formation of new church districts in states such as North Carolina. Tourism in some established Amish communities, especially in Lancaster County, has also raised land prices and spurred migration to less crowded sites. Thus, nonfarming occupations have increased in most Amish settlements, raising both economic and social challenges.

Agriculture

Despite recent changes, agriculture remains both a major way of making a living and a key element of collective identity for the Amish throughout North America. This continues a tradition begun in Europe, when persecuted Anabaptists fled to inaccessible rural areas in the seventeenth and eighteenth centuries. Legally, Anabaptists were prohibited from owning land, so most worked as tenant farmers for large landowners. The environmental pressures of farming on hilly, infertile land encouraged them to try novel methods of raising livestock, fertilizing, clearing land, and rotating and diversifying crops. Because leases passed from parents to children, families could improve land over long periods of time.[21] Agricultural innovation and success were reinforced and spread by frequent contact among scattered Anabaptist congregations. Church elders and members visiting other congregations communicated new practices, such as methods of fertilizing and feeding cattle, which had proved successful in another region. This fruitful contact was combined with separation from non-Anabaptist peasants. Anabaptist families provided their own labor, an independence, Jean Séguy writes, "further paralleled by an apparently almost complete autonomy of subsistence. Not only the food consumed by the Anabaptists, but also their clothing, their household linens, etc. came from their own hands as well. The Mennonite farm was an entity, as independent as possible, closed in upon itself."[22]

Preserving this autonomy requires constant hard work, thrift, and cooperation within the family and the larger community. Contemporary Amish farmers value the ability of their family and community to provide for themselves without depending on the outside world. This is one reason for the Amish rejection of electricity from public lines, which is seen as an "umbilical cord" to the world. Amish farms continue to rely heavily on family labor, and when additional workers are needed, farmers look to neighboring Amish families. This labor sharing is sometimes formalized, as in "rings" consisting of several neighboring families who help each other in jobs requiring many hands, such as threshing and silo filling. Even more common is spontaneous aid, especially in times of need such as illness and disaster. This aid may be offered by a single neighbor or, as in the case of barn raisings, by hundreds of Amish men and women from a number of church districts.

Today, both the farming methods and the social context of Amish agriculture remain relatively stable despite major changes in agriculture in North America. In the decades since World War II in the United States "farmers have become increasingly dependent on high inputs of commercial fertilizer, pesticides, heavy machinery and fossil fuel. . . . During this same time period, farm numbers have fallen sharply and average farm size has increased."[23] The causes of these changes include increased mechanization, public policies that favor certain farming methods and crops, and growing corporate ownership of farmland. Shifts in agriculture have transformed rural communities and small towns, with the loss of small businesses such as banks, grocery stores, and farm equipment dealers and the emigration of thousands of people.

Although not untouched by changes in farming and rural life, the Amish have largely defied these trends. The severe farm crisis of the 1980s "never hit Amish farmers," a recent article asserts.[24] A study of Amish farms in Iowa, one of the states hardest hit by overall changes in agriculture as well as by the recent farm crisis, shows a dramatic contrast between Amish and non-Amish farms. In Buchanan County, center of the second-largest Amish community in Iowa, only two Amish farms, out of about 180 total in the county, were sold during the years of the farm crisis. This represents "an incredible survival rate" in contrast to the numerous foreclosures of non-Amish farms in the same county.[25] The study concludes:

> In the midst of enormous economic instability, growing environmental dilemmas, and social upheaval (thousands of Iowa residents moving out of the state, countless farmers being forced out of farming and rural communities faced with decay), the Old Order Amish farmers and their communities were thriving. This type of success—keeping farm families on the farm, building the fertility of the soil for the benefit of future generations and earning a living on small holdings—was a reality often dismissed as irrelevant in an era when agricultural leaders believed a farmer must "get big or get out." The Amish example defied this popular belief and demonstrated a viable alternative.[26]

Amish farmers' economic resiliency rests on their rejection of the logic of mainstream agriculture: their farms are much smaller than average, they do not try to expand in size, they do not accept government subsidies, they reject many new technologies, and they use little fossil fuel. Their profits are higher per acre and per animal than conventional farmers, and their debts and expenses are much lower.[27] Gene Logsdon summarizes: "The fact is that Amish farms have mostly survived, if not thrived, right on through the current economic malaise despite the fact that, by the standards of the technocrats, small farms are supposed to be on the way out."[28] Or, in the words of another observer, "The survival of low-tech Amish farms in a high-tech society is significant; it cannot be dismissed as totally irrelevant. The success of Amish agriculture is a reality."[29]

Are Amish Farms and Communities Sustainable?

This success has encouraged environmentalists and others to explore the social, technological, and ecological dimensions of Amish agriculture. In this section, I explore the notion of Amish sustainability in economic, environmental, and social terms. To provide more detail, I illustrate some of the points with reference to an Amish farm in Holmes County, Ohio, site of the world's largest Amish community. The farm is owned by David Kline, who in addition to raising dairy cows is the author of two books and numerous essays, most on agrarian and environmental themes. He has become, as one interviewer points out, "somewhat of a poster child for environmentalists noting the sustainability of Amish farming practices."[30] Despite his unusual public profile, Kline is in most respects a typical Amish farmer. He and his wife, Elsie Kline, live on the farm on which David grew up, among extended family, and four of their five children farm with their own families within walking distance. The Kline family farm encompasses 123 acres, of which about seventy-five acres are tillable, twenty-nine are in permanent pasture, ten are forested, five are in orchard and gardens, and four are occupied by buildings. Most of their income comes from their small herd of dairy cows. Their farm and their community embody many of the environmental, economic, social, and religious factors that make Amish farming distinctive.

Environmental Sustainability

The environmental advantages of Amish agriculture begin with an extremely efficient use of energy. A 1977 study comparing the energy budgets of Amish and non-Amish farms in three states concluded that despite regional variation, overall the Amish farms had much better energy ratios of inputs to outputs.[31] One of the authors, Peter Craumer, conducted a more detailed study of the energy efficiency of dairy farms in two Amish settlements, conservative "Nebraska" Amish and more liberal "Renno" Amish, and non-Amish farms in Mifflin County, Pennsylvania. (The chief relevant difference between these two groups is that unlike the Nebraska Amish, Renno Amish permit diesel-powered cooling equipment and thus can meet standards for Grade A milk.) Craumer found that "the energy needed to produce a kg of milk . . . varies little between the Nebraska and the Renno A[mish] dairy farms, but approximately twice as much energy is required to produce a kg of milk on the smallest modern farms as on the Amish farms. Even the most efficient modern farms . . . require 65% more energy per kg of milk than these Rennos."[32] The greater energy efficiency of Amish dairy farms, Craumer found, stemmed not only from the use of draft animals and the lack of electricity but also from specific agricultural practices such as crop rotation, greater use of manure, and heavier reliance on hand cultivation and human labor. Even if they were to adopt tractors, he concluded, the Renno Amish would still use energy more efficiently than conventional farmers.

Because of their energy efficiency and limited use of nonrenewable resources, Amish farms produce less waste and contamination of air, soil, and water than do conventional farms. The advantages, however, extend beyond the natural environment, as avoidance of fossil fuels makes the Amish more self-sufficient and less vulnerable to national and global crises. While conventional agriculture depends on fossil fuels not only for transportation and machinery but also for fertilizer and pesticides, Amish farmers provide a model of energy independence that is especially relevant today, as our excessive use of nonrenewable energy exacerbates problems of urban sprawl, global warming, illnesses such as asthma, and international political conflicts. The Amish practice and preserve "a way of agriculture that may be needed when fuel runs out," as David Kline points out.[33]

In addition to efficient use of nonrenewable energy, other traditional Amish farming practices contribute to a relatively low environmental impact. Most Amish farmers use some commercial fertilizers and chemical herbicides, but in much lower quantities than conventional farmers, because most of their fertilizer comes from animal and green manures, and weed control is achieved mainly by crop rotation, cultivation, and crop diversity. One study found that when Ohio Amish farmers did use petrochemical fertilizer, they applied about half the recommended dosage, and they rarely used soil insecticides.[34]

In the conservation of topsoil, one of the most urgent problems facing farmers, especially in the Midwest, Amish farms also fare better than conventional farms. Most soil conservation experts today advocate no-till methods to conserve topsoil. In no-till agriculture, "soil disturbance is limited to the opening of small slots into which seeds are dropped. Crop residues are left on the soil surfaces, and weed control is accomplished with the use of herbicides."[35] In many cases, no-till crop production reduces soil erosion, but it requires significantly more herbicide than traditional cultivation. Traditional Amish farming involves intensive plowing, which in theory causes serious loss of topsoil year after year. In the mid-1980s, the Soil Conservation Service in Holmes County used the standard estimating tool, the Universal Soil Loss Equation (USLE), to estimate that Amish farms ought to be losing seven to fifteen tons of top soil per acre each year. Because many of the Amish farms have been under tillage for as many as 150 years, they have theoretically lost fifteen inches of topsoil. Thus, a researcher concluded, "These farms should have no topsoil left. This is obviously not the case." Without topsoil, farms become unproductive and require intensive applications of fertilizer to produce crops. However, "these Amish farms are very productive and continue to provide a substantial income to the families who live on them." Soil analyses found that not only did Amish farms have sufficient quantity of topsoil, but the soil was of excellent quality.[36]

The huge gap between estimates based on the USLE and the reality of soil on Amish farms stems from the analysts' lack of knowledge about traditional Amish farming and its effects on the soil. In Amish agriculture, "horse hooves replace tractor tires as compaction-generating forces. Velocity of tillage is reduced, which in turn reduces the force applied in displacing soil, the depth of tillage, and the extent to which residues are buried. Manure mixed with straw, and a 4-year rotation incorporating 2 continuous years of grass/legume hay are used instead of N[itrogen] fertilizers. Crop rotation and cultivation largely eliminate the need for chemical pesticides and keep the soil covered for all but 3 months in 4 years."[37] This means that Amish farms tilled with horse-drawn plows do not lose soil at anything approaching the rates of loss in fields that are conventionally tilled with large tractors and then planted with the same crop year after year. To the contrary, Amish farmers generally improve the soil, often taking exhausted farmland and, with intensive manuring and crop rotation, building up its fertility and other desirable qualities, such as capacity to hold water.

The soil erosion studies point to the inadequacy of conventional measures to evaluate Amish agriculture and perhaps other alternatives to the mainstream. They underline, further, the error of assuming that Amish farmers blindly continue practices that modern ways have rendered obsolete. Traditional Amish horse plowing, it turns out, is better for the soil than new no-till methods. Other studies have pointed to the viability, and even the cutting-edge quality, of other practices common among Amish farmers since the eighteenth century, such as crop rotation, the use of animal and green manures, and mixing production among diverse plant and animal species.

All these principles are evident on the Kline farm. The family practices a regular rotation between crops that use nitrogen, such as corn, and crops that fix nitrogen (produce it and leave it in the soil), such as legumes and hay. The Klines' current rotation is corn-oats-hay-hay, all raised mainly to feed their own animals. In some years, the rotation also includes wheat. The farm also has an orchard, beehives, chickens for eggs and meat, and a large vegetable garden. The garden, like their milk, is certified organic, and they usually sell garden shares during the growing season through a community-supported agriculture (CSA) program. Although few Amish farmers have joined the Klines in obtaining organic certification, most avoid the heavy dependence on chemical pesticides necessary in conventional and no-till agriculture, which kill songbirds and beneficial insects. Other common wildlife-friendly practices include leaving hedgerows, delaying harvests or plowing until birds have finished nesting, and placing bird boxes. All these are evident in the Klines' fields.

Many researchers argue that environmentally sustainable agriculture will have to combine new ideas and technologies with time-tested practices. This is standard among the Amish, who do not hesitate to learn about and sometimes apply more recent innovations. Amish craftsmen have created horse-drawn mechanisms as sophisticated as those that conventional farmers pull with tractors. At the same time, Amish skepticism about new technology means that innovations are not adopted simply because they are new but only when they have been shown to work better than time-tested models. Thus, the same farmer may use both a hundred-year-old hand or horse-drawn plow and a brand new horse-drawn thresher. Some Amish farmers also use wind or solar power. In some districts, Amish producers have adopted diesel-powered generators to power refrigerators due to government rules on cooling, storing, and transporting commercially sold milk. In sum, "the Amish are not opposed to incorporating new ways of farming which have stood the test of time and increase the economic self sufficiency of their families and communities without jeopardizing their religion. . . . Amish agriculture is a blend of old practices with new ideas."[38]

Amish farms provide a unique opportunity to study the results of sustainable practices over time. An Ohio study concluded, "Because the Amish have such a long history of experience as designers and practitioners of low-input sustainable agriculture, researchers and non-Amish practitioners of sustainable agriculture could learn a great deal from Amish farmers; not only in terms of determining what types of sustainable systems are economically and environmentally viable, but also in terms of understanding why they work." Amish farms that have been successful over many decades provide opportunities to examine the ecological, technological, and social processes that contribute to sustainability, which newly established experimental farms cannot offer.[39] Or, as another study puts it, "Low-input, sustainable agriculture is not new. Neither is it without precedent. Instead of reinventing the wheel, opportunities exist to examine the effects of alternative practices on farms that have already been using them."[40]

At the same time, while appreciating the unique strengths of Amish agriculture, we should not assume that Amish farming practices are ecologically without sin. A 1997 study of Amish farmers in St. Lawrence County, New York, notes that although there are real reasons to view Amish farming as a model for sustainable agriculture, at least some Amish farms are ecologically questionable. The researchers found, for example, a heavier reliance on chemical pesticides and fertilizers than is common among Amish farmers, probably due to specific characteristics of the Upstate New York community studied, such as its newness and the poor condition of soils that Amish farmers are reclaiming.[41] The differences among Amish communities, the relative scarcity of systematic studies, and the wide variations in methodologies and samples in the existing studies all suggest caution in generalizing about specific aspects of

Amish agriculture. Most researchers, however, agree on the socially and eco-logically sustainable aspects of certain distinctive traits of Amish farms: small scale, crop rotation, diversity of crops and animals, low reliance on fossil fuels, intensive use of manure, and the involvement of family and community.

This list raises the question of which, if any, elements of traditional Amish farming might be relevant to modern agriculture in North America and else-where. Craumer's study of the energy efficiency of Amish dairy farms offers some suggestions about the significance of Amish farming as a model for other agricultural systems. He does not find the more conservative Nebraska Amish system, which prohibits tractors, diesel equipment, and milking machines, very useful as a model for improving the efficiency of modern agriculture, although it might be helpful as a model for low-energy systems of agriculture in developing countries, where human and animal labor still predominates. Craumer points out that the more liberal Renno Amish dairy farms, which permit the use of tractors for pulling heavy loads on the farm but not in fields and which allow diesel for milk cooling equipment and hot water heaters, achieve productivity equal to or greater than many modern dairy farms. "The major penalty paid by the Rennos for this greater energy efficiency is in their greater labor requirements: 1.5 times as much labor per kilogram of milk sold as compared with the 20–29 cow modern farms and 3.1 times as much labor as compared with the largest modern dairy farms." The adoption of the Renno system throughout Pennsylvania, he calculated in 1978, would require 44,500 more farm laborers to maintain the same milk output, with an energy savings of 378,780,000 liters of gasoline per year.[42]

We may question Craumer's characterization of an increase in the number of farm jobs as a "penalty." This assumption reflects an uncritical acceptance of the dominant assumption that less labor, especially less manual labor, is always better. Especially in light of high rural unemployment rates, it is far from self-evident that fewer farm jobs are better than more. The Amish, cer-tainly, view mechanization and consolidation of farms and the resultant decline in labor requirements as distinct disadvantages, which scatter families and encourage young people to move away from home or to seek factory and service jobs. Such work strikes most Amish people as less fulfilling, healthy, and in-teresting than labor on the family farm.

Economic Subsistence

Amish tradition and culture define success very differently from the dominant society. This may be the key to the economic sustainability and stability of Amish society. Amish people understand success as the ability to work at home, spend time with their family, cooperate with neighbors and relatives, produce much of their own food, and have time for religious and community events. They do not pursue growth and ever higher profits as ends in themselves, and they reject expansion in farm or shop size when it contradicts other values. These principles keep Amish farms and businesses small, but they also limit debt and help to weather economic downturns such as the farm crisis of the 1980s.

Unlike most conventional farms today, but like the vast majority of farms in the United States and elsewhere prior to World War II, Amish farms are largely self-sufficient. This is true for the Klines, who produce most of the food for their family and their animals. Their fertilizer comes from their animals, and firewood comes from the woodlots on their property. The Amish strive for and largely achieve independence from mainstream society's food production and distribution networks and energy grid, as well as its insurance and social security programs and educational institutions. Many of the items they do not produce, or produce in insufficient quantity, they can borrow, buy, or barter from neighbors. This interdependence within the Amish community is what enables members to live in relative independence from the larger society; not individualism but a close-knit community undergirds their autonomy. Their security comes not only "in working beyond the grips of the money economy," as Kline puts it, but also in accepting their embeddedness within the local community.[43]

Like most Amish farmers, the Klines achieve a high per acre and per cow rate of profit, which stems less from greater per cow milk production than from lower spending on feed, medical care, machinery, and maintenance. Each year the family sells about 350,000 pounds of milk to a local business, making a profit of about $15,000 from their thirty to thirty-five Jersey cows, approximately double the $200 to $300 annual per cow profit common on industrial farms.[44] Their cows are completely grass-fed in season and periodically moved to new pasture for rotation. The only expense related to the cows is the small amount spent cleaning their udders. The Klines do not hire outside help but rely on extended family, friends, and neighbors to help with heavy farm labor and to loan machines, share seeds and manure, and otherwise support each other.

The economic stability of Amish communities also comes deeply in-grained values of frugality and thrift, which lead farmers, homemakers, and artisans to recycle, to make their own repairs when possible, and to use all sorts of resources wisely. (The local newspaper in Holmes County is *The Bargain Hunter*.) In addition, because the Amish do not accept government subsidies, they do not have to follow policies that encourage monocropping, constant expansion, and expensive machinery, among the major reasons that so many conventional farmers went bankrupt during the 1980s. Once again, by refusing the temptations of quick profit and expansion, the Amish largely avoid the risks of debt, bankruptcy, and foreclosure that have marked so many rural communities in the United States.

Social Justice

Sustainability involves not only environmental considerations but also social welfare and justice. I define social justice in relation to a society's ability to meet the needs of all members, reflected in access to land and other resources and care for the least well-off, including provision of social services such as health care, education, and housing. Success in these areas can be partly measured in quality of life indicators such as rates of infant mortality, literacy, access to shelter and potable water, and nutrition, though they also depend on relatively egalitarian distribution of both benefits and burdens. Widespread participation in decision-making processes is also important. Societies that repress or exclude segments of their population cannot be considered sustainable, regardless of their members' wealth or health. Economic subsistence is also crucial. Especially in the context of economic globalization, the question of how to combine sustainability with economic security becomes ever more pressing.

Amish communities take care of needy members in a variety of ways. The principle of mutual aid is embodied in informal practices, such as bringing food to a family with a new baby and helping harvest the hay of a farmer who is injured. In cases of serious need, the deacon ensures that community resources are mobilized, most famously in barn raisings to replace buildings lost in fires but also when a head of household is unable to farm or work due to illness or injury. Other forms of aid include interpersonal loans, labor exchanges, and sharing of machinery, animals, and equipment. Families take care of older and disabled members at home, never in institutions. Elderly people usually live in *dawdy* (grandparent) houses adjacent to the main farmhouses and are cared for by their children and grandchildren as well as by neighbors and church leaders. Amish Ordnungs prohibit both public insurance such as social security and private insurance policies because these would reduce members' mutual dependence. For members, the community is its own insurance, and in times of need no one falls through the cracks.

Amish settlements are not economically homogeneous, but they generally exhibit much less inequality than the larger society. Mutual aid, along with deep-rooted values of thrift and industriousness, help ensure that no one lives in absolute poverty or fails to have basic needs met. Other Amish principles prevent the emergence of huge gaps in wealth among members, including reluctance to make farms or other economic enterprises very large, to move away, to go into debt, or to put neighbors out of business. Parents' responsibility to help their children get started, preferably on a farm, and adult children's responsibility to care for elderly parents also prevent the accumulation of excessive wealth. More generally, "the community has an informal claim on a wealthy Amishman's resources. He is also protected from an all-out competition with other well-to-do families in purchasing and displaying the usual array of material status symbols. Prestige is also culturally tied in to the welfare of the community so that personal reputation can only reach fulfillment in the service of the kin and church community. The religious support for both cultural practices is strong teaching against high mindedness or pride and a conscious cultivation of the virtue of humility."[45]

Amish church districts are relatively egalitarian, due in part to the lack of a centralized bureaucracy, the small size of congregations, and the absence of church buildings. The Amish avoid hierarchy within the community by ensuring that all leaders, including the bishop, are chosen by lot, none are paid, and all have to make their own living. Although the bishop ultimately makes decisions on important issues, he does so only after all members, male and female, have voiced their opinions. Restrictions on the use of telephones and other media, plus the fact that church district members all live near each other, ensure that most communication is direct and face-to-face. This also fosters widespread participation and helps members hold leaders accountable.

Still, Amish communities are not free of inequalities, tensions, or conflicts. Although Amish women have an equal voice in church decisions, they cannot become ministers, and the division of labor tends to be traditionally patriarchal. Women have primary responsibility for child care, household maintenance, and kitchen gardens, whereas men work primarily in fields and animal care, on farms, or in workshops or factories. However, wives, sisters, and daughters often participate in plowing, harvest, and animal care. Elsie Kline, for example, has primary responsibility for the family's vegetable garden, including marketing shares through a CSA program. Single women also frequently work outside the home as teachers or in shops or factories.

The ban and shunning can also generate pressure to conform and intolerance of individual differences. Although Amish society may strike outsiders as harsh and inflexible, it has institutionalized a period of experimentation, *Rumspringa*, during which women and men in their teens or early twenties can experience aspects of the dominant culture: they can own cars, go to dances and movies, and work off the farm. Because church membership is voluntary, young people must be certain about their commitment and aware of the world they are rejecting before joining the church. These are practical consequences of the Anabaptist principle of adult baptism. Further, Amish-born people who decide not to be baptized remain connected to their family. In fact, Amish-born adults who were never baptized, and even those who leave after baptism, visit their parents about as often as do their Amish siblings.[46]

The Pursuit of Happiness

The sustainability of Amish farms and communities makes sense only in light of Amish values and goals. In particular, it is important to understand the differences between the Amish definition of success and that of mainstream

U.S. culture. "Amish economic aspirations," according to one scholar, "include the ability to provide food, clothing and shelter for a large family, sufficient profitability to service debt and taxes on the land and an excess to help others in time of need, including economic assistance for the next generation."[47] These and other, intangible goals, such as having neighbors who farm well, educating children in the tradition, having adult children live and farm nearby, providing food for the family, and living in a supportive, like-minded community, rank much higher than individual pursuit of profit.

Some see the heavy labor requirements of Amish agriculture as a drawback, yet for many Amish this is one of its major benefits. Their ideal communities consist of many small farms on which family members and neighbors can find useful and satisfying occupations while working where they live and living near each other. Having bigger farms would mean losing both neighbors who farm and the opportunity for adult children to continue farming. The dominant culture in the United States, including those practicing conventional agriculture, assumes without question that increasing efficiency, in terms of per person production, is always good. Amish people begin with different assumptions. They like the fact, as Stephen Stoll puts it, that they need every available family member, and often neighbors as well, to harvest their crops. "The work of the farm is the life of the family, so it must always embrace rest and pleasure." The principle behind this policy is that "anything that undermines their ability to cohere as a community of neighbors and linked families, anything that isolates them in their work or places production for profit ahead of the collective process, is prohibited."[48] This is not just an abstract value but an embedded practice with concrete consequences for work, family, and community life.

Successful and respected farmers are not just those whose land and animals produce well but, above all, those who help their neighbors and raise their children in the tradition—in sum, those who place adherence to the Ordnung and community well-being over private interest. Amish farmers also appreciate the relative independence and flexibility that their occupation makes possible, as Amish farmers in Illinois told interviewers: "First and foremost [among rewards] is the relaxation of being your own boss. . . . The change in seasons give[s] change to your life. In a factory [you have] the same thing day after day. . . . [On the farm] you can come and go as you like to. . . . We can take a day off if we want to for funerals, weddings. You don't have to ask the boss. You can go to help your neighbor . . . [or] spend time with your family."[49]

These values contrast sharply with the idea that success can be calculated in terms of monetary profit. Amish culture does not encourage ever higher levels of economic and social rewards but imposes clear limits on the pursuit of material goals. These constraints are not so rigid as to stifle all variation in wealth and social status in Amish society, and some families have greater economic resources than others. Few, however, fail to meet their basic needs, and, as Stoltzfus puts it, "The Amish dream is attainable for a much higher pro-portion of its dreamers than is the American dream."[50]

This poses the question of which model is more utopian: the Amish Ge-meinde or the American dream of affluence, freedom from want, and endless consumption, which so few people actually achieve. When it is attained, this material success not only fails to buy happiness but also demands excessive consumption of natural resources and habitats and frequently relies on the exploitation of poorly paid and treated workers in the United States or overseas who produce and sell what is consumed. Mainstream observers often dismiss the Amish as naïve idealists, unable to face the real world. However, their expectations are more realistic in their context than those of most North Amer-icans, and their social institutions are more able to help them realize their dreams.

A Model of Sustainability?

Amish agriculture makes sense and, in fact, is possible only in the framework of distinctive Amish approaches to family relationships, gender roles, educa-tion, mass media, entertainment, and transportation, as well as farming prac-tices. This kind of community cannot be reproduced easily, and many elements of Amish agriculture could not be sustained outside of the larger Amish cul-tural and geographic context. The Amish model of small-scale, diversified, horse-powered farming could not succeed, for example, without close neigh-bors who have the skills, time, and willingness to cooperate, without large families to provide labor, and without the fertile soils of their midwestern farms. And the Amish can rely on horse-drawn transportation only because most of them work at home or very close by, which is not the case for most North Americans.

Amish lifeways are sustained not only by a supportive community but also by government accommodations, such as their exemptions from social security and compulsory education. While these laws help enable the Amish to live as they choose, other laws and policies make it hard for non-Amish people to emulate sustainable dimensions of their agricultural and social practices. Cre-ating more sustainable societies will require knowledge of and changes in the ways laws, policies, and institutions affect styles of community interaction and resource use and thus the ways people can live their values. Current U.S. agricultural policies, for example, subsidize monocrop planting and the heavy use of chemical inputs. They rarely support and sometimes penalize farmers who seek alternatives. Beyond agriculture, laws, economic subsidies, and re-gional planning policies encourage a heavy reliance on automobiles and make alternatives such as bicycling, walking, and using public transportation difficult in many areas. In sum, just as laws and social structures enable the Amish to live and work sustainably, laws and structures encourage most North Americans to live and work in ways that are socially and environmentally destructive.

While policies and infrastructures are crucial for sustainability, so are values, attitudes, and worldviews. The success and stability of Amish farms, for example, depend on the willingness of Amish men, women, and children to live frugally, to do a great deal of manual labor, and to end formal education after eighth grade. Cultures that place a high value on individual achievement or material accumulation or that associate manual labor with low social status will hesitate to adopt Amish models of farming, regardless of their proven social and environmental advantages. Further, acceptance of particular agricultural and labor practices rests on Amish religious values, which are enculturated throughout the life of every member by means of frequently repeated historical and biblical narratives, hymns, sermons, and everyday experiences. Non-Amish values, including the American dream of individual success and material consumption, are similarly embedded in every aspect of mainstream culture, legitimizing and reinforcing dominant institutions and laws.

Transformations of structures and of values are thus intimately linked. It is impossible to achieve one without the other, and probably both kinds of change must take place at the same time. Simply knowing about the advantages of alternative models, in other words, will not ensure their successful or widespread adoption in the absence of larger cultural, religious, economic, and political transformations. Good ideas have to become, somehow, embedded practices. Thus, it is far from clear to what extent Amish social, economic, and agricultural practices, regardless of their sustainability, can be replicated in other contexts.

On the other hand, cultures do change constantly, and many Amish practices that are socially and environmentally sounder than the usual way of doing things can be effectively adopted by non-Amish people and communities. In agriculture, new practices are adopted or rejected not only because of policies, habits, and values but also due to the climate, rainfall, type of soil, and terrain of the region in which farms are located. For example, in less fertile areas, it is often necessary to farm larger areas to make a living, so the small scale dictated by horse-drawn equipment and family labor may not work. Here the Hutterites offer an interesting case. While sharing many characteristics with other Old Order Anabaptists, such as plain clothing, they permit the use of modern technology and transportation, in no small part because they live in much less fertile regions in the northern Great Plains (the Dakotas and Saskatchewan), where the community can support itself only by farming on a much larger scale than that of the Amish and Old Order Mennonites working the rich soils of Pennsylvania and Ohio.

Even farmers who must farm on a larger scale or who are not willing to give up their tractors for draft horses can benefit from some Amish practices. For example, they can save large amounts of energy by replacing petroleum-based fertilizers with crop rotation and use of green and animal manures. With favorable soils and climates, farmers may be able to reduce the size of their operations (and of their debts) and still make a living by concentrating on high-value products such as organic produce, herbs, flowers, and certain animal products, such as wool, milk, and eggs. If federal and state subsidy programs were changed to reward alternative agricultural practices, more farmers could care for a diverse array of animals and plants, thus avoiding the economic vulnerability and ecological damage caused by reliance on a single crop.

What about off the farm? A number of Amish practices not directly concerned with agriculture are also environmentally sustainable. Most significant are the bans on automobile ownership and public utility lines. These rules make Amish consumption of fossil fuels, and thus their contribution to air pollution and global warming, far lower than that of other North Americans. Few modern families would willingly give up their cars, especially in current suburban and rural settings. This might change, however, if we transformed our communities to make alternative transportation convenient, feasible, and attractive. Perhaps even fewer families would be willing to cut their link to energy grids, but again this could change if alternative energy sources, especially solar power, were more accessible. This could occur if people demanded it and politicians supported it. The problem is one of political will rather than technology.

Despite the limitations to what might enter mainstream culture, we can look even now to the Amish for practical ways that individuals, families, and neighborhoods can reduce energy consumption: outdoor clothes drying, greater use of bicycles and walking for local transportation, and carpooling for longer distances. (Amish families sometimes rent cars or vans and hire drivers to travel together to special events.) Other elements of Amish life that reduce ecological impact include recycling and reusing many items, preparing food at home, sharing such items as machinery and books among households, and patronizing local businesses and producers. Even nonfarming Amish families usually have sizable gardens, which enables them to grow food more ecologically and economically. Many other families, even in cities, can produce some of their own food this way, or they can purchase locally grown food through CSAs and farmers' markets, helping to reduce the huge amount of fossil fuels used to move food to large supermarkets, often across continents or even hemispheres. (The average mouthful of food in the United States travels 1,300 miles before it is eaten.)[51]

Although these practices yield clear ecological benefits, their primary intent for the Amish is not to protect the environment but to adhere to their religious vision and to preserve their communities. Even outside this religious and social context, however, people can reflect on the potential consequences, to the environment and the larger community as well as to their own household, of adopting new technologies and practices and challenge the conventional assumption that anything bigger, newer, faster, or more powerful must automatically be better. A contributor to the Amish magazine *Family Life* explained, "We ought to take a critical look before accepting every new invention that comes along. In the long run, how will it affect the family farm? Will it help to make more use of horsepower and family labor on the farm? Will it encourage working together as a family unit and as a community, to help each other? Or will we have so much money invested in expensive equipment that it may become necessary to take a job off the farm to pay for it?"[52] Mainstream culture rarely if ever poses such questions.

Even cautious and frugal Amish farmers presently face challenges to their way of life. High population growth has combined with suburban sprawl and tourism to raise land prices in Amish areas, especially in Lancaster County, Pennsylvania, making it difficult for many young Amish families to purchase their own farms. This problem was evident even twenty years ago, when a majority of Amish men interviewed said that the biggest problems facing young Amish men wanting to enter farming were cost and scarcity of land. One man said, "It used to be the case that a young man could buy a farm for a few thousand dollars and have his head above water. Now you can't even find a farm if you want to buy one. Before, if you wanted a farm in a certain area and if you were willing to wait for a few years, you would be able to buy one."[53]

Holmes County has witnessed a significant shift away from farming. In 1999, only 20 percent of Amish men in Holmes County were full-time farmers; most worked at least part time in construction, factories, or small businesses or shops.[54] Like many Amish farmers, David Kline laments the move of Amish families away from the farm into town, where they must buy their food rather than growing it.[55] He also worries about a related trend, the proliferation of large-scale agribusiness, in his region and elsewhere. "The mentality of corporate agriculture," he asserts, "is that they want cheap food no matter how many families or cultures will be disrupted. . . . We just operate in the shadow of agribusiness."[56]

Amish people have responded to the land shortage in various ways. Many couples, families, and whole communities have moved to areas where land is available at lower cost. Dozens of new Amish settlements have emerged in the past several decades outside the established areas in Ohio, Pennsylvania, and Indiana. Another common solution is for a father to subdivide land to make two farms out of one, which requires more intense cultivation (and perhaps some off-farm employment) to make a living. Growing numbers of Amish men, and some women, pursue full-time nonfarm employment as a temporary or permanent solution. Statistics vary from community to community, but in many settlements over half the men work in nonfarm occupations. Most of these work on or near their home, often making goods required by their neighbors, such as buggies, harnesses, or farm equipment, or providing services such as blacksmithing or milling lumber. This kind of work is less desirable than farming but still acceptable, especially if it enables the family to work together, does not involve much contact with outsiders, and is flexible enough to allow the worker to devote time to church and community events.

In these ways, many Amish families have shifted out of agriculture without violating the Ordnung or disrupting the community. Others, unable to make a living in home workshops or businesses, have sought work in factories. Factory work poses numerous problems, which are often summed up as "the lunch pail threat." First, factory work entails close, daily contact with non-Amish coworkers and thus unwanted exposure to worldly values and customs. Second, fathers who work far from home have less time to spend with their children and teach them traditional skills. Third, non-Amish factory owners often refuse the necessary time off for employees to attend weddings, help in barn raisings, and otherwise participate as full members of the community. For all these reasons, many Amish people fear that it will be very difficult, if not impossible, to maintain Amish values and customs working and living off the farm. As one Lancaster County man reflects, "That's our biggest problem, to keep our children on the farm. There's just no more room to grow. Lancaster County is my home. All the roots are here. Leaving would be like pulling a plant up by the roots. But I would do that, if that's what it takes, before we give up our faith. I would rather my children leave the county than see them work in a factory."[57]

Despite the challenges, predictions of the Old Orders' imminent demise have so far proven spectacularly wrong. They have grown numerically while continuing to thrive economically, to enculturate new generations, and to adhere to the core tenets of their faith. For all the changes, difficulties, and ambiguities they face, the Amish present probably the best North American proof that it is possible to live collectively by values that diverge in almost every respect from those of the mainstream. They also offer some unexpected lessons about just how this is possible. Sustaining local community, Amish experiences suggest, requires substantial participation in national and regional economies, a certain degree of political organization and allies, and cooperation from the state, along with neighborly support, careful farming, accumulated knowledge, and a great deal of hard work.

Even for people who have no intention of following any Amish practices, Old Order lives and values offer a deep and sweeping critique of mainstream society. Like other utopian communities, the Amish provide both a prophetic denunciation of the dominant culture and a radically different alternative.

2

Promised Land

Progressive Catholic Agrarians in Latin America

How Does God Want Us to Organize?

Efforts to create a utopian community in El Salvador, as in North American Amish settlements, emerge from deeply held and far-reaching religious convictions. In El Salvador, the major religious source is progressive Catholicism, a movement that emerged in the aftermath of the Second Vatican Council (1962–1965). The Council, a meeting of bishops called by Pope John XXIII, produced a wide range of documents addressing internal and external issues, including new, favorable interpretations of human rights, political democracy, and ecumenism. Especially important was the Council's final document, *Gaudium et spes* (Pastoral Constitution on the Church in the Modern World), which affirmed the importance of political equality for poor nations as well as poor individuals and urged the church to act in the world on behalf of the oppressed. The Council also called for changes in pastoral and liturgical practices and for increased lay participation in the church, which it defined not as the hierarchy but as the "people of God."

While setting a new tone and emphasis for the global church, Vatican II also encouraged regional and national churches to consider the Council's conclusions in light of their own circumstances. Following that suggestion, the Conference of Latin American Bishops (CELAM) met in 1968 in Medellín, Colombia, to reflect on the church in "the present-day transformation of Latin America in the light of the council."[1] The Medellín meeting inaugurated a new era for Latin American Catholicism in both ecclesial structure and the

church's social role. In key documents on peace and justice, the bishops de-
nounced the "institutionalized violence" of poverty throughout the region and
affirmed the church's commitment to work for the political and economic
transformations necessary to achieve the social justice demanded by the Bible
and the Catholic tradition. The Medellín documents also called for major
changes in pastoral work, including greater attention to poor neighborhoods
and rural villages and the development of new pastoral methods. In particular,
they promoted *comunidades eclesiales de base* (grassroots Christian communities, or CEBs), small groups of neighbors who met weekly to discuss biblical
readings and church documents in the light of their own experiences. CEBs,
the bishops asserted, were "the first and fundamental ecclesiastical nucleus,"[2]
the necessary foundationof a participatory and socially engaged church.

The Medellín meeting marked a turning point for Latin American Catholicism. Its advocacy of CEBs helped transform pastoral work in the region,
and its theological and ethical reflections gave major impetus to the theology
of liberation. Liberation theology, a term popularized by the Peruvian theologian and priest Gustavo Gutiérrez (a key advisor to the bishops at Medellín),
spread rapidly among Catholic (and a few Protestant) intellectuals and pastoral
agents throughout Latin America.[3] The new theology systematically analyzed
the biblical roots, doctrinal implications, and ethical imperatives of an emerging progressive Catholic vision of the church and the world. Liberation theology
and related pastoral and social programs received further support from CE-
LAM's 1979 conference in Puebla, Mexico. At Puebla the bishops first spoke
of the "preferential option for the poor,"[4] a term is now widely used in Catholic
theology and ethics to describe the church's special concern for the neediest
members of society.

Vatican II, the Medellín and Puebla meetings, and the theology of liberation all helped shift Latin American Catholicism significantly, though far from
unanimously, toward a new emphasis on social justice and popular participation. The practical consequences of these developments varied from country
to country and even from diocese to diocese. In El Salvador, the progressive
Catholic vision was embraced most fully in the Archdiocese of San Salvador,
under the leadership of Archbishop Luis Chávez y González, who served from
1939 to 1977. Chávez had promoted early reforms during the 1950s and early
1960s, and after Vatican II he issued pastoral letters applying the Council's
goals and concerns to the archdiocese. Because of Chávez's efforts, recalls a
Salvadoran diocesan priest, "The documents [of Vatican II and Medellín] were
like the air that we breathed at this time."[5] A group of young priests formed
in 1970 to discuss their work "within the historical movement forward of the
poor in our country."[6] That same year Chávez organized a National Pastoral
Week to discuss and strengthen pastoral innovations. In 1976 a second pastoral
week was held, this time limited to the archdiocese due to opposition from
conservative bishops in other dioceses. The aim of these various projects was

the formation of a "critical and liberating evangelization" along with concrete projects to combat "social sin."[7]

Two of the earliest and most influential projects took place in rural areas of the department of San Salvador. The first began in late 1968 in Suchitoto, when a young diocesan priest, José Inocencio Alas, returned to El Salvador after studying at the Latin American Pastoral Institute (IPLA) in Quito, Ecuador, a center for new pastoral and theological currents in Central and South America. Alas divided his parish into sectors, trained local lay leaders in two-month-long intensive courses (*cursillos*), and sent them back to the villages to help develop CEBs. In their courses and in discussions back in their villages, people focused on biblical themes that seemed to shed light on their own lives. Alas encouraged his parishioners to make connections between their faith and political and economic conditions—to challenge, for example, the assumption that infant deaths resulted from the will of God rather than inadequate health care. Increasingly, they criticized the ways that Salvadoran society and their own lives fell short of the way God wanted people to live. After reading the description of the early Christian community in the Acts of the Apostles, Alas recalls, some children "came and said to me, 'We have also studied the text of the Bible, and we think that here in our village it's not like it was in the first Christian communities, but we would like it to be that way.' I asked them why: 'Because our parents continue fighting over their things, my mother says the chickens are hers and my father says the cows are his; all this means that they are not working together, that they don't own things, collectively. We would like our parents to put their things together, own them collectively, and we would help them with it, too."[8]

A second early project was organized by four Jesuit priests who moved to the town of Aguilares in September 1972. They were led by Rutilio Grande, a native of El Paisnal, a village in the Aguilares parish. Like Alas, Grande had studied at the IPLA. He and the Jesuit team developed a plan for systematic development of CEBs based on extensive training of lay leaders. As in Suchitoto, a number of the men and women trained in these church programs went on to create agricultural cooperatives, advocate land reform, and participate in peasant movements.

Beyond the Archdiocese of San Salvador, which during this period encompassed the departments of San Salvador and Chalatenango, pastoral work proceeded less systematically. Even within the archdiocese, shortages of resources and pastoral agents made the development of CEBs challenging. Many of the principles behind the base communities, such as lay education and participation, biblical reflection, and community formation, were incorporated into other pastoral projects. The most important of these were peasant training centers (*centros de formación campesina*) or, more evocatively, "peasant universities" (*universidades campesinas*), developed by the archdiocese and several religious orders. The centers aimed to provide both religious and technical education in underserved rural areas. While similar projects existed in Guatemala and Nicaragua, the Salvadoran program was probably the most extensive. Each of the country's five dioceses sponsored a center, including the Centro Rural Itinerante, based in San Salvador, a traveling team that taught cursillos in rural parishes throughout the archdiocese.[9]

The peasant universities played a crucial role in the spread of progressive pastoral and social ideas throughout rural El Salvador. Although divisions among the bishops limited the centers' resources and ability to coordinate, El Salvador's compact scale facilitated contacts among pastoral agents and the diffusion of pastoral innovations. The centers shared materials and even personnel, as well as methods and an overarching goal, as described by a staff member from the center in El Castaño, San Miguel: "to develop leadership qualities in peasants, with knowledge of the value of mutual help and of cooperative work; to train men for change, ready to form part of parish and diocesan pastoral work, putting themselves at the service of bishops and priests. Briefly: the integral training of men for liberation."[10] The centers pursued these objectives through prebaptismal, prematrimonial, and child catechism; community development projects; and the purchase of land to help rural communities gain financial autonomy. Their defining activity, however, remained the cursillos, which enabled laypeople to learn about theology and social issues, to develop leadership skills, and to interact with other laypeople from their region.

The peasant universities constituted a supremely important means of spreading the ideas, practices, and goals of progressive Catholicism in El Salvador throughout the 1970s. Tens of thousands of peasants took courses, and thousands more came into contact with center graduates who worked as lay leaders in rural communities. "There was no catechist [in the region] who didn't pass through Centro Los Naranjos," recalls a priest who worked there.[11] Similar claims could be made for many of the other universidades campesinas. Together, the centers elaborated and extended an alternative vision of the realities and possibilities of life in El Salvador. They also helped bring together and mobilize a Christian peasant left that revolutionized not only the Salvadoran countryside but the entire nation.

Chalatenango

A number of important progressive Catholic initiatives took place in Chalatenango, a largely rural region whose poverty, low level of social services, and longstanding shortage of clergy made it ripe for new pastoral and social initiatives. Chalatenango was served by the Archdiocesan Centro Itinerante and also by the Foundation to Promote Cooperatives (Fundación para la Promoción de Cooperativas, FUNPROCOOP), founded by Archbishop Chávez in the late

1960s to apply the principles of progressive pastoral work to agricultural education. As one of its first tasks, FUNPROCOOP founded the Farm-School for
Agricultural Training (Granja-Escuela de Capacitación Agrícola, GECA) in
Nueva Concepción, Chalatenango. At the GECA, as at the diocesan training
centers, "peasants learned the principles of cooperativism and opened their
eyes to the reality of injustice and exploitation."[12] Chalatenango was also served
by priests and nuns working in individual parishes, such as a team of young
diocesan priests who arrived in Chalatenango in 1972. They held courses on
"Christian initiation," which addressed both the Bible and the "national reality,"
with a focus on rural issues. The various pastoral initiatives trained a number
of celebrators of the Word (lay preachers) and catechists (lay religious teachers),
who worked in villages and hamlets throughout Chalatenango, especially its
northeastern corner.

Progressive Catholic pastoral work transformed the lives of many peasants
in the region. Guadalupe Mejía, who lived near Las Vueltas, recalls that previously, "the people just suffered . . . and suffered. No one thought about how
to improve living conditions."[13] Pablo, a native of San Antonio los Ranchos,
recalls, "Before we began to organize, we felt pretty desperate, for there was
nobody to offer us any light, or the hope that we would be able to arrange
things so as to work better." New pastoral workers, however, encouraged projects such as establishment of an agricultural cooperative, explaining, "We'll
all work hard together in the regular way, but we're going to share what we
produce." Pablo's father joined and they gave him fertilizer and herbicide, "but
they had also given us the light, showing us how we would be able to get by."[14]

Magdalena, who lived in San Antonio los Ranchos in the 1970s, also highlights the break between old and new models of the church. Traditional religion, she says, preached that it was a blessing to be poor, that people who
suffered were fortunate because they would inherit the kingdom of heaven.
"In this sense our people were asleep, resigned to their situation." However,
she recalls, "there came a moment when the people realized that it was not
fair that we should go on living such a misery, that we had a right to live better.
For there were members of the Church who began to tell us that we should
prepare ourselves and work together so as to resolve our crises. There were
also other people who came from the city and tried to encourage people to
consolidate their efforts and work in a cooperative."[15] According to another
early participant, "We reflected on this question: How does God want us to
organize?"[16]

Cooperatives and other church-based projects in the early 1970s stimulated
interest in more organized peasant activism in San Antonio los Ranchos and
other communities in northeastern Chalatenango. Peasants felt, one participant explains, "that our people were growing stronger and more spirited every
day, and with the success of the cooperatives, that we would be able to overcome
our economic crises. Our people were overcoming so many obstacles, and we

felt that by joining together all the more in the cooperatives, and by opening up new sources of work through our own efforts, we would be able to move ever closer to the solution to our problems."[17] They took a major step forward in November 1974, when about seventy peasants met in the parish house in Chalatenango City to found the Union of Farm Workers (Unión de Trabajadores del Campo, UTC).[18] The founders of the UTC began with a vision of "our revolutionary goal: transform the unjust structures of the economy and political power." Inseparable from this political vision was a Christian foundation: "We were always motivated and inspired by the liberating message of the Word of God, which we integrated with revolutionary ideals." Other guiding principles included unity and solidarity, a rejection of selfishness, and a commitment to participatory democracy. The last principle entailed endless meetings as well as attention to political education, so that activists would be prepared to make informed decisions about their movement's direction. These values, which stemmed directly from the peasants' pastoral experience, help characterize El Salvador's peasant movement as a Catholic left, a new kind of movement in Latin America.[19]

El Salvador's other major peasant union also had explicitly Christian roots. The Federation of Christian Peasants (FECCAS), founded in 1964 with support from the Roman Catholic Church, the Christian Democratic Party, and the Latin American Social Christian Labor Organization. It began as a moderate response, based on Christian Democratic principles, to the intensifying crisis in El Salvador's rural areas. As the crisis intensified and Salvadoran society became more polarized during the late 1960s and 1970s, however, FECCAS shed its reformist aims for more revolutionary rhetoric and goals, largely under the influence of peasants who had been radicalized in base communities and other pastoral projects. FECCAS's increasingly militant tactics in the early and mid-1970s included land invasions and demonstrations to protest problems such as high prices for agricultural inputs, shortages of land, and unfair treatment from landlords and employers. In 1976, FECCAS and UTC created an alliance, called FECCAS-UTC, and in 1978 they merged to form the Federation of Farm Workers (Federación de Trabajadores del Campo), which then had between 10,000 and 12,000 members.[20]

Peasant activists adopted a wide range of political strategies, including land takeovers and demonstrations as well as innovative uses of popular theater and music. Significantly, the Christian peasant groups sought large-scale revolutionary change without losing sight of the "bread and butter" struggles (luchas reivindicativas) that dominated everyday life in the countryside, such as the payment of wages, proper meals for workers during harvests, better prices for fertilizer, and affordable land rentals.[21] This ability to combine visions of structural change with attention to immediate needs helps explain the success of the peasant movement. It addressed people's biggest dreams and also their everyday realities without opposing the two or demanding that one be sacrificed to the other. As Guadalupe Mejía explained, Chalatenango's peasant activists "thought not just of spiritual necessities, but also of material necessities, and how to help the people."[22] Activists were themselves peasants, keenly aware of the demands of everyday life as well as the aspirations awakened by church-based teachings and programs. In the words of another Chalatenango native, Pablo, the UTC "spoke very clearly to us, [and] it was true what they said. They told us that the problem for the rich was that they didn't want the poor people to wake up, so that they could keep us under their yoke. They told us that we had to wake up, but for that reason the rich did not want us to study, or to learn what they had been doing to us, because they wanted to keep us under their control."[23] After reading and discussing the Bible, Guadalupe Mejía adds, "we began to know what was the reality, and from there we opened our eyes more. . . . And from there, the repression began."[24]

By the late 1970s, the growing militancy of the campesino organizations made peasant leaders and activists targets of repression by the armed forces and paramilitary death squads (usually consisting of soldiers out of uniform). Many of the early peasant leaders in Chalatenango were killed, including UTC cofounder Justo Mejía. Mejía, who began as a catechist, was the chair of FECCAS-UTC in Chalatenango. On November 9, 1977, while attending a meeting in Dulce Nombre de María, he was picked up by the National Guard. The Guard tortured him, breaking his arms and gouging out his eyes before decapitating him and leaving him on a mountainside. "But the people love people like him," his widow, Guadalupe, recalls, and despite their fear, "after five days they started to look for him, and after seven days they found him." The National Guard arrived at his funeral and asked who knew the dead man. To save their own lives the mourners denied knowing him. "You have to make your heart hard," explains Guadalupe Mejía, who was left with nine children to support. "That's a sacrifice you have to make. But we know that it's through the gospel that we've discovered this, and this is where the persecution comes. Because they don't want you ever to know the reality."[25]

FECCAS-UTC joined with other opposition groups in the Revolutionary Coordinator of the Masses (Coordinadora Revolucionaria de las Masas) in January 1980. The unification of the left occasioned the largest demonstration in Salvadoran history, when 250,000 people, out of a population of less than 4 million, marched in downtown San Salvador. In December 1980, the country's five guerrilla armies united as the Farabundo Martí Front for National Liberation (Frente Farabundo Martí para la Liberación Nacional, FMLN).[26] The next month, the FMLN launched a major offensive which, although failing to bring the definitive victory the guerrillas sought, marked the beginning of an all-out civil war.

By the early 1980s, virtually every opposition movement in El Salvador was affiliated with one of the FMLN's member groups. The interlacing of political and military organization had begun during the 1970s, both as an organizing strategy and because activists could not survive, much less organize, without the protection provided by clandestine weapons, safe houses, and intelligence networks.[27] The repression was intense, as army units and death squads killed, captured, and "disappeared" thousands of peasant leaders, students, trade unionists, and Catholic lay leaders. The violence produced the images of El Salvador that the world knows best: soldiers machine-gunning unarmed demonstrators, terrified peasants being hauled away by helmeted National Guardsmen, and mutilated cadavers in body dumps. El Salvador in the 1980s, as anthropologist Leigh Binford writes, "stood in a metonymic relationship with murdered nuns, headless bodies, and mangled corpses."[28]

The government attacked civilians in part because they were easier targets than the well-trained and canny fighters of the FMLN, whom the U.S. government recognized as the most effective guerrillas in the hemisphere. Salvadoran government soldiers, many of whom had been forcibly recruited and who valued surviving more than winning the war, often avoided confrontations with the guerrillas.[29] A certain strategic logic also justified attacks on civilians. Salvadoran officials, along with their U.S. sponsors, recognized the left's strong popular backing. As an analyst for the Commission on U.S.–Latin American Relations wrote in April 1990, "Given the army's vast superiority in numbers and firepower, the FMLN could not survive—let alone operate as widely and freely as it does—without a substantial civilian base of support."[30] This meant that the only way to eliminate the guerrillas—the "fish"—would be to drain the "sea" in which they thrived: their dense network of ideological and logistical support. These webs of support compensated for the impossibility, in such a densely populated and deforested nation, of hiding in remote areas, as the Nicaraguan and Cuban insurgents had done. For the Salvadoran guerrillas, as FMLN leader Salvador Cayetano Carpio often claimed, "the people are our mountains."[31]

The government focused its attacks on the FMLN's zones of control, especially Chalatenango, the base for the largest guerrilla group, the Popular Liberation Forces (Fuerzas Populares para la Liberación, or FPL), and Morazán, headquarters of the People's Revolutionary Army (Ejército Revolucionario del Pueblo, or ERP). In a series of scorched-earth campaigns in the early 1980s, the government conducted aerial bombings, sent helicopters armed with artillery, and organized ground raids by army commandos, often with enormous civilian casualties. In Chalatenango, the army blocked every entrance to Chalatenango City and detained people traveling from the villages into town. Celso, a local resident, describes the situation vividly: "If someone was from Los Ranchos, they would put the finger on him and he would be killed, because our area was considered the most suspicious. They would simply drag him off the bus, take him away, and a moment later—bang, bang—he would be dead, he would never return to the village."[32]

As part of the effort to depopulate areas such as Chalatenango, soldiers traveled through villages killing "every living thing they found, whether animal or human," as Magdalena recalls. During this period, she continues, "the army was simply carrying out orders from the government to kill every living thing in our zone. For that reason, we could not afford to let them find us in any fixed place. We had to move around, because if they found us they would murder us, either with their planes or with the guns in their hands." In this situation, explains local resident Miguel Velásquez, "the only alternative left to us was to go to the hills, in fear, in poverty, in the rain. We lived off the things that others had left behind, knowing that they would now no longer be able to come back and get them." The civilians who remained in the war zones tried to plant corn and beans when possible and ate the few small animals that remained. Many people died from lack of proper food and medical care, and because, as Rigoberto, a Chalatenango native, remembers, they had "to endure the rains, without blankets, without clothing, without food. Our children were dying for lack of supplies. As we wandered in the mountains, we were always digging new graves and burying children."[33] Especially hard were the long marches called *guindas*, when groups or even whole villages would flee from soldiers, walking by night and hiding during the day. Entire communities often hid for days or weeks while the military occupied their villages. Knowing that the soldiers would kill anyone who was found, people went to desperate lengths to escape. Women continued walking immediately after giving birth, and in one of the most heart-rending consequences of the war, parents sometimes suffocated babies to prevent their cries from giving away the location of a group on the run.[34]

Government military operations and ongoing repression of political activists provoked a massive exodus of peasants from Chalatenango and other areas of guerrilla strength. By 1981 the war in the villages of northeastern Chalatenango was so intense, recalls Celso, that "I had to abandon all of my possessions and leave my house, leave everything I had worked for." People with some resources went to San Salvador and other cities, "but those of us who were poor, with neither money nor alternatives, we were obliged to look for other places and to flee the repression."[35] Most peasants fled to Honduran villages just across the border. Many were killed en route, including thousands in "hammer and anvil" operations in which Honduran soldiers fired from one side of the river dividing the two countries and Salvadoran troops fired from the other. During this period, countless villages were destroyed or abandoned, and the population in war-torn rural areas fell sharply. In 1971, Chalatenango province had 700,000 inhabitants. Ten years later the number had dropped to 350,000, and more left in the next several years.[36]

Local Popular Power

The few civilians who remained in the war zones concentrated around remote villages like Arcatao in Chalatenango and Perquín in Morazán, where guerrillas provided some protection from the government army. These civilians, often called the *masas clandestinas* (clandestine masses), struggled to make a living and keep their families intact. Their efforts to continue farming and to maintain community life in the *zonas de control* (zones of guerrilla control) faced constant threat of incursion by the Salvadoran army. In between guindas, air raids, and battles, peasants who remained in the war zones sought not only to survive but also to begin laying the foundations for a new kind of society, in accord with the values developed in the Catholic peasant movement. The most systematic and ambitious of these efforts was the construction of local popular power (*poder popular local*, PPL) in northeastern Chalatenango in the early 1980s. The PPLs emerged both because local residents desired a more permanent and organized way of life and because the increasingly effective FMLN was able to reduce the government army presence in much of the area, creating space for more sustained development.[37]

The most urgent tasks facing the PPLs were self-defense and the provision of material and moral support to the FMLN-FPL, whose combatants included many of the villages' young women and men. The guerrillas required multiple forms of support from civilians, especially food and other supplies, as well as places to store and hide supplies and assistance with transport. Some villages organized popular militias, which joined regular guerrilla troops in actions against the government army. Because the communities could rarely trade outside the FMLN-controlled zones, they had to produce much of what they needed, not only subsistence crops such as corn and beans but also clothing, shoes, soap, medicines, and other goods. Jenny Pearce points out that the organization of production, like other aspects of life in the controlled zones, reflects a dual reality of revolutionary war in El Salvador. On the one hand, the war made immediate demands of food and other goods necessary for both guerrillas and civilians in the face of destruction caused by army offensives and aerial bombardment. On the other hand, the residents wanted "to begin the revolutionary transformation of land tenure and forms of production." Central to the revolution that peasants hoped to create was "a more cooperative and collective spirit, which might in the future lay the foundations of more sweeping changes in the peasants' relations to the land."[38]

To meet the twin goals of providing necessary supplies and creating alternative models of production, the PPLs established new structures for landholding and labor. Collective work, to which every resident dedicated three days a week, provided for the whole community, especially old people and children. Two or three days each week, residents worked on small family plots, growing additional crops and vegetables to create an excess which they could sell to purchase nonfarm goods such as salt and sugar. Finally, all able community members contributed one day a week to centralized work producing corn and beans for the guerrillas.[39]

Because the war zones received no government services, the PPLs had to provide water, electricity, sanitation, roads, education, and health care. They strove to make services, especially education and health care, of high quality and available to all. Every community had a health promoter, usually trained by the guerrillas, along with emergency first-aid supplies, and ten communities in northeastern Chalatenango had clinics. The health promoters and clinics treated both war injuries and common diseases such as gastritis, diarrhea, and malaria.[40] Popular education in the war zones also achieved significant successes. Many civilians, children and adults, learned to read and write in projects developed by the PPLs. Activists from the national teachers' union trained some popular teachers, who were elected by their communities and had, ideally, completed fourth grade. Education in the war zones began with literacy programs for adults and youths and later, if conditions allowed, added elementary grades for children and adults. Classes were held beneath a tree, in an abandoned house, or, when there was danger of an attack, in gullies or bomb shelters.

Amid these pressing daily tasks, the PPLs created new forms of government, involving the active and democratic participation of the whole population in collective decisions and projects. Each village elected a community directorate (directiva comunal) to organize production, defense, health care, and education. The PPLs were not perfectly democratic, and some were riven by sexism, personalism, dependence on FMLN leaders, erratic participation, and uneven levels of development among different communities. Overall, however, they represented, as Pearce summarizes, "an experiment in popular democracy and political participation unique in the history of El Salvador."[41] They provided the first opportunity for poor peasants to organize their communities according to their own values and priorities, to govern themselves in a participatory manner, to learn from their own experiences, and to gain confidence in their ability to meet their needs and resolve their problems. The war zones were paradoxical spaces of freedom, where, despite danger and insecurity, people found unprecedented opportunities to remake their lives and communities according to their progressive Catholic vision. In the midst of crisis, explains one participant, "we got organized and found how, through the organization of the people, we could make changes. Here in the controlled zones there are more possibilities than ever in the past."[42] These possibilities, however, could not extend beyond their isolated mountain communities without major transformations in El Salvador's economic, political, and military structures, which seemed to require a definitive guerrilla victory. In pursuit of that goal, the FMLN reorganized its troops in late 1984 to emphasize small, mobile squadrons rather than extensive zones of control. This strategic change meant the end of most

PPLs, but many of their principles and specific projects were carried on in other settings, including, paradoxically, the refugee camps to which many peasants fled.[43]

Refugees

By 1981, only a small percentage of civilians remained, as masas clandestinas, in the war zones. Some left to live with relatives elsewhere in El Salvador, some emigrated permanently to the United States, and thousands ended up in refugee camps in San Salvador or Honduras. In the early 1980s, the United Nations High Commission on Refugees (UNHCR) established three large camps in Honduras, close to the Salvadoran border: Mesa Grande, which in 1987 held about 11,500 people, most from Chalatenango; Colomoncagua, with 8,400 residents, primarily from Morazán; and San Antonio, which housed about 1,500 people. A few smaller refugee settlements existed in Nicaragua and Panama. Conditions in the camps were harsh: residents crowded together in makeshift, often unsanitary houses; their freedom of movement was severely restricted; and they faced frequent harassment and sometimes violence from both Honduran and the Salvadoran armed forces, which characterized the camps as guerrilla training centers.

In forced exile, crowded and dependent on external aid for survival, some refugees responded passively. A large number, however, "were able to transcend their situation, drawing from it important lessons about how to live in community." Many refugees applied what they had learned about organization, education, and self-help in earlier peasant and church movements to their situation in the camps. They created new governing structures with representation from different sectors, such as women and children. Virtually every resident belonged to several different constituencies and had many opportunities to participate in the community's deliberations. The refugees' reliance on external aid enabled them to institute alternative incentives for labor and to devote themselves to "nonproductive" activities such as education, social welfare, and organizing. "People did not work for wages to support themselves or to win advantages for their families; they worked for the good of the community, so that everyone's needs would be met. Goods were distributed entirely on a per capita or per household basis, not according to how much work the individual had done."[44]

Religious life in the camps was spearheaded by lay activists, who had been trained as catechists or lay preachers (delegates of the Word) either in El Salvador or after arriving in exile. Some camps had relatively permanent pastoral care from a few Salvadoran and Honduran priests and a larger number of foreign missionaries who stayed in the camps for varying lengths of time. The number of pastoral agents was never sufficient to attend to all the laypeople in the camps, however, so they were left largely on their own, as they had been so often in El Salvador. The rituals and pastoral projects resembled the progressive Catholic models employed in El Salvador, including biblical reading and reflection, literacy classes, and cooperatives.

Like the zones of guerrilla control, refugee camps became "protected spaces" for learning both practical skills and less tangible lessons.[45] One resident of the Colomoncagua camp recalls, "There, you didn't work just for yourself or for your family, but for the community. All the work we did was collective, we were united by it. That time in the refuge has been a great help to us; we gained experience in many new things, and we kept on learning and working together right up to the time we came back to El Salvador. The communal life was a very different life, a beautiful life, because we all helped each other."[46] In the midst of scarcity, insecurity, and physical restrictions, the refugees sought to create communities guided by solidarity, sharing, and respect. Their communities represented, in many ways, "the incarnation of the values of liberation theology," as one study of the Meanguera camp puts it. "Here people lived together in harmony and equality, sharing what little they had to ensure that everyone's needs were met, encouraging each one's participation, and valuing each one's concerns."[47]

The camps were not perfect, of course, and they were a very artificial setting, with conditions that could not and should not be replicated. Still, they gave El Salvador's Christian left another opportunity to begin creating, on a small scale, the kind of society they wanted: a united community that cared for the most needy, that encouraged participation and open discussion, that sought to embody its values in every aspect of its social, economic, and political life. The refugees' achievement struck Jesuit sociologist Segundo Montes as a real alternative. During a visit to the Colomoncagua camp, he told the refugees, "I thought there was no future for El Salvador, but when I saw your model of organization and development, I changed my mind."[48]

Return

> I will bring about the restoration of my people Israel. They shall rebuild and inhabit their ruined cities, plant vineyards and drink the wine, set out gardens and eat the fruits. I will plant them upon their own ground. Never again shall they be plucked from the land I have given them, say I, the Lord your God.
>
> —Amos 9:14–15

Just as the Anabaptists define themselves in relation to the early Christian vision of faith and works expressed in the Gospels, many Salvadorans look to the narrative of exile and return described by Amos and other Hebrew prophets. In the words of members of a Christian community in the refugee camp in Colomoncagua, "We believe that we have lived in our own flesh the same circumstances that the people of Israel experienced in their Exodus, walking through foreign lands, suffering and crying out, but always having the help of God, and with very firm hope and faith. This same Liberating God is giving us a promised land, [which] we know by the name of El Salvador."[49]

Despite the many positive developments of life in the camps, most refugees were anxious for the war to end so they could return to their homes and rebuild their lives. However, five years after the first mass exodus from El Salvador, the war raged on with no end in sight. By the mid-1980s, "many of the displaced and the churches and nongovernmental organizations assisting them came to the conclusion that camps, settlements, and emergency assistance could no longer sustain this population. Longer term solutions had to be found. Large numbers of displaced persons had been in the camps for the duration of the war and could no longer tolerate the dependence, passivity, and forced idleness of the life there. By 1985, then, the opposite face of the army's depopulation campaign had fully emerged: the repopulation movement."[50]

A few families and small groups returned to some war zones in the early 1980s, mainly in northern and northeastern Chalatenango. These early, informal repopulations were rarely stable; residents would return seasonally, for planting and harvest, then scatter again when the armed forces came through.[51] The organized repopulations began in 1985, when 187 people who had been living in refugee camps in San Salvador and smaller cities returned, with support from the Archdiocese of San Salvador, to Tenancingo, in Cuscatlán province, which had been depopulated two years earlier.[52] The archdiocese also aided returns from camps in Honduras, as did the United Nations and other international agencies. The main organizers, however, were grassroots activistsinspired by progressive Catholic values and closely linked to the political opposition. The importance of religious values is reflected in the name of the largest refugee group, the Christian Committee for Refugees and the Displaced (CRIPDES), founded in 1984 by residents of a church-run camp in San Salvador. Most founders of CRIPDES were from Chalatenango, and like most activists from that region they were affiliated with the FPL. Working closely with residents of the refugee camps in Honduras, CRIPDES began to plan the first repatriations, or repopulations by people living outside the country.

The first mass repatriation was the October 1987 return of 4,000 refugees from Mesa Grande to Guarjila, Las Vueltas, Copapayo, and Santa Marta. The Salvadoran government had demanded that they go to places under government control, but refugees insisted on returning to their places of origin in the war zones,[53] including the heart of FMLN territory in Chalatenango. In preparation for their departure from Mesa Grande, the refugees had loaded 127 trucks with supplies, building materials, and everything else they could move from the camps. Then the people themselves filled 150 buses and traveled to the Salvadoran border, where they faced further government opposition. Eventually, the UNHCR intervened to end the standoff and the refugees crossed the border. After entering El Salvador, they divided into groups headed for the different villages to be reinhabited.

The first repopulators (*repobladores*) encountered daunting conditions. The bombings of the early 1980s and subsequent years of neglect had left the villages in shambles. In almost every village, most buildings had been destroyed, and those remaining consisted, for the most part, of a few partial walls, often marked by bullet holes, rockets, or fire. Almost none had roofs. The fields, never particularly fertile in this part of the country, were overtaken by shrubs and weeds, and most wells and water lines had been destroyed.

I visited Guarjila, the first village to be repopulated in Chalatenango, in October 1988, the first anniversary of its resettlement. During their first year, the returnees had built one- and two-room mud and straw houses for most families. These were usually constructed over the shells of the old houses and covered by tin roofs, with materials taken from their dismantled houses in the refugee camps. The construction of houses and community buildings continued around the more urgent tasks of planting and tending food crops. Harsh as they were, conditions in Guarjila were luxurious in comparison to those in San Antonio Los Ranchos, about a kilometer away, which had been resettled barely two months earlier. The residents of Los Ranchos were still spending most of their time clearing weeds from fields so they could plant corn, beans, and sorghum. They slept under plastic tarpaulins tied to sticks or spread over the walls or to the beams, which were all that remained of the prewar houses.

In their rudimentary shelters, the returnees established households with the few personal items they had brought with them on the buses, mostly plastic or tin cups and plates, burlap bags, rope, and hammocks. Some had also brought seeds or a few chickens. The only other domestic animals were the *perros aguacateros*, "avocado-eating" dogs who seemed to trail at the heels of every child and adult. The communities survived the first year largely with foreign aid from secular and church-based groups in North America and Europe, channeled through CRIPDES and other humanitarian agencies, which enabled them to purchase seeds, fertilizer, and building materials.

At that time, in October 1988, Guarjila and San Antonio los Ranchos were the only two inhabited villages in northeastern Chalatenango, apart from Arcatao, several kilometers further up the road. Arcatao was the one village in the area that had never been entirely abandoned during the war. A civilian remnant had remained, along with a semipermanent guerrilla presence. Never particularly rich in infrastructure, at the time of return northeastern Chalatenango lacked every basic service, including potable water, sewers, electricity, roads, schools, and medical services. Most village churches had been destroyed during the war, and makeshift chapels were among the first community buildings to be constructed in each repopulation, along with schools, health clinics, and spaces for storing the community's corn and grain. They also had to rebuild roads, dig latrines, and redig wells and install pumps. The residents, mostly women and children, joined by some old people and young men disabled by combat or land mines, accomplished these tasks with few resources but great organizational skills and determination. Virtually all the necessary work was accomplished in teams. To construct houses, for example, one team moved from site to site clearing away vegetation and rubble and leveling the ground. Other teams measured the sites, buried concrete blocks for foundations, built wooden frames, and nailed down sheets of corrugated tin for roofs. Still others collected rocks and branches to make the walls, which were finished off with mud. Working this way, the teams could build about seven two-room houses each week.

The repopulators faced not only the uphill work of reclaiming farmland and building shelter, but also constant harassment from the government military, including aerial attacks like the 1990 massacre in Corral de Piedra, ground incursions, and selective assassinations of teachers, health workers, and other community leaders. During an October 1988 visit, I stood under the tin roof of Guarjila's chapel and watched a plane repeatedly bomb a cornfield perhaps a kilometer away. We had no place to run, not even *tatus*, shallow underground bomb shelters used by many of the same peasants to escape army operations in the years before they had fled to Honduras. Watching the plane dive, drop a bomb, and circle around for another shot, I thought mainly about my immediate safety. For the scores of peasants around me, the destruction of their fields and crops posed an equally serious threat. Skirmishes between government and FMLN fighters also took place frequently in the villages and the hills surrounding them, although the government soldiers often chose to harass civilians rather than engage the guerrillas directly.

Despite the dangers and hardships, the repopulations quickly became known as a success story, both within El Salvador and among Salvadorans living in Mesa Grande and the other camps. As more refugees learned about the experiences of the first returnees, the repopulation movement grew. Rigoberto, who lived in Mesa Grande in the mid-1980s, recalls, "When we saw that [the first group of returnees] returned and were working the land, with their children happy studying, we stayed in close contact with them and decided to arrange for our return to San Antonio Los Ranchos."[54] He returned in August 1988 with 1,200 refugees from Mesa Grande, who settled in both San Antonio Los Ranchos and Teosinte in Chalatenango. A few months later, in October, 1,500 people from Mesa Grande resettled Santa Marta, Cabañas. In October 1989, another 1,200 refugees resettled in Teosinte, Tremedal, and Corral de Piedra in Chalatenango.

In March 1990, I accompanied one of the last mass repatriations, traveling with buses carrying hundreds of refugees from the Honduran border to several villages, including one in Chalatenango. This group faced the same harassment as earlier returnees, including delays at the border crossing, on the road, and at the army barracks in Chalatenango City, the last stop before the road into the repopulations. The refugees had left the camp before dawn; finally, well after dark, they finished a journey that should have taken a few hours. As the caravan of buses lumbered into Guarjila, the first village on the road through the repopulated region, we could make out long lines of people along each side of the dirt road; they were civilian returnees and, smiling and waving AK-47 rifles, dozens of uniformed guerrillas. A North American visiting El Salvador for the first time turned to me in alarm when she saw the guerrillas, but a wave of relief washed through the returning Salvadorans, who correctly interpreted the FMLN presence as an indication that government troops were nowhere near. When we finally reached San José las Flores, where the new arrivals would spend the night, we found many more civilians and combatants gathered. Despite the late hour, a party broke out, and it was hard to know who felt more like celebrating, the refugees who had finally completed their long journey or those who had waited for them. They had spent weeks clearing land and refurbishing houses to make it easier for the new arrivals to settle in. While later returnees such as this group still faced many challenges, their transition was infinitely easier than that of the first repobladores.

A number of repopulators eventually moved to other abandoned villages in search of more or better land or to be closer to family. Also during the period of repatriations in the late 1980s, many of the masas clandestinas who had remained in Chalatenango gradually joined with the repatriating refugees in the villages. With only a handful of refugees remaining, the Mesa Grande camp closed in 1992; San Antonio had closed in 1990. Thus, Chalatenango and most other conflicted departments were reinhabited in stages. The one exception was northern Morazán, which was resettled in a single mass repopulation by refugees in the Colomoncagua camp. In late 1989 and early 1990, all of the more than 8,000 residents of the Colomoncagua camp moved to the village of Meanguera (later renamed Ciudad Segundo Montes), north of the ERP stronghold of Perquín.[55]

Post-Guerra

The resettlement of Meanguera was delayed for several months by a major FMLN offensive that started on November 11, 1989. This was the largest FMLN operation since the "final offensive" of January 1981. Guerrillas occupied parts of San Salvador, including wealthy neighborhoods, and took control of many smaller cities. Their success gave the lie to the notion that socialist defeats in Eastern Europe and Nicaragua had weakened the FMLN, and the fighting in rich neighborhoods of San Salvador underscored the government's inability to control the war. In the most infamous event of the offensive, soldiers of the Atlacatl Battalion murdered six well-known Jesuit priests, their housekeeper, and her daughter at the Central American University. Their deaths prompted international outrage and a renewed push for peace talks.

Many Salvadoran civic and religious leaders, including the Jesuits, for years had been urging both sides to negotiate to reach a peaceful end to what had become a military stalemate. FMLN leaders had also expressed their willingness to engage in serious negotiations.[56] Despite hundreds of millions of dollars in aid from the United States, the Salvadoran government had failed to achieve a definitive victory over the FMLN. The pressure of the 1989 offensive, which demonstrated the FMLN's continued military and political strength, in addition to the outcry over the murders of the Jesuits, pushed the Salvadoran government, after years of resistance, to agree to negotiations.

After months of discussions, the two parties reached agreement on New Year's Eve 1991 and signed the treaty in Chapultepec Park in Mexico City on January 16, 1992. The accords called for eleven months of cease-fire, during which time combatants from both sides would remain in designated camps while the accords were enacted in a series of stages. The most important steps were to be completed by December 14, 1992, when the FMLN would demobilize completely, give up its weapons, and become a legal political party. In addition to this transformation of the FMLN, the peace accords specified the "purification" (*depuración*) of the government armed forces, including the elimination of the most notorious units, such as the "elite battalions," the National Guard, and the Treasury Police, as well as the removal of more than a hundred officers associated with human rights violations. The army would deal only with international conflicts, and internal problems were put under the jurisdiction of a National Civilian Police (Policia Nacional Civil), which was to include former combatants from both sides. Other former combatants were to be incorporated into civilian life, aided by a land-transfer program and educational opportunities. In addition to military changes, the settlement called for greater political openness, judicial autonomy, and respect for political pluralism and human rights.

These agreements aimed to restructure Salvadoran political and military institutions to establish the conditions under which change could occur through democratic processes. The peace accord represented a bargain in which "the Left accepted political inclusion at the price of economic moderation," as political scientist Elisabeth Wood puts it.[57] This compromise reflected debates within the FMLN during the late 1980s that redefined its goal as the construction of a pluralist democracy, in which military, police, electoral, and judicial reform would take precedence over socioeconomic issues. The accords thus failed to address most of the economic issues that had been the focus of peasant and labor protests before and during the war. The only serious redistributive element of the accords was the Land Transfer Program (Programa de Transferencia de Tierras, PTT), which provided land to former combatants of both sides and to organized supporters of the FMLN, particularly in repopulated communities. The PTT provided 3.5 *manzanas* (a manzana is an area equal to about 7,000 square meters [about 1.7 acres]) of land to each family or individual beneficiary. Land was granted to ex-combatants of both sides and to *tenedores* (landholders), people living and farming land that the owners had abandoned during the war. Initially the land was assigned as a whole to communities, based on the number of recipients in the community. Later, most of the land was divided into smaller plots and titles were granted to individuals, though some communities left substantial parts of their lands in collective ownership, often as forest reserves or watershed protection.

The land transfer plan has encountered numerous problems. First, some ex-combatants and tenedores had access to land under the PTT, but others did not. A large number of FMLN combatants, for example, were not recognized as combatants by the United Nations Observer Mission in El Salvador because they were under eighteen. Further, in many villages in northeastern Chalatenango, including Guarjila, there was not enough land to meet the demand, so some people were granted lands in other departments. Some moved permanently, others moved and then returned to their home villages, where they rent land. In the poor soils of Chalatenango, the small plots granted under the PTT often cannot provide for a family's subsistence, so some families have to rent additional lands. As one Guarjila resident put it, "Here the land is very tired and doesn't produce much."[58]

The land shortage has been exacerbated by the recalcitrance of some landowners. Much of the land distributed under the PTT involved property abandoned by the owners during the war and later inhabited by returned refugees or other residents of the war zones in "human settlements" (*asentamientos humanos*). People living in villages like Guarjila, San Antonio Los Ranchos, and San José las Flores were named the tenedores of the land. Under the peace accords, the state was to buy the land from the owners and transfer it to the people living there, but some owners refused to sell their land. Additional problems arose from the bureaucracy that oversees the process under which residents receive title to their land (Proceso de Titulación). Many transfers have been slow and disorganized, and some cases were still pending a full decade after the war's end.

A final problem involves the debt incurred by people who benefited from the PTT. Most recipients and activists believed that the peace accords granted land as gifts outright to ex-combatants and tenedores. However, after the war, the government defined the grants as a loan (to be paid in fifteen years at 5 percent interest). Many people rejected this debt, both because they could not pay it and because they felt they had earned the land. In 1995, the Democratic Peasant Alliance (Alianza Democrática Campesina), the largest peasant organization in El Salvador after the war, initiated a campaign for forgiveness of agrarian debt in 1995. Later that year, a parallel campaign was launched by the Agricultural Forum, a new coalition that included representatives of the FMLN and more than fifty other rural organizations, including CRIPDES, which works in repopulated villages in Chalatenango as well as those in many other departments. The peasant movements formed a temporary but effective alliance with medium and large landowners in eastern El Salvador, who also opposed the government's debt repayment scheme. After intense negotiations, the government agreed, in April 1998, to cancel 85 percent of the agrarian debt. As Adam Flint remarks, "This was a tremendous victory. For the first time since the end of the war, rural movements, the FMLN and their allies had defeated the government by their united efforts. Considering that rural movements looked as though they would die out after the peace accords, this victory is all the more impressive."[59] Flint sees the successful battle against the agrarian debt as evidence of a resurgence of social movements in El Salvador, especially those around rural issues, following several years of relative quiet after the war's end. In 2002 and 2003, social movements and unions engaged in major conflicts with the government over health care and social security. The Central American Free Trade Agreement (CAFTA) has also prompted intense protests.

Salvadoran social movements in the postwar era confront many of the same problems that faced activists in the 1970s and 1980s. El Salvador is still marked by severe economic inequities, poverty, and elite domination of politics. The country also suffers from widespread criminal violence, including the highest per capita homicide rate in the hemisphere. Many of these crimes are committed by former soldiers and by members of U.S.-influenced gangs.[60] Crime is exacerbated by high unemployment rates, a fragile judicial system, and the wide availability of weapons. Further, neoliberal economic reforms and "structural adjustments" have made life harder for poor Salvadorans in both rural and urban areas. Many Salvadoran families survive only due to the *remesas* (remittances) sent by relatives working in the United States, Canada, Europe, and Australia. The postwar era is marred not only by economic insecurity and criminal violence but also by failing infrastructure and deteriorating environmental conditions, including severe air pollution, soil erosion, and water contamination, all intensified by deforestation and urban sprawl. These problems were exacerbated by Hurricane Mitch in October 1998 and the devastating earthquakes of January 2001, which killed hundreds of people, displaced thousands, and badly damaged infrastructure and farmland.

Reinhabitation: Building Sustainable Communities

The successes of the repopulation movement are due to alliances, tactics, values, and solidarity forged in the base Christian communities and peasant cooperatives of the 1960s. Campesinos became radicalized in the mass organizations of the 1970s, and in the 1980s they survived brutal repression, guindas, refugee camps, and all the challenges of rebuilding abandoned villages. Once they returned, the repobladores faced harassment and violence from the government armed forces, including murders, arrests, and torture of individual residents, as well as mass attacks from both ground and air. They interpreted this violence using the same religious framework that had helped them make sense of earlier repression.

Following the tests and trials of the early repopulation period, the communities are now undergoing a process that might be called "reinhabitation." Whereas repopulation focused on reoccupying the land, reinhabitation is a slower, more complex process, which involves creating structures by which the residents can sustain and extend their vision of community. The repobladores aimed not just to come back to El Salvador and scrape out a living, as they did before, but to build a new society from the ground up. Ten years after the war ended and fifteen years since the first repopulations, not all their dreams are fulfilled and new challenges keep arising. Still, their achievements are astonishing. Here I focus on four areas in which they have made significant gains: environmental sustainability, economic subsistence, social justice, and political participation.

Environmental Sustainability

Protecting and restoring the natural environment cannot be separated from efforts to achieve social justice, economic security, and democratic political participation. Unsustainable exploitation of forests, heavy use of chemical pesticides and fertilizers, and many other forms of environmental damage are directly related to poverty and economic insecurity. As Ricardo Navarro, one of El Salvador's most prominent environmentalists, writes, "To speak of ecological problems is to speak about social problems, it is to speak about poverty, about relations of power, at a national and international level, and it is thus 'to get mixed up in politics' [meterse en política], as some would say."[61] Environmental projects cannot succeed unless and until rural residents stabilize their ability to provide for themselves and their families. Until that time, Navarro points out, people will continue to cut down trees for firewood and plant on exhausted soils. Most peasants realize that environmental problems exacerbate their struggles for economic subsistence, health, and equitable development, but few can implement more sustainable practices, individually or collectively. They cannot wait for the kind of ecological protection afforded by letting fields lie fallow for a season or leaving arable land in forest. Technologies such as solar- and wind-generated electricity cost less in the long run than high polluters such as diesel generators, but the long-term benefits cannot be reaped until communities make substantial initial investments.

On the other hand, most Salvadoran peasants know that if they exhaust the land, they have no source of survival. As a leader in Guarjila put it, "We live from the land, so we have to take care of it [Vivimos de la tierra, tenemos que cuidarla]."[62] Local governments and agencies such as CRIPDES and COR-

DES (Foundation for the Communal Development of El Salvator) must find the resources to develop alternative energy and organic fertilizers and pest controls and to restore forests and watersheds, and they must do so in a political and economic context that is acceptable to local residents and with methods that match their vision of their community's future.

A number of local, regional, and national organizations are pursuing this vision. PRISMA, an environmental organization in San Salvador, has worked with communities in Chalatenango to oppose the building of a new dam on the Lempa River in Nueva Concepción, which would have destroyed many communities. The united opposition succeeded and the dam plan was defeated. Another local group, the Unidad Ambiental del Cerro Alto, manages land in San Antonio los Ranchos and Guarjila for reforestation and water protection and to reduce landslides and erosion. The Comunidad Ambiental (Environmental Community) produces environmental profiles for projects and supports communities in their efforts to continue developing sustainably and to oppose environmentally and socially damaging projects. At the village level, many communities have ecological committees. To protect existing forests, the committee in Guarjila has planted trees that residents can use for firewood. The ecological committee has also helped distribute highly efficient wood-burning ovens, which are now used in almost all houses.

Of the various environmental issues facing the repopulated communities, the most important is agriculture, the main use of land in Chalatenango and the main activity of most residents. Navarro claims that El Salvador's major environmental problem is soil erosion,[63] which is especially severe in Chalatenango, where soils are poor to begin with and generations of intensive farming on steep hillsides have intensified topsoil loss. To control erosion, many communities in Chalatenango and other former war zones have begun reforesting and terracing. Thanks to intensive education programs by local leaders and environmental organizations, most farmers have stopped burning fields and now leave old crops and leaves for mulch. Some have also begun rotating crops, to the extent possible on their small plots. They have made less progress, residents admit, in reducing their reliance on chemical fertilizers and pesticides. People are aware of the damage that chemicals do to both ecological and human health but continue to use them to make the poor local soils produce. As a first step, people in Guarjila have undertaken a campaign to stop using insecticide containers for carrying and storing water. To strengthen sustainable agriculture and provide examples of success, CORDES and other organizations have supported a variety of projects. They have helped a number of families adopt *planes de finca* (land-use plans) which specify multiple uses of individual or family plots, some in fruit trees, some in perennial herbs, some in vegetable gardens, and some in trees for shade and firewood. CORDES also coordinates an initiative in which eighteen families will receive title to the land they now farm in ten years under the condition that they work with sustainable methods (e.g., not burning, minimizing insecticide use, preventing erosion, and pro-tecting watersheds). Another CORDES project is a women's "circle of integral education," which provides education about kitchen gardens and sustainable agriculture.

Some of the largest and most successful experiments with sustainable agriculture have taken place in the fertile soils of the Lower Lempa region (spanning parts of the departments of San Vicente and La Libertad), home to a number of repopulations. Here the war that caused so much human and environmental damage has created one advantage: the abandonment of fields and orchards for years has facilitated the process of organic certification, which enables local producers to take advantage of the more lucrative international market in organic products.

In addition to developing more sustainable ways to farm, communities are also working to set some land apart from intensive human use. Increasing awareness of the practical, as well as aesthetic, value of forests has led to nu-merous reforestation efforts, in both rural and urban areas. In Guarjila, the local *comité ecológico* and other organizations have provided fruit and shade trees to all the families in the village. This is strikingly evident from the hills surrounding Guarjila, now covered by a green canopy where before was only dust. Many native animal species recovered during the war. Residents of Chal-atenango report that when they returned to abandoned villages, many animals that had been locally extirpated had returned, including armadillos, deer, and squirrels. Although some residents still hunt these animals, there seems to be greater interest in protecting them, due partly to the increase in ownership of domestic animals that provide alternative sources of protein in milk, eggs, and meat. Residents also regularly see many formerly rare or absent bird species, which have returned due largely to reforestation efforts. During a recent visit, I saw a flock of parrots fly overhead, a formerly common occurrence that Sal-vadorans in other parts of the country talk about nostalgically and almost never witness. Old people take pleasure in seeing species they remember from their youth and sharing their knowledge with younger people, who interpret the birds' return in relation to concepts such as biodiversity, endangered species, and even wildlife corridors, with which they are increasingly familiar thanks to the work of Salvadoran and international NGOs and education efforts. One negative impact of the resettlement of the war zones lamented by residents has been a decrease in the population of seed-eating birds, due primarily to the use of chemical pesticides.

Economic Subsistence

Most families live primarily through agriculture but need to supplement what their small plots produce with additional sources of income. One major source of cash is remesas sent by relatives living in the United States. Another is permanent or seasonal wage labor in Chalatenango and other towns, an undertaking made easier by the paving of the main road into the former conflict zone and the extension of bus service to several villages. Some former combatants serve in the Policia Nacional Civil, the civilian police force created after the 1992 peace accords.

Most repopulations have a variety of cooperative micro-enterprises. These projects have multiple purposes: residents learn skills, produce goods needed by the communities and surrounding areas, and earn some supplemental income. In Guarjila, for example, a community-supported project dries locally grown fruit using a solar dryer; solar lighting is also used in the building in which the fruit is processed and packaged. Guarjila also has a carpentry workshop, embroidery and sewing workshops, and a bakery, all of which produce for local consumption and in some cases for markets in Chalatenango City and San Salvador. More recent ventures include bicycle repair and a community radio, Radio Sumpul, whose antenna now occupies a peak that served as a guerrilla lookout during the war. Other villages have similar projects. Not all these micro-enterprises are successful. Some have started and failed, others have undergone major transformations to survive economically, and still others manage only with substantial foreign aid, although international assistance has dropped off sharply since the war's end.

These community-owned and -run projects reflect the collective model that dominated the economy in the early repopulations and that has diminished since the war's end. Presently, for example, few if any villages designate a day for communal food production as they did in the early years. However, most still set aside collectively owned land, worked by community members, to provide basic crops for especially needy households, such as those whose heads are disabled, elderly, or single parents. Despite the move away from collective production, the rural communal movement remains committed to a mixed economy whose primary objective is meeting human needs. Although people farm mostly on privately owned land, other important resources, such as the workshops, stores, and other cottage industries, are collectively owned. Their profits, such as they are, are distributed throughout the community, and their workers are employees of the community. So are health care workers, who run clinics that serve surrounding hamlets as well as the resettlements, and schoolteachers, who constitute by far the largest number of community employees.

While striving to meet local needs, the communities must also find ways to survive in regional, national, and international economies. Especially as international aid has declined, the communities cannot fulfill residents' needs and realize their vision of sustainable and just development without participating successfully in larger markets. They face the considerable challenge, then, of combining sustainability with economic security. This task has become even more difficult with the growth of free trade zones and *maquilas* (sweatshops that produce export items) in El Salvador's cities. Job scarcity and low income remain chronic problems and have driven some young people away from the communities, a growing concern. Only if the communities achieve long-term economic viability can they both retain their populations and continue working to provide a model for the rest of the country. According to this model, the economic goal is not simply growth but an equitable distribution of both burdens and benefits and protection for the most vulnerable.

Social Justice and Services

After taking steps to meet residents' basic needs for food, shelter, and health care, the early repopulations began creating social, political, and economic structures that would embody their egalitarian values and their vision of a community modeled on the reign of God. In rural areas such as Chalatenango, greater access to and a more equitable distribution of arable land were crucial aspects of social justice. Despite its limitations, the PTT has led to a substantial redistribution of land in communities in the former war zones. Many families that previously owned no land at all now have titles to subsistence plots. This is a major, though imperfect, victory of more than two decades of struggle.

Perhaps even more impressive are the efforts to create a safety net that ensures all members have the basic goods, especially food, housing, and medical care, necessary for a "dignified" life. This commitment to social security is particularly impressive given that most people in the repopulated villages are poor even by Salvadoran standards. It is seen not only in the provision of communally produced food and health services, but also in the creation of senior citizens' homes in two villages to provide shelter, meals, services, and moral support to elderly residents, many of whom lost their children in the war and now have no younger relatives to care for them.

Education has been a major priority for the repopulation movement since its inception, building on experiences in the PPLs and refugee camps. Rigoberto recalls that the returnees' first priority was "to teach our children how to work the land. The second was that they should study."[64] In the early years, education in the repopulations resembled that in the PPLs and the camps: chronically short of supplies and training, with teachers who had barely finished one grade instructing those in next one down. Education was initially limited to grades 1 to 4, and many teachers were young people who learned to read and write in Mesa Grande. They received no support from the Salvadoran Ministry of Education, although teachers from ANDES, the national teachers union, sometimes traveled from San Salvador to offer teacher training. Today, the repopulated communities surpass most rural areas in El Salvador in educational resources. Almost all the village schools in the *repoblaciones* continue through eighth grade, and several villages, including Guarjila, have high schools. Thus, for the first time ever, local youths do not have to leave home to complete high school (bachillerato). Several communities offer technical and vocational training programs as well. Teachers are now certified and partially compensated by the Ministry of Education.

Similar success has met efforts to provide universal, high-quality health care. Most repopulated villages in Chalatenango have clinics staffed by well-trained lay health promoters, who provide prenatal checkups, childhood immunizations, and basic first aid. Several of the larger villages have more elaborate clinics with resident physicians. Many communities also offer insurance programs. In Guarjila, for example, 5 colones (less than $5) each month pays for a family's medical visits and medicines. The head of Guarjila's directiva estimates that 60 to 65 percent of the residents have the insurance and the rest use the clinic on a pay-per-visit basis and, in more complicated cases, go to the hospital in Chalatenango City. As a result of these services and of widespread health education programs, along with the guarantee of nutritious food for needy families, very few children in the communities die of the contagious diseases that killed a large percentage of campesino children before the war and very few women die in childbirth. Local residents point out with pride that Guarjila, previously a backward village in a backward province, now has schools and clinics that attract people from surrounding areas.

Political Participation and Democratization

To help institutionalize their values, the repobladores have created not only social services but new political structures and processes. Building on the experiences of poder popular local and the refugee camps, each village elects a directiva, or town council, usually with four to eight members.[65] Governance is not left to the directiva alone, however. Most repopulations are divided into sectors that meet regularly, and most have regular general assemblies open to the whole community. A foreign volunteer who lived in San Antonio Los Ranchos in the late 1980s called the discussions and planning that took place in the assemblies "nearly miraculous."[66] These structures reflect a definition of democracy that gives priority to participation and the ability to meet regularly with leaders.

Although popular participation appears to have declined in the repopulations since the war's end, it remains high compared to other rural and urban communities in El Salvador (and elsewhere). Local governments also maintain a significant degree of autonomy in relation to the national government. Many repopulations do not have mayors but rather elected directivas or consejos (councils), which are unofficial in relation to the national government. However, they usually have close links to other local officials and municipal councils, which are now dominated by the FMLN in most of northeastern Chalatenango. The close ties among the FMLN party, official local governments, unofficial community governing bodies, and organizations like CORDES and CRIPDES blur the lines between "oppositional outsider" institutions, in David Leaman's term, and the formal government. As Leaman argues, "While this kind of overlap raises questions about future community representation and governmental functions (Will community councils become redundant in FMLN electoral strongholds? What about individuals in those communities who are not FMLN partisans?), in this current period of historical transition, it has seemed to assist the integration of 'oppositional outsider' communities into the political mainstream, a positive development for Salvadoran democracy."[67] The innovative relations among local community institutions such as the directivas, NGOs such as CRIPDES and CORDES, local governments, and the FMLN party hold out the promise for combining pragmatic approaches to meeting local needs with a broad long-term vision of social change and sustainable development.

The struggle to realize this vision can now be waged in a context of relative political openness and physical security. Political intimidation and manipulation are not unknown, but soldiers no longer fire on demonstrations, movement leaders are not routinely abducted from their homes in the middle of the night, and mutilated bodies are not found in church yards and garbage dumps.[68] No one who lived through the horror of the late 1970s and 1980s takes these gains lightly. Salvadoran activists acknowledge that despite continuing political, economic, social, and environmental problems, the peace accords and the years of struggle leading up to them fundamentally changed El Salvador's political rules and institutions. The grassroots opposition forced the ruling class to make major concessions in what Elisabeth Wood calls an "insurgent transition." To institutionalize this transformation, the FMLN and its related organizations have had "to change the site of struggle from a military to a political stage," as a party official told me in June 1994.[69] This transition has been made much harder by divisions within the party, including the 1994 departure of the ERP and a smaller party, the Resistencia Nacional, which formed a separate party. While the FMLN still faces internal debates, notably between "orthodox" and "renovating" wings, it has begun to recover from the sharp divisions and strategic confusion of the immediate postwar years. The party has increased its presence in municipal government and in the national legislative assembly with every election since 1994. The March 2001 elections gave the FMLN the mayoralty of San Salvador and other municipalities, including most mayoralties in Chalatenango. Local and municipal gains stem from leaders' recognition that they needed to pay more attention to local issues in both urban and rural areas. FMLN mayors have tried to follow local electoral victories with effective governance, including coalitions with social movements and with progressive leadership in other locales to address problems such as failing infrastructure. The success of local FMLN mayors in paving the road from Chalatenango City to Arcatao is one example.

Nationally, the FMLN has substantially increased its power in the Legislative Assembly. In the 2001 elections, for the first time, the FMLN won more seats than the rightist ARENA party, which had led the country since 1989. Out of eighty-four total seats in the Legislative Assembly, FMLN legislative candidates won thirty-one seats and ARENA won twenty-nine, despite ARENA's far superior financial resources and media presence. The next national elections, in March 2003, solidified the FMLN's position as the country's largest party, as the left held its thirty-one seats and ARENA dropped to twenty-seven.[70] The FMLN also controls the city governments of San Salvador and other key municipalities, although ARENA retained its hold on the presidency in the March 2004 presidential elections.

The 2004 elections disappointed FMLN supporters, who had hoped that their presidential candidate, former guerrilla commander Schafik Handal, would prevail. Up until the elections on March 21, polls had shown a tight race between Handal and the ARENA candidate, Tony Saca. However, in the end, Handal received only 36 percent of the vote, compared to 57 percent for Saca, in an election with the largest turnout (63 percent of registered voters) since the war's end. A number of factors contributed to the election results, including some dissatisfaction with Handal, who, at age seventy-three, was perceived as inflexible, tied to the past, and generally less attractive than other potential FMLN candidates, especially the popular mayor of San Salvador, Oscar Ortiz. Campaign tactics by ARENA also played a role, especially its claims that if the FMLN won, the United States might deport the 2.5 million Salvadorans living there and end the flow of remittances, which total $2 billion a year and help 28 percent of Salvadoran adults. For example, an ARENA television advertisement portrayed a middle-class couple in El Salvador speaking on the telephone with their son in Los Angeles. "Mom, I wanted to let you know that I'm scared," the young man tells his mother, "because if Schafik becomes president of El Salvador, I may be deported, and you won't be able to receive the remittances that I'm sending you."[71] U.S. government officials reinforced ARENA's fear campaign by asserting that the United States might indeed reconsider the 300,000 temporary work permits issued to Salvadoran workers if the FMLN won. As the assistant secretary of the U.S. Bureau of Western Hemisphere Affairs put it, "We know the history of this political movement, and for this reason, it is fair that the Salvadoran people consider what type of relations a new government could have with us."[72] Given the long history of U.S. influence in El Salvador, such statements could not help but affect many voters.

Despite the disappointments of March 2004, overall the FMLN has established itself solidly in Salvadoran electoral politics. Along with events such as the 2002 election of Luís Inácio da Silva (Lula) to the presidency of Brazil, this trajectory can be read as part of a reconfigured and perhaps resurgent Latin

American left that is both pragmatic and utopian.[73] Like Lula's Workers' Party, the contemporary FMLN has achieved electoral success with a platform that remains "distinctly anti-neoliberal (if no longer expressly socialist), as distinguished from opposition center-left parties elsewhere that have sought to moderate the excesses of the neoliberal formula."[74] In El Salvador, the neoliberal economic policies imposed by the World Bank and International Monetary Fund are increasingly unpopular in the face of the deepening postwar economic crisis. The steady economic growth in El Salvador in the decade since the war ended has benefited only a small elite; 40 percent of the national population still earns less than a dollar a day, and the social problems associated with poverty—including malnutrition, illiteracy, and criminal violence—remain widespread.[75]

In this context, it is not surprising that many Salvadorans, in both rural and urban areas, continue to desire substantive social changes. The dreams of more equal distribution of wealth and land and improved social services, especially health and education, remain powerful. Many activists believe, however, that the changes they seek must emerge out of feasible proposals, shaped by the experiences and interests of local communities and constituencies, rather than the sometimes ideologically driven or top-down projects offered in the past. As an FMLN leader explained, "The challenge of the left is to broaden itself, adapt itself, modernize itself, and especially to develop its capacity for making concrete proposals." The opposition cannot merely protest against what it does not like, he added, but must present specific projects and proposals "in order to have the democracy that we want."[76]

Efforts at local change and development are hampered by chronic underfunding of municipal governments (which was somewhat improved but not resolved by a recent law giving municipalities 6 percent of the national budget). This lack of public aid is exacerbated by a sharp decline in international assistance since the end of the war. Further, the little aid now flowing into the country goes mainly to technical and development projects disconnected from political struggles and ideologies. "While such projects can benefit the recipient population on an individual level," Flint argues, "one common result is that if individuals or isolated communities perceive that their immediate material problems can be resolved via a particular NGO-financed project, they may decide not to put time and energy into what is perceived as the riskier long-term strategy of political mobilization. This can depoliticize communities and discourage them from holding the state accountable for the social welfare of its citizens."[77] This approach challenges both the communal solidarity and the commitment to structural change that have characterized rural struggles in El Salvador since the early peasant federations.

A Promised Land?

The story of Chalatenango's peasant movements spans more than three decades of struggle to create a society in which all people's material needs are
met and members are united in their commitment to the common good.
Today, many people complain about the loss of unity and willingness to put
aside personal interests for the sake of larger goals, values that carried
them through repression, war, exile, and return throughout the 1980s. In
the repopulations, residents sometimes look back on the years of war and
exile with a certain nostalgia, recalling the closeness and sense of purpose
that marked their lives in the refugee camps and in Chalatenango during
the war. Soyapa, who has lived in Guarjila since returning from Mesa
Grande with the first repatriation in 1987, explains, "Since the peace accords, it isn't so necessary to be so tightly connected." Before, she says,
people had to work together because of the military threat. Now, greater
physical security has meant the end of most collective farming, among
other activities. Another Guarjila resident, Mauricio, echoes her evaluation:
"Collectivity [la colectividad] is what we've lost."⁷⁸

In addition to this self-critique of the communities and movements themselves, peasant activists have a number of serious complaints about the peace
accords. A community leader in Guarjila summarized the disillusions of many
when he explained, "People struggled for twelve years for a different society.
The Peace Accords don't fulfill those yearnings." One of his neighbors agrees
that the settlement "fell short in relation to [our] dreams." The disillusionment
is especially acute for former guerrillas and their families, and in villages in
Chalatenango and other rural areas in northern and eastern El Salvador, almost
every family had someone fighting with the FMLN. Their expectations were
high, an ex-combatant in Guarjila explains, because "we put all our future and
youth into the struggle."⁷⁹

A campesino from Usulután suggests what this struggle was not about
with an ironic question: "We shed blood all these years in order to buy land at
market prices?"⁸⁰ Most peasant activists did not fight for a free market in land,
or even for judicial and legal reforms. Rather, they struggled to construct an
entire society like the communities they built in the peasant cooperatives and
CEBs of the 1970s, in the refugee camps and the PPLs during the early 1980s,
and, most ambitiously, in the repopulations. This new society would be politically democratic and free of repression. Most important, it would be egalitarian, it would protect the most vulnerable, and its members would be united
around their shared values. These goals, more than free elections, judicial
reform, or new political parties, define the utopian vision for which thousands
of peasants in Chalatenango and elsewhere fought, and for which many died:
the promised land they dreamed of during long years of war, exile, and bare

survival. As one ex-combatant summarized, "We were all going to be equal [Todos íbamos a ser iguales]."[81]

The failure to achieve this goal has tempted some to declare the repopulations and the entire peasant movement a failure. This conclusion errs, first, by ignoring the real material and political gains that the Christian left has achieved in three decades of struggle. Second, it confuses the communities' present with their future. If there is any lesson to be gained from El Salvador's recent history it is, above all, that the future is open.

3

Nature

Rich and poor nations join today in a headlong rush to environmental destruction. Both ecological integrity and human health face threats from global warming, deforestation, and poisoned land and water, among many other problems. The most frightening indicator may be the daily loss of plant and animal species, due primarily to habitat destruction. The ever accelerating pace of biodiversity loss around the world has led one eminent biologist to declare, "We literally are standing on the edge of the end of biological history."[1] An August 2002 news article explains:

> Expanding human settlements, logging, mining, agriculture and pollution are destroying ecosystems, upsetting nature's balance and driving many species to extinction. There is virtual unanimity among scientists that we have entered a period of mass extinction not seen since the age of the dinosaurs, an emerging global crisis that could have disastrous effects on our future food supplies, our search for new medicines, and on the water we drink and the air we breathe. Estimates vary, but extinction is figured by experts to be taking place between 100 to 1,000 times higher than natural "background" extinction.[2]

This is indeed, as the United Nations puts it, "A Global Picture of Death, Damage and Destruction."[3]

The death, damage, and destruction result directly from the ways we live on Earth. This is especially true for affluent residents of Western industrial societies, whose reckless consumption of natural resources threatens both humanity's common good and the nonhuman world. On a planet that provides 4.5 productive acres for every person, by 1997 the average U.S. resident consumed natural resources equaling an "ecological footprint" of 24 acres. In contrast, the average Ethiopian uses about 1.6 acres, the average Chinese about 2.3. The current total human environmental impact exceeds the Earth's biological capacity by 20 percent.[4]

The overall ecological impacts of rich and poor nations still differ widely, yet affluent Westerners' destructive ways of life are increasingly shared by small but influential minorities in Third World nations, who drive sports utility vehicles to shopping malls, own the maquilas (sweatshops) producing consumer goods for First World consumers, drink bottled water, and employ their compatriots at less than living wages. Their impoverished fellow citizens also contribute to environmental destruction, often because their only hope of survival rests in cutting down the few remaining trees for firewood, catching the last fish for dinner, or spreading chemical fertilizers and pesticides on worn-out soil to make it produce one more season's worth of corn and beans.

We urgently need less destructive ways to live with nature. Scientists, philosophers, policy analysts, and many other "experts" have imagined countless means of reducing the damage caused by human populations and proposed remedies, including better technology, greater ecological understanding, moral education, economic incentives, and coercive laws. Sometimes these measures help. In the wake of California's 2001 energy crisis, for example, what the *New York Times* called "surprisingly effective conservation efforts," such as rebates for consumer purchases of efficient appliances and lower thermostats at government offices, contributed to a major decline in demand for energy in only a few months.[5] In other places, public investment in high-quality public transportation or alternative energy has achieved similar results, "surprising" mainly to those who cannot imagine alternatives to familiar ways of moving people and producing power or who fear that pursuing such alternatives will result in lives marred by poverty and sacrifice. However, some parts of the world have achieved standards of living equal to or higher than those of middle-class North Americans with much lower ecological impacts. In Belgium, the average ecological footprint is under 10 acres per person; in Italy it is 8.2. And two Latin American nations, Costa Rica and Chile, have achieved a high quality of life with less than 5 acres per person.[6]

It is worth asking how Belgians and Costa Ricans achieve results similar to those of the United States in infant mortality, life expectancy, literacy, and nutrition at a much lower ecological cost. Much of the difference stems from less reliance on automobiles and more compact urban areas. Higher energy efficiency standards for vehicles and appliances, smaller living quarters, and lower meat consumption also contribute, as do more locally oriented food production and distribution networks. A great deal can be learned from studying these national examples and pursuing economic and energy policies, urban models, and technology that would enable the United States to lower its overall impact.

Despite the availability of less destructive options, global and national per capita consumption of natural resources has increased sharply in recent decades, far outstripping the rate of population growth. And even though a vast majority of people in the United States repeatedly tell pollsters that they care deeply about the environment, this country has implemented few efforts to conserve resources. For example, Congress has for years refused to increase miles-per-gallon standards for automobiles, easily achievable with existing technology, even though such increases would significantly reduce our national contribution to global warming. In this and many other cases, industry leaders and politicians have overcome environmentalist arguments, in practice if not in theory, by appealing to Americans' attachment to a way of life that depends on high consumption of natural resources. During national debates in 2001, for example, the Bush administration argued against stringent conservation measures on the grounds that energy policy must protect "the American way of life," which presumably entails no limitations on personal consumption.[7] Even many environmental activists shy away from challenging consumption patterns. They share with conservatives a "production-oriented logic," according to which production, rather than consumption, is the root problem. Thus, "regulation of producers becomes the answer. Producers must internalize the cost of pollution or simply cease their abusive activities."[8] For example, environmentalists campaign to require higher miles-per-gallon standards for new cars rather than urging people to drive less and working to make it easier to drive less.[9]

The unwillingness of both environmentalists and their opponents to challenge consumption results, in large part, from deeply ingrained worldviews and values. Our cultural and religious traditions often isolate individuals from larger social and environmental contexts and encourage us to separate our practices from negative ecological impacts. We buy bigger cars and drive them more, live in bigger houses in sprawling suburbs, and fail to connect these practices to our declared concern for global warming and habitat loss. Even when we do make the connection, we assume that we cannot reduce ecological destruction without diminishing our quality of life. Again and again, we choose convenience and comfort over any potential sacrifice on behalf of the natural environment or even other human beings.

Here the communities described in this book have something to show us. Not only do people in Amish settlements and the Salvadoran repopulations hold different values and assumptions about what makes for a good life and moral behavior, but, perhaps more important, they organize their communities in accord with these values. In this chapter, I examine the ways that these communities view and live with the natural world and how their experiences and practices might shed light on problems and possibilities for the rest of us, including some of the roots of environmental destruction and some obstacles to possible solutions in both the First and Third Worlds. I aim in particular to explore the links between their practices and the value systems rooted in Anabaptist and Catholic views of nature.

Nature in Roman Catholic Thought

Because Roman Catholicism has long been the religion of small farmers, in Europe and Latin America the tradition's ritual practices, annual calendar, and many beliefs are closely linked to natural cycles and landscapes. However, the church has also served as the religion of empire in both Old and New Worlds, a pillar of cultural imperialism and territorial greed. In any guise, Catholicism does not have an especially long tradition of explicit theological and moral reflection about the natural world. On the other hand, Catholics can lay claim to the "patron saint of ecology," Francis of Assisi. Environmental historians and Pope John Paul II have acknowledged Francis's central role both in making the natural world and nonhuman animals significant issues for theological reflection and in advocating for their inherent moral worth.[10] Francis's writings and the legends about his work show a sense of unity with the natural world, seen in his use of the terms "brother" and "sister" for nonhuman animals and the moon and sun and in his gentle treatment of creatures from wolves to sparrows. Beyond these reported actions, in his writings Francis argued that animals have value to God above and beyond their usefulness to humans.[11]

Still, St. Francis stands as an exception in a tradition that concentrates on human good and sees nonhuman nature mainly as a backdrop for human action or as a means to human ends. Because humans were created in God's image, Catholic social teaching asserts, they possess unique dignity and inviolable rights. This humanistic emphasis has given rise to sharp economic and social critiques. For example, numerous modern Catholic documents, including the U.S. bishops' 1985 pastoral letter on the economy, assert that economies are to be judged not by the wealth they create but by their capacity to fulfill the basic needs of all and especially the poorest members of society.[12] Pope John Paul II brought Catholic social teaching to bear on capitalism in his encyclical *Laborem Exercens*, declaring that "man alone, independent of the work he does, ought to be treated as the effective subject of work and its true maker and creator. Precisely this reversal of order ... should rightly be called 'capitalism.' "[13]

This argument undergirds a powerful social critique, but its flip side is the danger of justifying almost any exploitation of natural resources that appears to serve human well-being. In contrast to humans, nature appears to have little intrinsic value and is appreciated insofar as it contributes to collective human well-being. The long-established Catholic conviction that God intended creation to serve the common human good has one set of moral and practical implications when used to oppose the individual pursuit of profit and a different set when contrasted to the notion that the natural world has value and ends apart from its use by humans. This is an instance of the more general point that the political consequences of religious ideas vary according to the context, and even within the same culture they change over time.

Recognizing some of the tensions in the Catholic humanist approach to nature, in recent years Catholic thinkers have been reworking their tradition's attitudes toward the natural world, applying central values to nature. First and most important, they contend that God created all of nature to serve human dignity and the common good, not individual profit. This assertion of the social purpose of created goods suggests a strong connection between environmental and social problems. In their 1991 pastoral letter *Renewing the Earth*, the U.S. bishops stressed the need to avoid "false choices between the people and the planet. It is the poor, here and in the developing countries, who suffer first and most from damage to the environment; they are the prime victims of a global system that degrades them and the rest of God's creation."[14] Along similar lines, a pastoral letter issued in December 2000 by the Apostolic Vicariate of Petén, Guatemala, titled *El grito de la selva en el año jubilar: Entre la agonía y esperanza* (The cry of the forest in the jubilee year: Between agony and hope) contends, "It is not possible to speak of ecology without taking justice into account. It is not possible to defend the conservation of the forest apart from the advancement and life of the poor."[15] Excessive consumption by some harms both poor people and the natural world; the solution will entail more restraint in human use of natural resources and a better distribution of the goods they make possible. In El Salvador's former war zones, these values are reflected in efforts to distribute land relatively equally, in concern for protecting water and soil for future generations, and in critiques of government policies that exploit natural resources to benefit only a few. A few other communities in Latin America, including in Ecuador, Brazil, Costa Rica, and Chiapas, Mexico, have also tried to embody their environmental values in and through distinctive institutions, agricultural practices, and community governance. Many of these also share religious roots, mostly in progressive Catholicism but sometimes in Protestant traditions.

A second core theme of Roman Catholic thinking on the environment is that people should serve as wise and careful stewards of the natural world. In his encyclical *Redemptor Hominis* (1979), John Paul II argued that exploitation of the Earth and the uncontrolled development of technology often bring "a threat to man's natural environment, alienate him in his relations with nature and remove him from nature. Man often seems to see no other meaning in his natural environment than what serves for immediate use and consumption.

Yet it was the creator's will that man should communicate with nature as an intelligent and noble 'master' and 'guardian,' and not as a heedless 'exploiter' and 'destroyer.' "[16] Ultimately, the church calls on people to be good stewards of the Earth and its resources because all of creation is a gift from God, intended for the well-being of all of humanity. Greed, expressed in consumerist culture and unrestrained capitalist economics, leads to overexploitation of nature and of persons, ultimately destroying human and natural communities. Progressive Catholicism has consistently attacked this consumerism and its destructive consequences for both affluent and impoverished groups. In El Salvador, activists criticize the unwillingness of elites to share the nation's wealth and resources with the poor majority—their failure, as Archbishop Romero put it, to "take the rings from their fingers before they lose the hand."[17] In the present context, this short-sighted selfishness includes not only refusal to redistribute land and wealth but also reckless exploitation of natural resources.

The Radical Reformation and Nature

Although Catholics differ in their views regarding the natural environment, the centralized character of the Roman Catholic Church makes possible a wide, though perhaps not always very deep, agreement. Protestantism has followed a different course. The Reformation theological emphasis on the "priesthood of all believers" and the primacy of individual salvation combined, not coincidentally, with a rejection of a centralized bureaucracy and leadership hierarchies. This means that doctrinal differences among Protestant leaders or groups could, and very often did, lead to the creation of new churches and denominations. This fragmentation began soon after Luther's first steps away from the Roman church and continues today. Despite decades of ecumenical initiatives, significant disagreements on both theological and practical issues persist even among closely related mainstream (or "historical") Protestant denominations, such as Methodists, Lutherans, and Presbyterians. The differences increase on those rare occasions when peripheral groups such as Anabaptists are taken into account.

The marginalization of the Radical Reformation tradition within the larger body of Protestants continues in discussions of Protestant environmental thought.[18] This exclusion is unfortunate, because the Anabaptist tradition offers a distinctive understanding of the relationship between humans and nature. Although the Radical Reformation began as a primarily urban movement, persecution quickly forced believers to small villages and farming communities, where Anabaptist affiliation became associated with agrarian identity. Anabaptist attitudes toward nature were also shaped by the experiences of believers who took refuge from persecutors in mountain caves and other wilderness areas. "Early Anabaptists," David Kline suggests, "looked at the earth not as an adversary but as a friend." The forbidding Jura Mountains sheltered those fleeing persecution in the Emmenthal area of Switzerland; even bad weather had advantages, because it kept the Anabaptist hunters at home, thus enabling believers to meet, often in caves and forests. "Perhaps that reliance on nature's protection," Kline continues, "is one of the reasons Anabaptists never much cared for purging from their everyday lives what today would be considered pagan practices."[19]

These historical experiences, in interaction with theological convictions about nonviolence, nonresistance (Gelassenheit), and discipleship, have helped shape Anabaptist environmental perspectives. Many Anabaptists see nonviolence and nonresistance as central to the construction of their tradition's distinctive view of nature, forging an attitude of peaceableness, acceptance, and reconciliation toward nonhuman nature as well as within human society. An Amish prayer echoes this theme in its request to God to "help us be gentle with your creatures and handiwork so that we may abide in your eternal salvation and continue to be held in the hollow of your hand."[20] Nonviolence is part of a larger vision of Christian discipleship, an insistence on following Jesus' teachings and example in everyday practice and community life. Many Anabaptists believe that discipleship and Christian community also encompass relations with and use of nature. The creation and maintenance of the church requires attention to the ways the natural world both supports human efforts to live ethically and itself requires transformation to match the harmonious and peaceful vision of the reign of God.

Discipleship undergirds an Anabaptist stewardship ethic that demands careful, respectful, and conservative use of natural resources and places. Like Roman Catholicism, the Anabaptist tradition acknowledges that people must use natural goods to survive while also insisting that they not consume excessively, waste, hoard, or deny those in need. They believe, as Kline writes, that "God gave man 'dominion over the fish of the sea, and over the fowls of the air, and over the cattle and over all the earth, and over every creeping thing that creepeth upon the earth.'" This power, however, requires people "to be wise stewards" and not to "exploit, abuse, and exterminate His Creation."[21] The principle of stewardship has guided traditional Mennonite and Anabaptist practices of thrift and frugality, as well as charity and mutual aid. Old Order groups voluntarily limit their own convenience and profit in order to follow religiously based rules in farming and other aspects of their lives that have an impact on the natural world. The Amish do not always explicitly link their agricultural and household practices to environmental stewardship, but many do view their commitment to plain lifestyles in that light.

Sustainability and Agriculture

How are these religiously grounded, locally based ways of life and community organization related to larger projects of environmental protection at national, even international levels? We can begin to answer this question in relation to an overriding aim of environmental advocates and movements today: the effort to develop sustainable practices in agriculture, forestry, fishing, industry, housing, and transportation. An activity is sustainable if it can be continued for an indefinite period of time without destroying or depleting natural resources beyond their capacity to regenerate. The term gained currency in relation to the notion of sustainable development, which first appeared in the Brundtland Commission report *Our Common Future* in 1987 and gained further prominence after the 1992 Earth Summit in Rio de Janeiro. Sustainable development combines environmental and social goals, as a World Bank–commissioned report on natural resource management in Latin America explains, in an effort "to seek, develop, and implement . . . intensification strategies that will provide increased yields, that are sustainable (that is, they will not degrade the natural resource base in the long term), and that will contribute to the preservation of biodiversity."[22] This definition suggests that it is possible, through careful use of technology and expert knowledge, to avoid long-term harm to natural habitats and species while achieving social and economic objectives such as increasing agricultural and forest production and reducing poverty. The concept of sustainability has influenced everything from United Nations declarations to local city planning guidelines. Its appeal stems largely from the suggestion that we can "have it all," both economic growth and a cleaner environment.[23] Despite attempts to implement sustainable development projects, however, in recent years ecological degradation has intensified, while income gaps have grown both within and between nations. It has become increasingly clear that we *cannot* have it all and that in fact dominant practices provide neither ecological protection nor social development.

Agriculture plays a central role in discussions of sustainability. Often it is seen as part of the problem, especially by those who view the rise of agriculture as a turning point in human conceptions and treatment of nature. Environmentalists who focus on wilderness protection, as is common in North America, attribute many, even most contemporary environmental problems to the domestication of plants and animals and the practices and attitudes to which this gave rise, especially the fact that it enabled people to live beyond the limits of a local ecosystem. Thus Paul Shepard proclaims, "If there is a single complex of events responsible for the deterioration of human health and ecology, agricultural civilization is it."[24] For Shepard, only a return to hunting and gathering lifestyles can resolve contemporary ecological problems. Because hunter-gatherers could never forget their vulnerability and dependence on nature, he argues, they treated nonhuman animals, natural objects, and the land with respect and restraint. Agriculture, in contrast, fosters an instrumental view of nature, which appears valuable only insofar as it is useful for humans. In this view, wild species are at best irrelevant, at worst competitors or threats to be eliminated, and the land itself should be managed and manipulated to maximize production.

This criticism highlights the intrinsic value of nature, the importance of saving wild places and nonhuman species regardless of their actual or potential utility to humans. However, given the current human population, in the short or medium term we cannot live as hunter-gatherers. We may therefore want to frame the problem not as domestication and farming per se but rather as the more recent emergence of a particular type of agriculture. The traditional family farm in Europe, the United States, and Latin America was small in size, used simple technology, relied primarily on human and animal labor, and produced a variety of plant and animal products primarily for home consumption, with a surplus that was sold mainly in local markets. This model of agriculture was relatively benign environmentally. It respected natural cycles and events, allowed room for wildlife at the margins of cultivated land and in woodlots, did not contaminate air or water, preserved topsoil, and consumed few fossil fuels and chemical inputs. Small farms also supported diverse local economies, widespread ownership of land, and neighborly cooperation.

It is important not to idealize traditional small farmers, of course, either as consistently attentive to ecological and social values or as consistently happy, secure, and prosperous. Even preindustrial farmers caused environmental damage, sometimes minimal and sometimes more serious, as in deforestation in parts of Asia and predator extermination throughout Europe and North America. And farming has often been a difficult, dangerous, and unstable way to make a living. The problems may arise, however, less from "the nature of farming," as Brian Donahue contends, than from the fact that "farmers have been ensnared in political and economic systems designed to extract what they produce, leaving them barely enough to survive. Especially in the United States, Donahue continues, "our economic system has made it impossible for most farmers to thrive. The market economy has consistently encouraged and rewarded farming that is exploitative of land and people, and has steadily driven farmers off the land. As it has operated in America, the market has systematically undercut all other agrarian values: care for the land, and healthy family and community life."[25]

The social and environmental harm wrought by the market increased markedly with the industrialization of agriculture since World War II. This modern agriculture is characterized by crop and animal specialization, increased use of chemical inputs, and reliance on fossil fuel–driven machines rather than human and animal labor. This new type of farm has had devastating environmental consequences, including erosion of topsoil, water and soil contamination from chemical fertilizers and pesticides, air and water pollution due to the use of fossil fuels, loss of genetic diversity in domestic plant and animal species, and destruction of wildlife habitats. Social and economic problems have also grown, including declines in rural population fueled by high out-migration, especially of young people; increased concentration of ownership of land and equipment; a smaller number of larger farms; and the failure of many locally owned businesses that depended on the agricultural economy. The harm has been multiplied by the aggressive exportation of this model to the Third World during the "green revolution" of the 1960s. More recently, economic trends toward free trade, embodied in treaties such as the North American and Central American Free Trade Agreements (NAFTA and CAFTA), have discouraged U.S. farmers from practicing conservation by forcing them to compete with cheap labor in poorer countries. To compete, U.S. farmers buy expensive labor-replacing machinery and fuel and increase their use of toxic chemicals and exploitation of people as well as land.

Despite the damage wrought by agriculture, nonagricultural methods (hunting and gathering) can supply food for only a small fraction of the world's present human population, or even a substantially smaller one. Agriculture in some form seems to be necessary for the survival of humans as a species, even assuming population decline in the medium or long term; thus, we need to ask how it might be possible to farm without exploiting or exterminating non-human plant and animal species. Residents of urban, industrialized societies cannot afford to ignore their dependence on agriculture, even though many have been shielded, so far, from the negative effects of unsustainable farming. Our thoughtless consumption has destructive environmental, social, and economic consequences, and these problems demand solutions that not only change the way most people eat and farmers produce food but that also reconnect food production and rural communities with the cities and suburbs.

The problems of agriculture have given rise to endless discussions, meetings, and studies about the possibility and characteristics of environmentally and socially friendly ways to farm. The names vary; the most common is "sustainable agriculture," although some critics dislike this phrase because of its association with the problematic concept of sustainable development. A host of other terms are also used, including "agroecology" and "natural systems agriculture." Just as the names of the different approaches differ, so do specific elements of their proposals for solving not just problems within agriculture but the larger problem *of* agriculture, as Wes Jackson terms it: the notion that humans can impose their own systems and standards on natural processes. For example, one important stream in natural systems agriculture is Jackson's ambitious program to transform the large-scale commercial production of basic crops by developing perennial varieties of basic grains and legumes such as corn, wheat, and soy. Jackson, a plant geneticist by training, aims ultimately to replace fields full of annual monocrops with a "perennial polyculture," modeled after the midwestern prairie, which needs no tilling and little, if any, fertilizer and pesticide. Jackson's approach, targeting the large-scale production of grains and legumes, complements alternative agricultural models that aim for more organic production and local distribution of vegetables, fruits, herbs, and animal products. Small-scale, diversified subsistence farmers such as the Amish and Salvadoran repopulators could benefit from innovations developed in all of these diverse programs, and the innovators, in turn, can learn much from traditional practices such as Amish methods of crop rotation.

Despite the diversity of approaches under the category of sustainable agriculture, some common themes emerge. One is a return to a smaller scale of production. Smaller farms are more likely to be diverse in their crops, to use fewer pesticides and artificial fertilizers, and to be tied to local economies and cultures.[26] They are also highly productive, when productivity is measured by yield per unit of land or per unit of energy used. As Jack Manno summarizes, "The most productive farming turns out to be small labor-intensive, gardenlike cultivation systems with mixed crops, shifting cultivation, and a high degree of nutrient recycling." Such farms produce up to three times more per unit area than highly mechanized capital- and energy-intensive agricultural production.[27] The productivity of bigger farms and ranches, in contrast, is high only when judged in relation to the labor, especially skilled labor, required. Large farms harm the environment not only through their greater consumption of energy and land in relation to production but also because they often grow single crops, thus requiring more pesticides and reducing biological diversity, and usually rely on fossil fuel–based fertilizers. They also generate negative social consequences because they are likely to be owned by large corporations and to produce for national and international, rather than local, markets.

Although small farms have a potential for high productivity and more positive environmental and social contributions, economic trends and government policies in the United States and beyond make it very difficult to earn a living through small-scale agriculture. The experience of Amish farmers is especially important, therefore, because they are among the few groups that have remained economically successful on small farms. Their success stems from a variety of factors: general frugality, reliance on inexpensive horse and human labor, and especially a supportive family and community context. In Ohio, Pennsylvania, Indiana, and elsewhere, the Amish have managed to create communities in which small farmers and rural craftspeople can make a living producing goods needed by their neighbors. In Latin America, most farmers also work on a small scale, but in very different conditions and with very different economic outcomes. Severe shortages of land and capital limit the scale of farming in repopulated communities in Chalatenango, and it is much harder for them to employ sustainable methods due to the poor quality of their land.

A second important feature of sustainable agriculture linked to small scale is local orientation: production is primarily for local markets and intended to meet the needs of local consumers. Production for distant markets is destructive not only because it requires energy for transportation and storage but also because it discourages production of diverse, locally specific species and varieties and reduces the local community's food self-sufficiency. Despite recent changes, Amish communities remain largely self-sufficient and locally oriented in food and other necessities. In Chalatenango, repopulated villages have sought to produce more for local markets, recognizing that they cannot compete nationally with imported products. The Salvadoran government's policy of supporting export-oriented crops and importing basic foods makes it harder for subsistence farmers, in Chalatenango and elsewhere, to sell their small surpluses locally and make an adequate cash income. The stable, relatively self-sufficient local economies of Amish settlements might serve as a model for villages in Chalatenango and elsewhere in Latin America, but national policies and poverty make realization of this goal unlikely in the short term. Larger structural changes, in other words, must complement local efforts to achieve economic security.

A third characteristic of sustainable agriculture is that it follows, rather than destroys, natural processes. This means using domestic plants and animals adapted for local conditions and respecting ecological principles such as diversity and interdependence. Rather than working against the ecosystem in which it is placed, the farm uses its existing strengths and possibilities, asking both what is possible in their particular place and also, as Wes Jackson puts it, "What will nature require of us?"[28] Ecologically sound farms include a variety of plant and animal species. They do not rely heavily on external inputs such as chemical fertilizers and pesticides, and preferably they employ organic methods that not only reduce air, soil, and water pollution but also promote the farm's self-sufficiency. Self-sufficiency and low ecological impact are also facilitated by another lesson of natural processes: intensive recycling. The use of animal manure, for example, reduces the expenses associated with purchasing fertilizer and disposing of waste.

In this regard Anabaptists have been pioneers, developing ways of using green and animal manure that are widely employed by contemporary sustainable farmers. Whereas conventional farms rely on external resources such as fossil fuels for machinery, chemical fertilizers, and artificial pest control, Amish farms have a relatively closed cycle: most food needed by animals and humans is grown on the farm, most crop fertilizer comes from animal and green manures produced on site, most labor comes from resident animals and humans, and most energy is provided by renewable sources such as wind (to pump water), wood (for heating), and the sun (to produce food and fertilizers). Many Amish farms use some fossil fuels, for example, for diesel generators and tractors used around the barn, but their consumption of nonrenewable resources is vastly lower than that of conventional agriculture, which consumes fossil fuels not only to run tractors, trucks, and other machinery but also in fertilizers and animal feed.

Fossil fuel consumption is also low in Chalatenango, as in much of Latin America, due primarily to poverty and lack of access to machinery and fuel. Most work is done by people and domestic animals, although under conditions of hardship rather than deliberate design. The use of sustainable practices is increasing in the repopulations, particularly when national and international environmental NGOs provide technical and financial assistance. In Chalatenango, a number of residents have experimented with waste recycling, use of compost and organic fertilizers, and alternative methods of pest and weed control. The most extensive experiment in sustainable agriculture, or agroecology, in Chalatenango is La Montañona, a postwar community discussed later in this chapter.

Finally, sustainable agriculture should leave room for wild nature, for example, in hedgerows, woodlots, and wild areas on the edges of cultivated land. Aldo Leopold defined a good farm as one where the wild flora and fauna have lost ground without losing their existence.[29] This has been a guiding principle for David Kline, who contends that traditional Amish farming practices, including allowing some grasses and fence rows to become overgrown, leaving substantial areas in woods and wildflowers, and diverting the plow or even delaying the harvest to protect birds nesting in the fields, all help make land more attractive to wildlife.[30] In El Salvador, intensive restoration efforts will be required to re-create habitat for wildlife. Although many native species no longer survive in the country due to habitat loss and hunting, the depopulation of rural areas caused by the war made it possible for some species to return. Repobladores now face the challenge of sharing limited land, water, and vegetation with wild animals. They have had some success, most notably through reforestation projects that have expanded habitat for bird species.

The values listed above arise most commonly in discussions of sustainable farming, especially in the United States. The list could be expanded with other principles that have emerged as particularly important for Third World experiences and perspectives, many of which can also be applied to the United States. These additional guidelines for agricultural sustainability might include national self-sufficiency in the production of basic foodstuffs or at least a reduction in reliance on imports; the preservation of native domestic and wild plant and animal species and varieties as well as indigenous and traditional cultures that have learned to cohabit with these species; fair wages, benefits, and safety conditions for agricultural workers; and avoidance of unequal trading relationships, regionally and internationally.[31]

An additional element of sustainable agriculture is the relationship between the countryside and the cities, where most people, in the United States and throughout the world, live. It bears pointing out, first, that "the eating habits of urbanites have an enormous impact on the viability of good farming."[32] Agriculture will change, in other words, if consumers demand organic foods, seek out local products, reduce their meat consumption, and demand products from free-range and grass-fed animals rather than those produced in concentrated feeding operations. More specifically, agricultural methods have immediate impacts on nearby urban areas, just as urban and suburban development affects neighboring rural areas. Despite this mutual influencing, which affects quality of life in both cities and countryside, very few urban areas maintain a sustainable balance with their surrounding regions. Local products are mostly exported, and locally consumed foods are mostly imported. This is true in the United States and most developing nations. One way to begin moving toward more sustainable cities is to increase the amount of food that city consumers purchase from farmers in the local countryside. With a more locally centered food economy, Wendell Berry predicts, "local farming would become more diverse; the farms would become smaller, more complex, more productive; and some city people would be needed to work on the farms."[33] (Like most Amish people, Berry does not count a growth in the need for rural labor as a disadvantage.) Increased connections between cities and their rural sources of production would ultimately help transform people's values and ways of thinking, thus making possible changes toward even greater sustainability and local economic self-sufficiency. In the long run, it will be impossible, in the United States and elsewhere, to create more sustainable agricultural practices without major economic and cultural changes in urban and suburban, as well as rural, areas. In fact, new models for rural and urban planning share similar goals, including most generally "a proliferation of small, relatively self-sufficient communities, populated by people with intimate knowledge of their place and their neighbors."[34]

These changes will not come easily. Small, diversified, locally oriented farmers face serious challenges in their efforts to integrate into markets at regional, national, and even international levels. In Latin America as in the United States, producers cannot survive unless they sell their products in sufficient numbers and at an adequate profit. Small-scale, locally based producers cannot easily compete with corporate-owned farms and ranches which produce in vast quantities and have the capacity to advertise, market, and export their products across the world. One strategy adopted by a number of farmers in both the United States and Latin America has been to seek out niches for high-value products, such as organic and specialty produce.

Chalatenango has less land devoted to sustainable agriculture than the more fertile regions where other repopulated communities are located. This is partly because farmers in Chalatenango continue to produce mainly for themselves and their families, with the small surpluses available going to local markets. On the other hand, some repopulated communities in the lower Lempa River region in the San Vicente and La Paz departments in El Salvador have had success selling organic cashew nuts in the United States and Europe. At one end, communities in the lower Lempa region export 95 percent of what they produce, including high-value products, while at the other end, Chalatenango's agricultural production is almost all for internal consumption.[35] El Salvador has virtually no internal market for organic products, and even the international market is small at present, so organic produce cannot provide a large-scale solution for El Salvador's rural development at this point. Further, the Salvadoran government offers no economic incentives for organic production and no technical assistance with sustainable methods such as integrated pest management. Currently, only 1.6 percent of the national budget (including debt payments) goes toward agriculture, and most of that goes to large- and medium-scale export-oriented production. Government agricultural policy asserts that the country should no longer produce many basic foods for internal consumption but instead should import them, especially corn and sorghum for animal feed, which are produced more cheaply in the United States, in large part because of government subsidies. Salvadoran policymakers and economic elites see no future for the production of basic foodstuffs, especially by small farmers.

In the United States, government support of agriculture, though much larger in scale than in El Salvador, similarly reinforces the existing distribution of wealth and influence and encourages unsustainable farming practices such as monocropping, confined animal feedlots, and heavy use of chemical pesticides and fertilizers. Even the main alternative practice encouraged by government policies and experts, no-till cropping intended to reduce soil erosion, has a high cost in terms of increased reliance on herbicides, which damage water and even the very soil the practice is meant to conserve. The U.S. government provides virtually no subsidies or support for small-scale, diversified, or organic crop production. Even conventional family farmers find it difficult to survive in the face of growing corporate ownership of land and machinery and increased global free trade.

Because of what and how they produce, most Amish farmers are ineligible for government support or subsidy programs. In most cases, they would not accept the subsidies anyway, due to religious rules against depending on government support. Some Amish farmers do use information from agricultural extension agencies, although many view such services with suspicion. In some areas, local land-use regulations have also helped Amish families continue farming and protected their land from highways and other development. This protection is often achieved with support from non-Amish neighbors or environmental groups, who value the ways the Amish farm and live, their contribution to local economic stability, and the preservation of a diversified, healthy rural landscape. Many Amish people feel ambivalent about these alliances with the contemporary equivalent of the Treuherzige who aided persecuted Anabaptists in the sixteenth and seventeenth centuries.

Rejecting most government programs, some Amish farmers have pursued organic certification for dairy products and vegetables, which allows them to sell at higher profits and often requires little modification of their practices. In both Latin America and North America, farmers have found that cooperatives or networks increase their ability to advertise, market, and transport their products. In the United States, in addition, a number of Amish and other small farmers have turned to community-supported agriculture, which provides farmers with necessary capital during the planting and growing seasons and helps them survive episodes of drought, floods, and frosts that otherwise would have meant disaster.

Community-supported agriculture (CSA) producers often sell their surplus products at farmers' markets, which have grown tremendously throughout the United States in the past decade or so. At farmers' markets, producers sell fresh produce, plants, and value-added items such as jam, cheese, salsa, and baked goods directly to shoppers, who congregate in parking lots, downtown plazas, and parks. As a September 2002 *New York Times* article notes, "With no subsidies and no middle men, farmers' markets have increased by 79 per cent since 1994, to 3,137 in all 50 states, and the number of farmers who sell at them has more than tripled to 67,000." About 3 million Americans a week now shop at farmers' markets, helping thousands of small producers survive. Many small farmers, in fact, have stopped selling to big wholesalers entirely because their profit margin is so much higher when they sell directly at farmers' markets.[36]

Farmers' markets resemble the traditional village markets that have long been central to rural and small-town life in most of the world. Weekly or daily open-air markets at which producers sell directly still survive in many parts of Latin America, but they have lost ground to supermarket chains and fast-food restaurants. In El Salvador, some small producers have organized *días de mercado* (market days), similar to farmers' markets, in which farmers from a certain area bring their products to a designated village on a particular day of the week. The market days help both producers and village residents, who gain access to fresh, diverse food without having to travel to larger towns.

These local initiatives operate in the shadow of larger trends and without government support. Much but not everything can be done at local levels. We cannot solve the problems in and of agriculture with only small-scale local initiatives. In both the United States and El Salvador, regional and national policies and institutions mostly ignore or actively obstruct small-scale sustainable farming. On occasion, however, laws and political programs have helped small agrarian communities survive. More of these initiatives are necessary, in all countries, if communities are to survive economically without shortchanging their commitments to environmental sustainability, popular participation, and equitable and harmonious social relations. Where governments have invested in sustainable agriculture and forestry, as in some Latin American and European countries, the results have been impressive in both economic and environmental terms. The Costa Rican government, in particular, has achieved significant success with policies encouraging sustainable use of forests and promoting nonchemical crop protection. In France, national and regional programs have helped preserve village economies and local cultures, preventing the sort of rural-urban migration that has devastated the midwestern United States. One bright spot in the United States is the presence of some limited incentives for farmers to conserve wetlands, although these programs have come under threat in recent agricultural appropriations bills. Much remains to be done, and even locally focused activists must remember that national policies and investments affect how small farmers and communities move toward more sustainable practices.

Sustainable Agriculture in Collective Practice

There are many possible ways to trace the history of sustainable agriculture in the United States and elsewhere. Some observers point out that the characteristics necessary for more sustainable agriculture—small, diversified, self-reliant, and locally oriented farms—characterize most of the family farms that dominated Europe and North America after European settlement until quite recently. From this perspective, "alternative" farming is really just a return to what was mainstream for most of agricultural history.[37] Contemporary sustainable agriculture also draws from the ecological orientation of the organic food movement that began in the 1960s.

One major difference between traditional diversified family farms and contemporary alternatives to corporate agriculture is the latter's social and economic isolation. In the United States today, most people attempting to farm sustainably do so by themselves, as a family or a small group of friends organized into a cooperative. Few live immersed in a community of like-minded farmers doing similar things: either they work isolated farms in mainly urban or suburban areas, or they live as eccentrics in rural communities surrounded by conventional farmers.

In the absence of natural communities that farm sustainably, some advocates and farmers have worked to create networks that can expand alternative models of agriculture. One of the most important is the community-supported agriculture movement. CSA involves

> a relationship of mutual support and commitment between local
> farmers and community members who pay an annual membership
> fee due at the first of the year or in quarterly installments to cover
> the farm's production costs, and in turn receive their share of the
> harvest each week during the local growing season. This arrange-
> ment guarantees the CSA farmer financial support, which enables

many small- to moderate-scale organic family farms to remain in business, despite increasing pressure from larger organic or conventional farming operations. Ultimately, CSA creates "agriculture-supported communities," where members receive a wide variety of foods harvested at their peak of ripeness, flavor, and vitamin and mineral content.[38]

The CSA concept began in Japan in 1965 and spread to North America in 1985. Presently, more than a thousand farms participate in CSA networks in the United States and Canada, making available an increasingly broad spectrum of farm products to more than 100,000 members. Most of the farms that participate in CSA programs produce certified organic or otherwise sustainable products and use ecologically sensitive practices such as intercropping, crop rotation, cover crops, green manure, companion planting, biological pest control, integrated pest management, composting, and seed saving. Further, most CSA farms are small and family-owned, and they usually produce a diverse array of vegetables, fruits, and sometimes animal products (such as eggs and dairy products). There are economic as well as environmental benefits. When members buy shares of a farmer's crop, they eliminate the middlemen required for wholesale marketing, enabling farmers to receive better returns on products and keeping food expenditures in the local economy. Further, the fact that members share risks and production costs reduces the economic pressure on the farmers, allowing them to use more ecologically sound methods. Finally, CSAs link consumers directly to local food producers and increase their knowledge of the local "foodshed."[39] These advantages are countered by a major drawback: while supported by local consumers, most CSA farms are not linked to other agricultural producers or larger rural communities, which makes it difficult to transform farming and rural life on a large scale.

If contemporary organic farmers employ ecologically beneficial agricultural methods but often lack community, many Mennonite farmers find themselves in the opposite situation. Rural Mennonite communities retain many traditional features, such as mutual aid, collective accountability, shared religious values, deep roots in local history and places, and the presence of extended family. They share, especially, a conviction about the need to leave things better for the next generation. "We are immortal," explains one Kansas farmer, "because although individuals die, the race goes on." However, the group will continue only if each generation restrains its own consumption and avoids the "audacity" of consuming without giving anything back. Anabaptist humility counsels against assuming that technology will always solve the problems people cause, including soil erosion and pollution.[40] In their farming methods, however, few Mennonites diverge from the mainstream. Some Mennonite farmers are experimenting with organic production, and many try to preserve wooded areas, protect watersheds, and provide habitat for wildlife.

Overall, however, a relatively small number employ unconventional farming techniques and technologies. Their farms, more often than not, are indistinguishable from non-Mennonite farms: they encompass hundreds, even thousands, of acres; they grow only a few crops (usually wheat, soy, sorghum, or corn); they use chemical fertilizers and pesticides; and they rely on tractors and other heavy machinery. They participate in government subsidy programs and follow advice from the U.S. Department of Agriculture and agricultural extension services. On the recommendations of these agencies, many have adopted no-till methods in an attempt to conserve topsoil. In all these features, their farms resemble other conventional farms in the Midwest.

What distinguishes Mennonite farming is the social setting: farms stay in families and are not sold to large corporations, sons and daughters return to rural communities to farm or to work in the local economy, and neighbors know and help each other. The Anabaptist tradition of mutual aid continues, part of what one farmer calls the difference that being Mennonite makes to his work. As an example, he points out that Mennonite farmers break the rule against working on Sundays only when their neighbors need help. They also hold each other accountable for their use of the land and its impact on the community. He recalls severe local disapproval of a man who rented out his land for an intensive hog farming operation. If that farmer decides to sell his land, neighbors will buy his barns, even though they have no plan to raise hogs, to prevent a large corporation from buying it.[41] In such cases, a long-standing Anabaptist emphasis on community responsibility holds individualism in check. Unlike most North American farmers, in short, these Mennonites live and work in the context of tight-knit, supportive, and stable rural communities.

The Amish have this sort of community to a more intense degree. Their settlements are more close-knit, more mutually dependent, more stable, and more homogeneous than those of mainstream Mennonites, and even more so than corporate farmers. "Probably the greatest difference between Amish farming and agribusiness," contends David Kline, "is the supportive community life we have." This community makes the Amish way of life possible, and in turn their way of farming reflects a commitment to "nurturing and supporting all our community—that includes people as well as land and wildlife."[42] Amish farmers pursue these goals through agricultural practices that are decidedly unconventional by mainstream U.S. standards although deeply traditional in their own context. Along with other Old Order groups, the Amish are the only substantial and enduring population in North America who farm in a community setting, using mostly sustainable methods; who keep farms in the family and grown children on the farm (or at least in rural communities); who have survived and often thrived economically; and who, in consequence, live in healthy and stable rural communities. Despite the ongoing challenges they face, their experience cannot be ignored in efforts to uncover and extend more sustainable ways of farming and perhaps of making a living in any environment.

The villages in Chalatenango, like Amish settlements, are intentional communities, with a strong religious orientation. Unlike the Amish, however, they are poor communities in a poor region of a poor nation. They have faced political violence, state neglect, and resource shortages that limit their ability to build the kind of agriculture and the kind of society toward which they aspire. Mainstream agriculture in El Salvador, as in most of Latin America, is no more and possibly even less environmentally sustainable than in the United States, relying on heavy doses of chemical fertilizers and pesticides, including some, such as DDT, that are banned in the United States and Europe. They rely heavily on human and animal labor, but many workers are exploited and endangered. Often farmers recognize the damage their practices cause to human and ecological health but cannot use alternative methods, even when they are aware of them. For example, organic fertilizers may be insufficient in soils exhausted by years of overuse or unsuitable for cultivation; in such cases, farmers have to use chemical fertilizers if they hope to feed their families.

This dilemma offers an important perspective on the philosophical distinction between instrumental and intrinsic value in nature and also on the tendency (at least of some environmental philosophers) to believe that people who use nature instrumentally do not appreciate its intrinsic value. Many people in Chalatenango appreciate the noninstrumental value of species and landscapes that are not particularly useful for humans. Community members speak animatedly about formerly rare or absent bird species they now see regularly as a result of reforestation efforts. Sometimes people have to override these "nonanthropocentric" values, as in their continued use of some pesticides that are dangerous to seed-eating songbirds, but this does not mean they do not hold these values, nor does it mean they do not want better alternatives.

The most extensive experiment with such alternatives in Chalatenango is in La Montañona ("big mountain"), a village in a former war zone that was created not through the resettlement of an abandoned village but through the postwar Land Transfer Program (PTT). The community encompasses 136 plots spread over 503 hectares of land, at the peak of a "soil protection zone" and within the infiltration zone for the nation's largest reservoir, the Cerrón Grande. Most of the land is unsuitable for traditional agricultural production, even by the desperate standards of Chalatenango's highlands. Thus, the new residents, mainly former FMLN combatants and their families, had to find ways to provide food for themselves without destroying some of the last remaining forests in El Salvador. Working with Salvadoran and international NGOs, residents of La Montañona developed a series of village and regional plans adapted to local ecological and economic realities, including a shift from grain to vegetable production, development of local trade and market networks, and medium-term credits to develop a small wood products industry, all in an effort to protect natural resources and at the same time meet community needs. The environmental standards include minimal use of chemical pesticides; efforts to limit erosion and to protect water and forests; adaptation of agriculture to local environments (thus the move to vegetable crops adapted to local conditions); economic diversification; holistic management of local agricultural and ecological systems across different scales of household, village, region, and nation; and long-term ecological sustainability and social stability. Finally, the community's plans aim to keep local people in control of their community's development and direction. This requires NGOs and technical experts to work closely with local residents so that knowledge is shared and decisions are based on mutual agreement rather than outside imposition. According to one researcher, La Montañona represents

> an example of how researchers, NGOs and communities can form alliances that facilitate exchange of information, knowledge, and power to promote environmental and social well-being rather than operating under a top-down development model. In Montañona, the community sought consultation and financial support from national and international governmental and non-governmental organizations, but they were particularly careful to insure that the decision-making processes remained within their control. When development projects are firmly rooted in locally identified priorities for improving livelihoods and environmental quality, communities can *coordinate* outside assistance in such a way to insure that development is appropriate in socio-economic and ecological terms. When people who are commonly the objects of the development process have access to tools and systems of knowledge—ranging from local knowledge of soil fertility to GIS [geographic information system]—better-informed decisions on land and livelihood are made, and concerns for ecological integrity can be better represented.[43]

La Montañona's residents have also engaged national politics, especially through efforts in collaboration with other municipalities and NGOs, to require El Salvador's water company to pay farmers for water conserved by improved soil protections. This is part of a larger movement in Latin America toward payment for environmental services (*pago por servicios ambientales*), spearheaded by national environmental groups as a way to link environmental protection and rural livelihoods. Though not all repopulations have the same environmental focus as La Montañona, most are trying some environmentally oriented projects on various scales. They are aware that their long-term survival depends on a transition to more sustainable ways of making a living. As a member of the directiva in Guarjila explained, "We live from the earth; we have to take care of it."[44]

What is significant about the still unfolding experience of La Montañona is not only the emphasis on environmental protection but the effort to integrate economic and ecological considerations within a larger commitment to local self-governance and social justice in accord with Catholic social thought. These principles govern other repopulations, although most communities cannot yet allow ecological considerations to play as determinative a role as they have in La Montañona. The postwar origin of the community and the high level of support and involvement from Salvadoran and international NGOs have helped make possible its success to date. If this success continues, it may encourage other villages to undertake more ambitious environmental protection and restoration measures, including but not limited to sustainable agriculture. To pursue such projects, however, local groups will require outside funding from the Salvadoran government or international conservation and development agencies.

Many agencies involved in Chalatenango and elsewhere in El Salvador's former war zones share a conviction that environmental protection can succeed only when grounded in the experiences, interests, and priorities of local communities. This reflects a growing conviction, in Latin America and elsewhere in the Third World, that conventional approaches, usually elaborated by experts working in isolation from local residents, have been shown repeatedly and in different parts of the world to fail to protect the environment or to achieve a better quality of life or greater justice for human communities. As an alternative, many scholars, policymakers, and activists advocate community-based conservation plans, which are developed with the input and active involvement of local residents and leaders.

Common Ground

Despite the historic, ideological, and institutional differences between Catholic and Anabaptist traditions, the two share several important features in relation to social and environmental ethics. First, both Catholic and Anabaptist views of the social world and the natural environment are oriented toward a particular theological vision, in which God's power, grace, and creative work are central. They are thus theocentric, or God-centered, rather than anthropocentric, or human-centered. In regard to environmental ethics, this unites them with many mainstream Protestant (and Eastern Orthodox, Jewish, and Muslim) believers and distinguishes them from nontheistic religious traditions such as Buddhism and also from secular environmental philosophies. For Catholics and Anabaptists, nonhuman animals, plants, wild places, and other aspects of the natural world have special worth because they are created and valued by God. Respectful treatment of nature thus reflects respect for God; mistreatment of nature is not just morally bad but a sin against the Creator and the divine will.

Similar themes emerge in thinking about social justice. It is God's intention for people to live in particular ways, both Anabaptists and Roman Catholics argue, and failure to do so represents not just a social lack but a religious sin. Thus, progressive Catholic theologians in Latin America speak of "social sin," which points to the ways that oppressive political and economic policies and institutions offend against God and not just people. This theological approach dictates a particular treatment of nature, understood most generally as careful stewardship of God-given resources. This perspective, common to Catholics and Anabaptists, differs from some radical ecological views in its assertion that creation is given for human use; it does not have to be left alone as wilderness, or at least not all of it does.

Catholics and Anabaptists also share a conception of humans as social beings who can live full and proper lives only as part of a community and who can be saved only collectively. The social community is necessarily a natural community as well. Humans depend on each other, on God, and on nature. This mutual interdependence is part of an overarching natural and divine order, and what happens between humans has real and lasting effects on what happens in the natural world and vice versa. Similar principles guide both natural and social realms, and human behavior in both areas ought to be consistent. Creation is one, a single God rules over it, and the same rules apply to all believers. This belief rests on natural law for Catholics, and on the principle of discipleship for Anabaptists. In both cases, the foundational ethic stems from the model of the reign of God as an ideal community in which all members adhere to the same high standards.

Further, contemporary Roman Catholics and Anabaptists share a conviction that social, economic, and environmental problems are connected in their causes and potential solutions. This reflects a resistance, common among both Third World and Christian environmentalists, to ecocentric perspectives that see solutions to environmental problems in keeping humans out of wild areas. Many Third World environmentalists believe this perspective reflects the self-interest of wealthy North Americans who want to enjoy nature for its aesthetic and recreational possibilities. In contrast, they argue, poor people who have to make a living from the land cannot afford to set aside parcels of wilderness. If the poor majorities in countries like El Salvador are to survive, then environmental protection must take place in the context of human habitation and use of nature. It is also worth recalling that the high-consumption practices of wealthy elites, in both developing and industrial societies, create more environmental damage than the subsistence lifestyles of poor peasants.

This political critique agrees with Catholic and Anabaptist arguments that God intended creation for the use of all and Christians should use it in respectful and conservative ways. Some human use of natural resources is necessary, but overexploitation leads to environmental destruction and deprivation for other humans. The good life does not require excessive consumption. The

Amish and many Mennonites keep consumption low because they do not want consumerism to penetrate their culture and displace more important values such as community well-being and faithful discipleship. In El Salvador, consumption is also low, due in large part to extreme poverty; few people have cars or telephones because few can afford them. Still, Salvadorans seeking to create alternative communities explicitly reject mainstream U.S. values of individualism and the pursuit of comfort and profit at the cost of survival for the poor. The adoption of these values by Salvadoran elites led to social inequity and political violence. In contrast to this consumerist ethic, progressive Catholics insist that both hardships and goods are to be shared, so that all have what they need. This concern for the least well-off rests on a deeply rooted belief in the priority of community.

4

Community

Defining Community

The idea of community is central to many of the issues at stake in this book, such as how religious traditions are embodied in people's everyday lives and in institutions, how humans relate to the natural world, how social change occurs, and how local practices are linked to larger structural, even global, processes. What exactly constitutes a community, however, is not always clear. People often use the term unselfconsciously, as though it means the same thing in all times and places and requires no explanation. For example, we frequently think of a community as a fairly small geographic space (a town, village, or neighborhood) with clear boundaries, inhabited by more or less similar people, most of whom know each other personally. This homogeneous, compact, physically rooted, and personally connected social group often serves as a sort of default definition of community, what people assume when they use the term without defining it explicitly. At the same time, many people—sometimes the same people—believe that this sort of community no longer exists. This paradox emerges, for example, in David Kirp's recent book about "America's love-hate relationship with community." Kirp explores the dangers and benefits of community without ever spelling out what he means by the key term. He admits, "The word *community* itself is a Rorschach blot upon which myriad hopes and fears are projected" but assumes that everyone will know what he means by it.[1]

Many contemporary discussions begin with this vision of community as Rorschach blot. The concept is so varied and fluid, many scholars argue, that it resists all permanent or universal definition. In this perspective, community, like most of the important categories we use to think about ourselves and our world, is socially constructed. It is neither objective nor self-evident, in other words, but is invented, shaped, and maintained by specific social groups, with their own histories and values, in particular times and places. Communities are socially constructed because they are not given by God or nature but are established, by both members and outsiders, in relation to a broader cultural and social context. Every definition involves choices about what to include and exclude. As Mitchell Thomashow points out, definitions of community always pose certain questions to those doing the defining, such as "What space and time boundaries are you using and why have you chosen them?"[2] Further, people construct and shape communities not only and not necessarily with reference to spatial and temporal borders but also according to subjective and symbolic traits, such as shared language, religion, values, and history. A community may be defined by how its members make similar sense of things, different from other ways of thinking and seeing, rather than by geographic boundaries and physical characteristics.[3] Thus people living in the same neighborhood may not identify themselves as a community, whereas people sharing certain traits—Swedish ancestors, the hobby of stamp collecting, or belief in the teachings of Mary Baker Eddy—can feel joined in community although they live far from each other and rarely, if ever, meet face to face.

This attention to the symbolic dimensions of community underlines the fact that community is a normative as well as a descriptive term. A community is defined by what the group aspires to be and not only by what it actually is. Of course, no real community fulfills all its goals, and most of the time members know that their community fails to live up to its own ideals. Speaking of the community in idealized terms need not indicate ignorance or deceptiveness. It may instead reflect hope for what the community should be and could become, despite recognition that it currently falls short and perhaps always will. Many Christians, for example, see the early church as an ideal for which contemporary believers should strive, even though they may never realize it fully. This is particularly true for progressive Catholics and Anabaptists, who explicitly relate the forms and values of their contemporary religious communities to the practices and teachings of Jesus' first disciples.

Even communities such as these, based on what members believe are divinely given values and traditions, change over time. For example, Amish communities are often stereotyped as living exactly like their nineteenth-century ancestors, yet they continually adapt in response to changes generated from within and outside their settlements. Most of the time, Amish leaders manage to direct and restrain the changes so that they do not threaten the core values of unity and discipleship. This success is possible not because the Amish resist all change, but because they have developed and nurtured effective ways of recognizing and dealing with change, grounded in knowledge of their own history and in educated reflection about the probable impact of changes on the community and its values. The repopulations in Chalatenango and elsewhere in El Salvador are still working out their responses to the dramatic changes in their communities since the war's end, including not only national and international economic and political events but also the loss of the intense unity that prevailed during the war years. Community members generally recognize, as do most Amish people in North America, that even situations that appear threatening cannot be met with simple denial or blanket resistance to change. For the community to persist, members and leaders must recognize what has changed and why, how it has affected the community, and what can and should be done about it, which may entail further changes in community institutions or practices.

Even small and tight-knit communities, including the ones discussed in this book, face not only changing circumstances but also internal differences and disagreements. The histories of the Amish and the Salvadoran peasant movements suggest that community survival depends not on the absence of disagreement but on the presence of effective mechanisms for recognizing conflicts and resolving them in ways that most community members accept. This is institutionalized in Amish disciplinary practices for members who violate the Ordnung, as well as in the local governmental bodies of the Salvadoran repopulations. Informal processes, ranging from gossip to mutual aid, also help prevent conflicts from growing to dangerous levels. Such formal and informal mechanisms, built on guiding principles and knowledge of human weaknesses, enable community members to address problems in ways that, most of the time, avoid deep divisions and enable desired projects and the community itself to continue.

Awareness of the social construction, fluidity, and internal complexity of all communities provides a necessary context for reflection on the understanding and experience of community in the cases explored in this book. While agreeing with the social constructionist claim that no definition of community can hold universally or permanently, I still believe it is possible to specify what we mean by community in particular cases and, on that basis, to compare, contrast, and evaluate. Examining the common features of these or any communities will not lead to a generic definition of community. However, in this case, comparison can help us identify which shared features of these communities help them to shape their institutions and everyday lives according to their ethical principles and also to live in ways that are more environmentally and socially sustainable than in most other Western societies. Careful comparisons leave us with as many particularities as commonalities, and both can increase our understanding of how we might move our own particular communities toward a more sustainable future.

To move toward an understanding of what these communities have in common as communities, I propose a provisional definition, sketched as a set of shared characteristics. I begin with the notion that these communities, like any, consist of "a group of interacting individuals."[4] The individuals in the Amish and Salvadoran communities I discuss interact not only in subjective and symbolic ways. They embody concrete realities, groups of people who live and work in close physical proximity. Further, these people live in rural villages and are mostly small farmers, although this is changing as new forms of livelihood become necessary and sometimes desirable. The communities are also fairly homogeneous in terms of religion, culture, and ethnicity. For the Amish, this homogeneity is especially great, as the church includes only baptized adults. Children and nonbaptized adult relatives of Amish church members, however, still belong to the larger community. The Salvadoran re-populations encompass some, although not much, religious diversity. A few Pentecostal families live in Guarjila, for example, but they represent less than 1 percent of the population. Further, the members of these communities know each other and interact face-to-face all the time. These are small communities, with a few dozen or, in the largest repopulations and church districts, a few hundred families that live and work in close proximity. A final common feature is a deep attachment to particular places, including the landscape, to native species, and to natural and cultural histories. Despite the histories of exile that mark both groups, members are defined by their knowledge of, history in, and close identification with their place of residence.

These qualities characterize Salvadoran peasants and the North American Amish as a kind of community that sometimes seems obsolete: several hundred or several thousand people sharing common histories and values, living in physical proximity, and experiencing frequent face-to-face interactions. They appear to exemplify a premodern "folk" society, the kind of traditional community that we both assume and dismiss, in sharp contrast to contemporary societies in which large populations of diverse people interact via technology, move frequently, and have few long-lasting ties to either their neighbors or their place of residence. Many people assume that such communities must always be narrow-minded, repressive, hostile to outsiders, and ignorant of the world beyond their borders—literally parochial. However, a few caveats are worth keeping in mind. First, intolerance and xenophobia are hardly in short supply in urban areas of the United States, Europe, and other cosmopolitan societies; it is unfair, as well as inaccurate, to assume that these negative qualities are never found in cities and suburbs but always in the country. Second, although openness to novelty and diversity are good, they are not all that a pluralistic and democratic society needs. We also need commitment to mutual aid and a willingness, on occasion, to set aside self-interest for the common good. These are not exclusively rural values, any more than tolerance is an urban one, but they may receive more social and institutional support in small towns and villages. In short, it is no more intellectually justifiable or politically helpful to dismiss local values and small communities than to romanticize them.

It is also worth noting that in many ways the communities described here are far from premodern, if we understand modernity not in terms of particular practices or artifacts but "as the perception of choice between different paths of social development." By this definition, the Amish are highly modern, insofar as they self-consciously manipulate their path of social development, selectively replacing some technology and forms of social organization and accepting others.[5] The same can be said for the carefully planned and organized repopulations. They are small, locally rooted, and religiously based, but they are not holdovers from premodern culture. Nor do they exist in a vacuum. However self-contained and stable these communities appear, they live in the world and cannot be understood or experienced in isolation from other social processes, institutions, and forces. They know about and interact with regional, national, and global institutions and actors with whom they have multiple, mutual influences.

These communities also share a social understanding of human nature. Their members understand themselves first and foremost in relationship to the larger collective. Persons are not conceived of primarily as autonomous, self-sufficient individuals but as social beings who can develop and thrive only in the course of mutual interactions and dependencies with others. For both Catholics and Anabaptists, humans are social creatures because they are related to and dependent on God. As the Mennonite *Confession of Faith* puts it, "We believe that God has created human beings in the divine image. God formed them from the dust of the earth and gave them a special dignity among all the works of creation. Human beings have been made for relations with God, to live in peace with each other, and to take care of the rest of creation."[6] This echoes the Roman Catholic position, expressed in *Gaudium et spes*, the final document of the Second Vatican Council: "God did not create man for life in isolation, but for the formation of social unity."[7] The divine act of creation endowed humans not only with inviolable dignity and rights but also with a social nature, which makes human fulfillment impossible outside of a healthy and harmonious community. Even ultimate salvation requires a social setting, because the believing community, rather than the individual, is the locus of God's salvific activity. In this framework, it is natural to believe, as David Kline puts it, that "when an issue comes up between self and community, you should always choose community."[8] Such conflicts, in fact, may be illusory, for ultimately no self can survive apart from a supporting community.

This view of personhood dictates certain principles for the organization and distribution of social and natural resources. Both are intended, Catholic and Anabaptist traditions insist, for the common good. This means that a society's success is defined not primarily by the fate of the most privileged but rather by the well-being of the larger collective and especially the least well-off within it. Former refugees in El Salvador put this value into practice when they set aside land to produce food for needy community members and dedicate scarce resources and their own time to projects such as clinics and schools. In Amish settlements, similarly, farmers and business owners base economic decisions, such as whether to expand an operation or adopt new technology, on their potential impact on the larger community rather than on the promise of individual profit. In both cases, the driving goals are that the community as a whole be strengthened and that no member be left without the basic requirements of a dignified life.

This commitment appears hard, if not impossible, to live out in the complex and diverse society in which most North Americans live. However, Amish experiences demonstrate that it is possible to set up a community so that people live their values even when they conflict with larger cultural patterns and institutions. This is most evident in transportation. While most people in the United States could never get along without cars, the Amish do so very well, because they have deliberately constructed their communities and institutions and directed their aspirations so that they can live their values. Structures and individual behavior cannot stand, or be understood, alone. Herein lies a crucial lesson for building sustainable communities. The Salvadoran repopulations also have high levels of face-to-face relations and independence from cars. These are not so clearly the result of careful planning, although such planning may become necessary in the face of increasing mobility and road construction. In other spheres, the repopulations have deliberately established and maintained institutions that make it possible to live out their values, such as collective ownership and production, participatory decision making, universal health care and education, and social security for the least well-off.

People act on these commitments and place the common good ahead of private interest because they share an identity forged by a common history. Their visions of an alternative future, as well as their critique of present realities, rest on collective, religiously based knowledge and values as well as practices and institutions. Although communal traditions can suffer from many shortcomings, including intolerance and inflexibility, they can achieve consistency, endurance, and enforcing power lacking in individualist philosophies. In the particular communities at stake here, the Roman Catholic and the Anabaptist traditions have advantages over many other religions, especially mainline Protestants, and also over many political groups, because their basic unit is not the individual but the church or congregation. This is institutionalized in the Catholic principle of holding scripture and church tradition as equal authorities and, in a more informal but no less binding fashion, in the Anabaptist practices of collective biblical interpretation and mutual accountability and aid.

Both Catholic and Anabaptist churches constitute "communities of memory," as Robert Bellah and colleagues describe them in *Habits of the Heart*. These contrast with the many communities in the United States today that rest on superficial common interests and are merely transitory "lifestyle enclaves." Communities of memory are built on shared history and deep-rooted values and a common vision of the good life and the best means to achieve it, for the group as well as individuals. Collective narratives nurture and maintain both this future vision and the past experiences of the contemporary community. As the authors of *Habits of the Heart* explain, "A 'community of memory' is involved in retelling its story, its constitutive narrative, and in so doing, it offers examples of the men and women who have embodied and exemplified the meaning of the community. . . . The stories that make up a tradition contain concepts of character, of what a good person is like, and the virtues that define such a character."[9] Communities of memory do not deprive their members of individual identity. Rather, they make possible the fulfillment of individualism *in* rather than *against* community.

The Anabaptist tradition is especially instructive in this regard, due to its combined emphasis on personal choice and community solidarity. In Kansas, a young farmer told me that Mennonites may appear to be individualistic because of their nonconformity, especially on military issues. However, he argues, members of the Mennonite community are parts of a larger whole that can take precedence over private interests and desires. Interestingly, this farmer criticized other Mennonites who want to give to the community but hesitate to receive aid or be dependent. He offers a distinctively Anabaptist critique of this position as "another kind of individualism," the failure to acknowledge mutual dependence.[10]

Communities of memory contrast with the utilitarian individualism that dominates contemporary U.S. culture and that defines selves by reference to needs and desires, even by the pursuit of what *Habits of the Heart* calls a "contentless freedom." According to the dominant worldview, substantive commitments, especially to a larger group or an enduring moral tradition, appear hostile to the individual. Communities of memory, on the other hand, are built on shared history, deep-rooted values, and a collective vision of the common good and the best means to reach it. Members develop their sense of self by reference to long-term commitments and virtues passed on and modeled by others, nurtured and maintained through social narratives. This is true for the people described in this book, for whom both historical memory and future vision are, further, religious. They are religious, moreover, in a particular way: they share a sense of historical continuity with the historical Jesus and his early disciples. This leads to a vision of the ideal society modeled on the early Christian community, an embodiment of the virtues of unity, cooperation, and brotherly love, of considering the common good above their individual interest. In both the Amish and the repopulated settlements, it is widely agreed that this is how people are and how God calls them to be.

This commitment makes them willing to sacrifice, if necessary, for their convictions and for the community. They believe, with the writer of the second letter of Timothy (3:12), that "all who desire to live a godly life in Christ Jesus can expect to be persecuted." For both Anabaptists and progressive Catholics, history has borne out this expectation of persecution. Experiences of sacrifice and persecution mark the collective identity of the two groups. Since their origins in the early 1500s, Anabaptists have faced physical violence as well as legal sanctions from religious and secular powers. Seeking refuge, they have moved again and again, across Europe and to the Americas. *The Martyrs' Mirror* grounds a deeply rooted sense of the community as a small minority that continually challenges the dominant ideas and institutions, religious and secular, of every period. They believe, as the Mennonite *Confession of Faith* puts it, that "conformity to Christ necessarily implies nonconformity to the world."[11] Or, as a sixteenth-century Dutch Anabaptist woman immortalized in *The Martyrs' Mirror* wrote, "If they have persecuted the Lord, they will also persecute us."[12]

Because Catholicism became a dominant, state-sponsored religion with the Spanish conquest, Latin American Catholics do not share a generalized minority identity. Progressive Catholics, however, make explicit parallels between the violence they have suffered since the late 1960s and the martyrdom of the early church. They understand themselves, as did the early Anabaptists, as purifying the corruption of the established church, re-creating a Christian community modeled on Jesus' own values and aspirations. Salvadorans describe clandestine base communities of the 1970s and 1980s as the "church of the catacombs," paralleling the experiences of Christians in the Roman Empire.[13] They see themselves as a pilgrim community, striving to embody a certain kind of social vision against the dominant values and institutions of their time.

Experiences and recollections of exile and migration affect people' ties to their place of residence. For Anabaptists in the United States and for Salvadoran refugees, finding a place where they can settle down and make a home has cost them, and they remain aware that exile could happen again. For all these communities, attachment to and knowledge of place is deep-rooted but also self-consciously vulnerable. Like other agrarians, as Wendell Berry suggests, they "value land because somewhere back in the history of their consciousness is some memory of being landless. . . . People who have been landless know that the land is invaluable; it is worth everything."[14] The experience of intertwined attachment to and loss of the land also shapes their moral values. Their ethics are both cosmopolitan and provincial, rooted in particular places and experiences but capable of looking outward, to the experiences of others or the possibility of a different future. For these communities, further, social and natural histories mingle. Natural landscapes are marked by memories of happy and tragic events. Their value systems embody a dictum of environmental philosopher Holmes Rolston: "An ethic is not just a theory but a track through the world."[15] Amish and Salvadoran agrarians track their ethics in the dynamics of persecution, exile, and coming home.

Memories of suffering and of the first Christian community are connected to aspirations for the future, to a larger vision of the common good. These ultimate values, for Anabaptists and progressive Catholics, hold up the reign of God as an ideal way of life for humans, a model that should shape present social organization and not remain merely a future aspiration. This goal fulfills an additional important function of communities of memory: to "turn us toward the future as communities of hope . . . that can allow us to connect our aspirations for ourselves and those closest to us with the aspirations of a larger whole and see our own efforts as being in part contributions to the common good."[16] Religious communities are especially able to forge these connections, as members understand themselves as part of a larger movement, continuous across times and spaces beyond their own immediate circumstances. Their values and aims precede and outlast any particular manifestation and are linked by their common origins and ends in a transcendent source.

Religion also serves practical purposes by shaping everyday patterns of behavior, forms of interaction among members and between members and outsiders, economic and political organization, and priorities for social agendas. For example, every group's understanding of what it means to be a community is linked to a particular understanding of what it means to be the church. This is especially true for the Amish, for whom community and church district are largely identical and both overlap heavily with extended family. Amish communities have been able to survive despite the divergent, often hostile context in which they live largely because of their religious convictions and shared submission to spiritual authority.

Progressive Catholics in Latin America also build their vision of an ideal society on an understanding of the church's proper shape and social role. For both Anabaptists and progressive Catholics, again, the early Christian communities provide an important model. They believe the church should resemble the small, egalitarian, and participatory intentional communities of disciples described in early church documents. Progressive Catholics and activist Mennonites believe, further, that these values should be embodied in larger social institutions as much as possible. Part of their religious identity is the requirement to reach out in diverse ways to these larger wholes.

Community, Social Justice, and Quality of Life

We saw in other poor people what we were suffering. When we went looking for work, we saw the poverty in which some people were living in their little farms with all their children, everything wet inside, without enough to support their families. And seeing all that, your heart felt pretty soft, wishing for a solution to these problems. When you are poor, you think of other poor people, so that you see many things. But the landowners don't look upon us as their own people, they only use us when they need us to do their work. We saw that it is necessary to unite in struggle for the good of all, so that one day we can all be free and that we might live a more happy life as human beings, as brothers and sisters, as sons of God. All of us must achieve this, not just a few.

—Tomás, Chalatenango resident[17]

No real human society can embody its religious or philosophical ideals perfectly in its social life. Further, most societies are guided not by a single ideal but by a wide variety of beliefs, which in turn are shaped by historical, economic, political, and environmental factors. The fact that there is no direct correlation between a community and a particular doctrine, however, does not mean that religious and philosophical values fail to influence social forms, processes, and institutions. They do, in ways that are concrete and often momentous, if not always predictable. The mutual shaping of religious ideas and social factors generates distinctive religious cultures, which in turn interact with their own social contexts. This is true for the communities discussed in this book, in which core elements of Roman Catholic and Anabaptist doctrine, carried down and transformed in the course of each tradition's history, are embodied and transformed again in particular settings. The result is communities that are distinctively Anabaptist or Catholic but not generically so. They share certain core beliefs and convictions, as well as practices and customs, with coreligionists in other times and places, at the same time that their religious lives are shaped by their own regional and national as well as personal histories, cultures, and landscapes.

The Catholic option for the poor and the Anabaptist understanding of mutual aid undergird a belief that no community member in need should be left unaided. As Tomás puts it, the goal is to "live a more happy life as human beings, as brothers and sisters, as sons of God. All of us must achieve this, not just a few." Thus, community institutions and practices in the repopulations prioritize care for the most vulnerable community members, such as small children, the elderly, disabled, orphans, and widows. This reflects a central principle of Catholic social thinking, according to which a society's health and success are measured not by how many people become very wealthy but by how few lack the basic requirements of life, with special attention to the least well-off.

Anabaptist communities do not participate in a centralized institution like the Roman Catholic Church, in which key statements express principles applicable to all members. However, the Anabaptist tradition provides clear-cut and distinctive guidelines on social welfare and justice, which can be traced back to the principles outlined in the Schleitheim Confession and other early Anabaptist statements, in turn inspired by biblical teachings. The guiding principle for contemporary social life, according to this vision, is the community Jesus brought together, which strove to embody the values of the coming reign of God. It is not possible to create a perfect society on earth, Anabaptists admit, but it is possible and necessary to create communities that take God's kingdom as a model. The church is to be, as John Howard Yoder puts it, "a restored society . . . a sample of the kind of humanity within which, for example, economic and racial differences are surmounted."[18]

Anabaptist and progressive Catholic theological ethics both demand that the ultimate values of the reign of God be enacted in social life here and now. This principle distinguishes them from the mainstream Protestant perception of a wide gap between the two cities or kingdoms (as Augustine and Luther put it) of "true Christians" and "the world." According to this model, no truly Christian community can survive in the real world; values such as disinterested love and self-sacrifice must be relegated to interpersonal relationships and occasional acts of charity. Because the world is unavoidably and permanently fallen, any attempt to replicate the reign of God or create a truly Christian society on earth must fall short. Those who do not share this skepticism are naïve or perhaps fanatical. In contrast to this dualistic vision, both Anabaptists and progressive Catholics have insisted that Christian criteria such as the well-being of the least well-off and mutual aid can and should undergird real social policies and institutions. Our common life here and now can be judged by the standards of the reign of God, including sufficiency of material goods, solidarity, and peaceableness.

Meeting Needs and Distributing Resources

The Amish and Catholic Christians described here have tried to create communities that live up to their religious values. How well have their efforts fared? Certainly, they have not met all their members' needs, eliminated injustice, or transcended the limitations of their economic and political conditions. They are, however, far ahead of mainstream U.S. and Latin American societies in their attention to the needs and wants of their most vulnerable members. For example, as noted earlier, refugees who returned to Chalatenango and other war zones placed the construction of schools and health clinics among their top priorities upon arriving back in El Salvador. Only planting crops necessary for survival took precedence. That done, they built schools even before permanent houses for individual families. Today Guarjila and several other repopulations have centers for elder care as well. Needy community members, such as single parents, orphans, and the elderly, also receive collective support in the form of volunteer labor, food, and other supplies. All these projects, initiated and sustained at significant cost by community members with few resources, attest to a collective commitment to caring for the most needy. These values took shape in the progressive Catholic pastoral projects of the 1960s and 1970s and survived, even grew stronger, throughout the years of war and exile.

The Amish do not live in the profound poverty and scarcity that shape the lives of most people in Chalatenango. Still, in the midst of demanding lives that allow for little spare time and money, the Amish also aid their less well-off community members—not just out of their excess but out of their very necessities. John Hostetler elaborates: "The Amish view personal property, expressed in farms and family dwellings, as a form of stewardship, but they carefully avoid any ostentatious display of wealth. The fruits of their labor are used to perpetuate community life through sharing, hospitality, stewardship, and underwriting the cost of an expanding population."[19] Amish and larger Anabaptist practices of neighborly mutual aid and lifelong care for the elderly and disabled embody these traditional values. The Christian community, set apart from mainstream society, demands that all its members take responsibility for the welfare of all others.

Economic Subsistence

Alternative communities and agriculture must be capable of providing stable livelihoods or, regardless of their environmental or social benefits, they will fail. A certain degree of economic success is necessary not only for individuals, families, and communities to survive but also for their work to offer plausible alternatives to mainstream values, models, and institutions. This is a major challenge for the communities described here, all of which face, in different forms, the difficulties of enduring in the midst of local, national, regional, and international economies that are changing rapidly and are inhospitable, even hostile, to the efforts of small, subsistence-oriented agrarian communities.

Although it has rarely been easy to make a living as a small farmer in the United States or anywhere else, recent global and national trends have made it much harder. In addition to the environmental costs detailed in earlier chapters, the trends have many negative social consequences. Since World War II, the number of farmers in the United States has declined sharply, while the number of acres that each farmer works has increased, as has production per acre. Most farmers' debt has also increased, due in large part to the rising cost of machinery, fuel, and chemical inputs. Today there are fewer, larger farms, and they tend to be owned by corporations rather than families. These social and economic trends have transformed rural life, especially in the midwestern United States. The resulting farm crisis entails bankruptcies and failures of many family-owned farms, related failures of small businesses, severe population declines in many rural counties, and the loss of community institutions such as banks and schools.

With their retention of small, diversified, family-owned farms that rely on human, animal, and solar power rather than fossil fuels, the Amish represent a remarkable exception to national and global trends against subsistence farming. Their farms are less lucrative in good times but much less vulnerable to failure in bad times than larger, more specialized operations. Amish farmers generally maintain modest but steady profit levels, undergirded by highly efficient use of energy and low household and farm expenses. Farms stay in the family, and adult children remain close to home. As the Iowa study cited earlier documents, Amish communities, including not only farmers but the small businesses that serve them, have continued to thrive during periods when other farmers and rural communities have suffered and often collapsed.

Small farmers in Latin America face some of the same challenges as those in North America, as economies of scale and reliance on expensive petroleum-based inputs have increased. In El Salvador, small producers of staple foods such as corn and beans must compete with both large corporate producers in their own nations and with imports from other parts of the world. The exodus away from small towns in Latin America may be even greater than that in the midwestern United States, as young people seek outside opportunities for education and employment. Many migrate to the United States or other wealthy nations, and the remittances they send home provide crucial income for many families and many villages. However, reliance on remittances can generate dependence and a loss of productive capacity in the receiving communities, as well as exacerbating internal conflicts. The challenges of retaining young people and surviving in an often harsh global economy are faced by all rural communities, perhaps especially by those deliberately trying to establish different models of farming and social organization.

When the repopulation of El Salvador's conflict zones began in the mid-1980s, solidarity, development, and religious groups in the United States and Europe funded economic, agricultural, and social development in the villages. In the absence of government support, international aid made possible the construction of houses, roads, and community buildings, the funding and staffing of training programs, and the establishment of economic enterprises such as bakeries and carpentry shops. Some repopulations, especially those outside guerrilla strongholds, received much less attention and assistance, and as a result they have far poorer infrastructure and services. Although it was vital for the repopulations' initial survival and subsequent development, foreign assistance generated problems, including conflicts among villages and between community members and the organizations working with them; a tendency to direct community development as desired by funding agencies; and a general dependence on external subsidies for all projects, including enterprises that failed to achieve economic self-sufficiency even years after their founding.

Since the war's end, foreign aid to nongovernmental projects in El Salvador has declined sharply, partly due to changing interests of funders and activists, many of whom have concentrated on other parts of the world since the late 1990s. Economic downturns in the United States and post-9/11 changes have also limited the capacity even of interested funders to support large-scale projects. In addition, a number of agencies that have worked in El Salvador throughout the 1980s and 1990s are urging and in some cases demanding that the repopulated communities and organizations working with them become economically self-sufficient.

Community leaders and organizations such as CRIPDES and CORDES share the goals of efficiency and autonomy but recognize the serious obstacles to achieving them. Most rural Salvadorans have few savings or other sources of capital to initiate individual or collective income-generating projects and keep them going until they break even. Without loans or grants, they can do little more than subsistence farm, and many go into debt to purchase seeds, fertilizer, and machinery. In Chalatenango, the poor soils, hilly terrain, and limited infrastructure make local economic self-sufficiency even more difficult than in some other former war zones, where industrial or agricultural development, fertile land, access to larger markets, or other advantages provide a head start or buffer for local community development. It is particularly difficult to practice ecologically sustainable farming without an economic safety net, as the demands of survival make it hard to exercise restraint in the use of the few resources available. In the words of agricultural economist René Rivera,[20] farmers in El Salvador are "immediatist": their resources are so limited and their economic situation so critical that they cannot plan beyond the urgent needs of the present.

Despite all the challenges, the repopulated communities have achieved significant victories. Most important may be the land acquired through the Land Transfer Program. Another victory of the 1992 peace accords, the legalization of the FMLN as a political party, has created important political changes in areas where repopulations are located. In Chalatenango, for example, local FMLN leaders have worked together to bring electricity and bus service to a number of repopulated communities. To the extent that it consolidates its national power, gains legislative and municipal experience, and overcomes internal divisions, the party promises to become a more effective ally for grassroots activists and communities, not only in improving local conditions but also in extending their vision nationally. Success in this effort may hinge on the party's capacity to articulate and put in practice a dual approach, similar to that which galvanized peasants and other activists during the 1970s and 1980s, which combines a utopian vision of large-scale, long-term change with attention to local, bread-and-butter issues.

Popular Participation and Democratization

Both progressive Catholics and Anabaptists value popular participation in the decisions and processes that organize their communities. The two traditions approach issues of governance and democracy, however, in very different ways. Long-standing theological and ethical principles continue to shape Anabaptist and Roman Catholic attitudes toward politics and especially toward the relationship between the local religious congregation and the larger society, the ways their small communities might help create a society that more closely resembles their ideal.

Since its origins, the Anabaptist movement has rejected the hierarchical structure of the Catholic Church. In the Radical Reformation tradition, all baptized members have a full and equal voice in decisions affecting the community. Not all members have equal access to leadership positions, however, as some churches, including most Old Orders, limit ministry positions to married men. These limitations resemble those in the Roman Catholic Church to some extent, although the pool of candidates among Anabaptists (married men) is much larger than the Catholic pool of celibate men with years of seminary training. Further, Anabaptist churches permit and even demand a much greater degree of lay participation by both women and men in congregational activities and decisions. This participation is especially meaningful given that local congregations exercise full control over their own policies, activities, and personnel.

Anabaptists reject hierarchy of rank within the community of believers and insist on mutual decision making and discipline, as well as unpaid, community-mandated leadership. Far more than mainstream Protestant denominations, Anabaptists, especially the Amish, seek to follow Luther's principle of the priesthood of all believers, a vision of the church as a community in which all members have the right and the obligation to participate in making and carrying out collective decisions. Amish settlements sharply restrict the growth of institutions, limiting them to the family and the church district. Together these fulfill almost all the functions that mainstream society delegates to various public and private institutions. In an Amish church district and family, all members are responsible to each other and to the group as a whole. For example, Amish communities address violations of the Ordnung in a collective manner. Not only bishops but the entire church considers the violation and the consequences, which are mild in the beginning, arriving at the ban only after repeated attempts at reconciliation have failed.

Despite their commitment to participatory and egalitarian practices in the local church, Anabaptists rarely work for political democratization at larger levels. The Amish in particular continue the early Anabaptist desire for physical as well as spiritual separation from the brutality and corruption of "the sword." Believers are to create their own beloved communities, embodying the harmony, cooperation, peacefulness, and equality preached by Jesus and promised in the coming reign of God. While refusing to divide their secular and sacred loyalties, as Luther preached, Anabaptists also believe that a true Christian community can never be anything other than a small "remnant." Convinced that they cannot convert or transform the world beyond their doors, they focus on helping it by providing an example and by practical projects such as mutual aid and disaster relief.

The Catholic tradition holds a more positive view of the potential for secular political processes and institutions to contribute to the construction of a Christian society. Catholic social thought contends that believers can cooperate with secular leaders and institutions to remake the larger society into a more Christian form. In many circumstances, this conviction has led the church hierarchy to collaborate with less than ideal governments and to uphold undemocratic, often repressive political and economic establishments. This history has led Anabaptists to accuse Catholicism of participating in a Faustian bargain, or more precisely a Constantinian one, in which ecclesial elites gain prestige, wealth, and power at the cost of relinquishing the critical core of their faith. Spanish colonization of the Americas represents one among many cases in which the Catholic Church reinforced an exploitive political project in pursuit of its institutional self-interest.

Since the late 1960s, progressive Catholic theologians and activists have taken up this critique, describing much of the church's past as the creation of a Christendom in which the church has supported an unjust status quo in order to preserve its own status. For progressive Catholics, this situation demands not the Anabaptist answer of separation from the secular world but a critical reevaluation of the church's political mission and responsibilities and efforts at democratization in both church structures and the larger society. Their efforts have helped make human rights, social justice, and political democracy central to Catholic social and political positions vis-à-vis the secular world. In official documents, pastoral offices, and even its liturgy, the church holds up these values as vital to Christian belief and practice. Church leaders from the pope down call on national governments, corporations, and other secular institutions to democratize, to protect human rights, to practice economic justice. At the same time, however, most church officials strenuously resist efforts to democratize the church's own policies, procedures, and leadership. They see a qualitative difference between public life and the holy church, in contrast not only to Anabaptist theology but also to the progressive wing within Catholicism, especially in Latin America.

Progressive Catholic pastoral agents and laypeople have sought more widespread and meaningful participation in decision making at various levels of the church to parallel expanded participation of all citizens, especially the poor, women, and people of indigenous and African descent, in secular political institutions and civil society. For example, when Father José Inocencio Alas began training laymen in Suchitoto to perform pastoral duties in 1969, he hoped that some of them would ultimately become priests when, as he expected, Pope Paul VI permitted the ordination of married men.[21] The ordination of married men, like the ordination of women, has long been discussed by different sectors within the Roman Catholic Church. Both advocates and opponents of expanding ordination recognize that it would not merely increase the numbers of priests but radically transform the nature of authority and decision making within the church. In El Salvador, many activists desired the expansion of ordination as an integral part of the larger democratization of church leadership and structures. Although lay leaders have taken on new and expanded roles in many activities, however, to this day the Roman Catholic priesthood remains limited to highly educated, celibate men.[22]

Although these democratic values and goals were never extended to the institutional church, they were practiced successfully in local religious projects and in political organizations and structures. Base communities, in particular, embodied as well as advocated a social ideal in which democracy was central, priests were partners rather than patrons, and the diverse gifts of all members were valued. These values emerged from innovative pastoral projects that gave many laypeople their first taste of democratic political processes in meetings in which anyone could speak, in expanded access to education (e.g., in literacy campaigns), and in opportunities to speak publicly, to hold leadership positions, to organize collectively, or merely to advocate policies other than those of the status quo. The Catholic peasant movement applied religiously grounded values of equality and democracy in the PPLs, in refugee organizations, and in the repopulations. Community members developed institutions and procedures to spread leadership and decision-making power among different groups. The structures have changed since the war's end, but the principles of full participation and equity remain. For example, they hold frequent open meetings to discuss and decide policies. Further, none of the elected council members are full-time professional politicians; they are immersed in the community and its work, and they are accessible to community members. These organizational structures, leadership patterns, and decision-making procedures are far from perfect, but they are infinitely more open, participatory, and responsive than anything Salvadoran peasants experienced, on any scale, prior to the religious and social movements of the 1960s and 1970s.

The problem, as many activists realize, is that there is no straightforward link between the practice of local democracy and the establishment and consolidation of democratic practices and institutions in the larger society. This issue preoccupies many of the activists and scholars who held out great hope that religiously based, grassroots movements beginning in the 1970s would shape not only new kinds of citizens but also new social, economic, and political structures. Many progressive Catholics also believed that their local experiments would have an impact beyond the parish or village level, not only as a model for a more democratic social life but also as an agent for change in national institutions and policies.

Problems of Scale

According to some observers, these movements would help create change because they were not only democratic in character but also attentive to local and personal interests. CEBs, peasant federations, and similar movements of the Catholic left mobilized people where they lived and enabled meaningful participation in civil society for groups that had long been marginalized. They empowered women, peasants, and shanty town residents and brought their voices and interests into political debate. Many of them improved the quality of life for people in their villages and barrios, installing health clinics, schools, sanitary systems, and street lights where none had ever existed. In their most impressive successes, the repopulations, they created whole new communities in the midst of war.

These achievements were made possible not only because of political commitment and organization but also because of attachment to particular places. Refugees insisted on returning from Honduras to their place of origin because of a strong regional identity and personal and collective histories rooted in particular places, war-torn and despoiled as they were. Many refugees insist that they never felt at home in exile, even in other parts of El Salvador. Some even left land they owned elsewhere in order to return to their place of origin. They have a sense of "settlement," as Raymond Williams terms it, that draws "on many deep and persistent feelings: an identification with the people among whom we grew up; an attachment to the place, the landscape, in which we first lived and learned to see."[23] For former refugees, this identification and attachment is tempered by experiences of life elsewhere, a keen awareness of the larger geographic, political, and economic contexts in which they live. They understand their work to build local communities as the construction of a basis for radical changes at larger levels. Their localism, then, is complex, cosmopolitan, and radical. They are settled in places that are at once traditional and new, a setting into which they were born but that they have now deliberately chosen, aiming to transform a whole society.

The Amish also have a complicated local attachment. Many Amish communities and families have roots in a particular settlement, often on a single farm, which go back generations, even centuries. In the mobile and rootless culture that dominates the contemporary United States, the Amish may indeed be, as David Kline declares, "the only ones who really know where they are."[24] On the other hand, few ethnic groups have as mobile a history as the Amish, whose ancestors were propelled across most of Europe and North America by persecution and the need for land. Even thriving Amish communities today

retain a sense of vulnerability, stemming not only from the possibility of persecution but also from suburban sprawl and occupational changes. Their commitment to specific places is deep, but it remains always subordinate to their
religious values and the collective way of life that enables them to live out these
values.

Thus, larger contexts—religious, historical, and cultural—frame local attachments for both Anabaptists and progressive Catholics. This contextuali-
zation and the sense of vulnerability and critical awareness that it fosters can
help people avoid the dangers that sometimes arise when long-term residence
is viewed as an end in itself. Perhaps most important, they realize that local
communities never exist in isolation. Even the smallest farm or village is affected by international flows and by the continual movement of people, information, and resources across borders. Religion often plays an important part
in facilitating these flows and people's awareness of connections and identities
beyond the local and contemporary.

The interactions between local loyalties and larger contexts provide a necessary corrective to certain streams within bioregionalism, a prominent school
of environmentalist thought and activism that gives center stage to local knowledge, experience, and commitment in efforts to preserve wild places and make
human communities more sustainable. Bioregionalism's central ethical claim
is that people who are knowledgeable about and well-adapted to their particular
places are more likely to want and be able to care for those places. Environmental and social destruction results as scales—especially of production, ownership, and governance—become larger and as decision makers are removed
from the places where their decisions have most impact. Thus, bioregionalists
reject many forms of globalization and prioritize local solutions to environmental and other problems and place their faith in those who are (or who
become) "native" to particular places. Bioregionalist principles have not only
influenced environmentalist thought and practice but also interacted with other
social movements, where local commitments play an increasing role in fram-
ing, planning, and carrying out action. The emphasis on small scales and local
commitments provides important correctives to top-down, overly general approaches to social and environmental problems.

Attention to the local, however, is no panacea. Attachment to a place does
not, by itself, guarantee ecological sensitivity, just distribution of resources, or
economic security. In the Salvadoran repopulations, deep local roots and loyalties are challenged both by the communities' own lack of resources and by
the constraining context of national and international policies, institutions, and
forces. Many returned refugees, like other peasant activists, face an uphill battle
to "go on living where they are," as Raymond Williams puts it. Williams describes the problems facing the border region between England and Wales,
where he grew up and which "has been steadily and terribly losing its people,
who can no longer make a living there." Because of this experience, he writes,

"When I hear the idealisation of settlement, I do not need to borrow the first [positive] feelings; I know, in just that sense, what neighbourhood means, and what is involved in separation and leaving. But I know, also, why people had to move, why so many moved in my own family. So that I then see the idealisation of settlement . . . as an insolent indifference to most people's needs." He goes on to point out that "settlement is indeed easy, is positively welcome, for those who can settle in a reasonable independence. For those who cannot— and under the pressures of change from a new mode of production these became the majority—it can become a prison: a long disheartening and despair, under an imposed rigidity of conditions."[25]

Williams puts his finger on the unacknowledged class bias of much bioregionalist activism and thinking. Loving a place does not guarantee the ability to make a living in it, and sometimes only the privileged can afford to stay put. Poor people, regardless of their history in or feeling for a place, must go where they can sell their labor. This is as true in the midwestern United States and northern El Salvador as it is in rural Britain. Further, commitment to a place may be harder to generate when life there has been characterized by scarcity and hardship or by intolerance and division, or when the place itself is despoiled and unlovely. In such cases, one can hardly blame residents for pursuing broader, or at least different, horizons. Their situation contrasts sharply with that of prominent bioregionalist advocates and writers in North America, many of whom have settled in areas of exceptional beauty, often far from where they were born. They advise others "Don't move," as Gary Snyder once summed up the bioregionalist message,[26] at the risk of losing credibility due to the inconsistency of their own positions and to their insensitivity to the needs of people with fewer resources and options.

While bioregionalism may be vulnerable to charges of elitism on the one hand, it is also subject to charges of provincialism and tunnel vision on the other. Paeans to localism strike many political analysts and activists, in particular, as unrealistic and ineffective. Social and environmental problems have global causes and ramifications, they argue; efforts at change that are purely local in scope and small in scale will have little real impact. In response to such critiques, some thinkers have begun to articulate what Mitchell Thomashow calls a "cosmopolitan bioregionalism," which looks for "the connections between place-based knowledge and global environmental change, the interdependence of local ecology and global economies, and the matrix of affiliations and networks that constitute ecological biodiversity and multicultural and multispecies tolerance—allowing different people to understand all the different places that may be considered home. This is the basis of a local/global dialectic and emphasizes the necessity of a cosmopolitan bioregionalism."[27] This approach values local knowledge and attachments without forgetting the larger web of causes and effects in which not only places but also practices and ideas are embedded.

For bioregionalists and for anyone interested in environmental and social sustainability, the challenge is not just to appreciate complexity but to link scales. In ecological terms, this requires integrating the ecological concepts of bioregion and watershed with knowledge of the social, political, and economic conditions that determine how people live with nature and with each other. In political terms, the problem is how to extend local achievements to larger structures. Reaching these goals will require not only the institutionalization of principles of ecological sustainability, social justice, and political democracy in all levels of government and civil society but also transformations in personal identity and gender and family relations. Earlier generations of radicals, both secular and religious, did not always appreciate how extensive or slow this process might be—how much must be reworked, in both intimate relations and public institutions, to achieve deep and lasting social change. To accomplish revolutions, or even significant reforms, activists must learn to negotiate the problem of *levels* of struggle, the boundary between the grassroots and the "big structures" of the state and the economy.[28] The possibilities for making these changes might depend on the middle range between local and the global levels.[29]

At this middle level, the challenge is how to bring together universal aspirations to democratization and social justice with personal and local values, histories, and what Williams calls "militant particularisms." Instead of erasing or ignoring particularity, Williams suggests, a larger progressive movement needs to "make real what is at first sight the extraordinary claim that the defence and advancement of certain particular interests, properly brought together, are in fact the general interest."[30] Because no single, overarching vision captures every participant's values and goals, there is a need to respect particulars while also transcending parochial visions of change. This is no easy task. The implementation of democratic, participatory practices at the grassroots does not automatically generate structural changes, just as national processes such as a transition from military to civilian rule often do not transform authoritarian and unjust relations in everyday life. Local activism cannot be seen simply as an "alternative" to national projects but can succeed only as a complement to and component of larger changes.

The mutual shaping of local and larger processes is evident in El Salvador, where peasants' everyday lives have long been influenced by forces beyond their control and even knowledge. In particular, national and international dynamics related to the civil war, including government and guerrilla strategies and the postwar Land Transfer Program, had profound effects on local communities, destroying some, creating others, transforming many more. In the United States, government policies such as exemptions from compulsory education and social security laws have helped Amish communities thrive while many other rural towns decline. Policies, institutions, and laws affect communities at multiple levels between the local and the national, and communities and community-based movements make diverse demands on these different levels of government. Similarly, national and international markets, as well as local and regional ones, help shape and continually affect local conditions. Even communities that strive for greater self-sufficiency cannot achieve complete isolation. Both the Amish and the repobladores have sought and achieved a great deal of autonomy, but none live independent of national and international processes.

Even the Amish, who seek separation and cannot by any stretch of the imagination be called activists, are linked to and shaped by national institutions and policies. Acculturated Mennonites have pursued connections among levels more explicitly, aiming for a balance between Anabaptist nonconformity and a desire to bring their values into the public sphere, between attachment to home and a sense of connectedness extending beyond local and even national borders. Thus, many tight-knit Mennonite towns, where everyone knows everyone else, are populated by well-educated, well-read, well-traveled people, informed about and interested in national and international events. A certain kind of internationalism is increasingly part of contemporary Mennonite identity, as evidenced by a strong interest in international events and by donations and volunteerism to help those in need elsewhere in the world, especially Africa and Latin America. Many Mennonites travel to the Third World for missions, which focus more on self-help and sustainable development projects than on religious conversion. Although Old Order Anabaptists do not send missionaries, they often work with Mennonites to raise funds for victims of natural disasters and wars and on issues such as legal protection for conscientious objectors and local land use problems. Widespread commitment to such projects, along with high levels of reading, means that rural Anabaptists often know more about world events than urban residents with better access to mass media and more formal education.

The effort to combine local rootedness and global engagement generates what might be called a "cosmopolitan localism" that increasingly marks Anabaptist identity, especially for liberal Mennonites but also in many Old Order communities. Anabaptists and progressive Catholics share a sense that knowledge of the rest of the world constitutes the necessary context for understanding their own local places and communities. Their histories, shaped by wars and international religious movements, have made this knowledge central to their values and cultural identities. They recognize, and their religious leaders remind them, that what happens at national, regional, and international levels profoundly affects what happens locally. These communities continually negotiate the tension "between the idea that the local is not always good, that you have to go outside your 'own' place in order to learn, and, on the other hand, the idea that the local has enough of everything to teach us."[31]

This tension resides not only in personal consciousness and experience but also in political processes and institutions. Attachment to places and people—militant particularisms—may well be the most effective force to motivate activism, but local movements face serious limits in their capacity to change larger systems. This is true for both social and environmental problems. The dilemma is illustrated in the bioregionalist contention that people in a given ecological region are most likely to protect it. However, for local communities to live sustainably in their own places, much larger political and economic changes are necessary. Laws and policies relative to land use, transportation, and many other issues make possible some practices and prohibit others. Individuals and communities cannot construct ecologically sensitive ways of life without a fundamental reorienting of the larger society, both in the United States and in El Salvador. And of course many ecological problems, such as global warming and biodiversity loss, do not respect national or local borders. Making local commitments politically efficacious requires not merely individual decisions to live "in place" but also collective activism leading to changes in policies, infrastructures, and the means of production.

The moral of the story so far might be summarized thus: local communities are much more complex than idealized and abstract images allow, and they are intimately involved in and shaped by what happens at larger scales, just as large institutions are affected by small ones. Even the most apparently self-sufficient communities are enmeshed in larger policies, structures, histories, and social relations, and they cannot be understood or experienced in isolation from other social processes, institutions, and forces. These interactions may be more intense now than ever, especially in the face of increasing globalization via economic treaties such as NAFTA and CAFTA, new communications media, and other contemporary complications.

Tied to the empirical task of understanding the interactions between local and larger levels is the normative problem of embodying what people value locally in larger institutions and structures.[32] Alternative communities face a challenge: they can look only to their own private survival, or they can seek to extend their vision of a good society beyond their own borders, to the nation and even the human community as a whole. The possibility of such an extension poses the question of utopia.

5

Utopia

The most utopian moment I have experienced came on January 16, 1992, when I joined thousands of people in San Salvador's *plaza central* to celebrate the signing of the peace accords. We watched an endless series of individuals and groups step up to a makeshift stage, some to lead songs praising the guerrillas' success in forcing the government to negotiate, others to remember the tens of thousands killed before peace came. Over the crowd loomed the skeleton of the national cathedral, unfinished since the late 1970s, when Archbishop Oscar Romero halted construction because, he insisted, the church ought to spend its money helping the victims of violence rather than building monuments. After Romero's assassination in 1980, his body was placed inside the half-finished church that symbolized his dedication to the poor.

All afternoon and evening, young people climbed up and down the front of the cathedral to hang flags with images of Farabundo Martí, a Salvadoran communist executed in 1932, and the letters FMLN, acronym of the guerrilla organization bearing his name. Even more than Farabundo Martí and the armed opposition, however, Romero dominated the celebration. Inside the cathedral, flowers, candles, and handwritten notes of supplication and thanks covered his tomb. Outside in the crowd, his image (pastoral, serene) and his words (agonized, prophetic) appeared everywhere, on flags and bandanas, posters and shirts.[1]

Even though progressive Catholicism was probably the dominant ideology among the Salvadorans celebrating peace in the plaza, the institutional church distinguished itself by its absence (*brillaba* por su ausencia, as Salvadorans say). Neither Arturo Rivera y Damas, Romero's successor as archbishop of San Salvador, nor any other member of the Catholic episcopacy attended the celebration. The only bishop present was the Lutheran Medardo Gómez, sharing the stage with Baptists, Episcopalians, lay Catholics, and a few priests who had split with the hierarchy over their work with the political left. The martyr Romero alone represented the official church, one of many ambiguities of that utopian moment.

The Salvadoran peace celebrations embodied a uniquely Latin American intertwining of Christian and socialist visions of a better world. I first encountered this synthesis in the mid-1980s in Nicaragua, where the Sandinista government and popular organizations, strongly influenced by progressive Catholicism, sought to create "open a doorway toward the Kingdom of God," as Nicaraguan activist Carlos Manuel Sánchez put it.[2] The Sandinistas achieved a great deal, but their utopia was always ambivalent, encompassing huge gains in quality of life indicators such as literacy and infant mortality but also accusations of corruption and neglect of minority populations. The Sandinistas' loss in Nicaragua's 1990 presidential election led many commentators to declare the death of the Latin American left, or at least of that part of the left that still harbored dreams of radical change.

In El Salvador, the FMLN never achieved a definitive military triumph. Unlike the Sandinistas, the Salvadoran guerrillas did not march triumphantly into their capital city to erase the images of past dictatorships and begin building a new society from the ground up. The Salvadoran revolution led instead to a negotiated settlement that demanded cohabitation and continued negotiation with a brutal, corrupt, and intransigent national elite. The FMLN's transition from guerrilla army to electoral party since the war's end has been neither easy nor smooth. At the national level, the party has been divided within and challenged from without, unable to pursue the sweeping reforms that the Sandinistas achieved, albeit temporarily. At local levels, however, decades of organization and struggle are bearing fruit.

The greatest challenge faced by the opposition today may be finding the balance between an expansive vision of change and attention to people's concrete needs, the balance that peasant movements before and during the war often achieved so well. Those earlier movements made certain values nonnegotiable, including collective unity and care for the least well-off. These values, along with a sense of themselves as participants in a sacred struggle, constituted the utopian vision that made El Salvador seem a promised land to so many activists. Perhaps the greatest challenge faced by revolutionaries in the postwar period is to retain a utopian vision while at the same time engaging in the practical give-and-take of local and national politics and efforts to attend to people's concrete needs.

In different ways, both the Salvadoran and Nicaraguan revolutions suggest that unambiguous utopias are hard to come by. Their experiences inject a necessary note of caution and critical awareness into movements for social change, but do they necessarily discredit utopian visions? Is there still value in talking and thinking about utopia? These questions push us toward a revaluation of particular forms of utopianism, the worldviews and values they affirm, and the histories they have shaped. Both the FMLN and the Sandinistas had their roots in a socialist left that, across many variations, has held as its core a conviction that political struggles, mostly class-based, sometimes nationalist or antiracist, will create a qualitatively better society, the "splendid city" of which the Chilean poet Pablo Neruda wrote.[3] The struggle for this society was rooted in a conviction, as Neruda's comrades in the Popular Unity movement sang, that "the life that is coming will be better [será mejor la vida que vendrá]."[4] What would be better about it? Woody Guthrie put it as concisely as anyone:

> There's a better world a'comin', can't you see, see, see
> There's a better world a'comin', can't you see?
> When we'll all be union and we'll all be free.[5]

Guthrie (like Neruda, a lifelong socialist) captures the twin values at the heart of the old left imagination: human solidarity and liberation from exploitation, universally extended. It is crucial to this vision that we are both united *and* free. Against liberal individualism, the socialist left declares that freedom does not require separation and protection from others. Rather, freedom can be achieved only in and through community. Utopia is a collective life, the social context necessary for people to pursue their potential. This potential can be fulfilled only when material needs are met, when no member of the corporate body is crippled by hunger, poverty, homelessness, lack of education, or failures of health care. These and other social demands spell out the vision crystallized in Marx's famous phrase: "From each according to his ability, to each according to his needs!"[6] The satisfaction of material wants, however, does not in itself constitute a utopia. Rather, it creates the necessary foundation for a society in which the values of freedom and solidarity might thrive, in which, as Marx and Engels put it, "the free development of each is the condition for the free development of all."[7]

Critics of Utopianism

Utopianism is presently out of fashion in politics, academia, and even the churches. The current wave of antiutopianism takes many different forms, as do the aspirations it rejects. One variant is Christian realism, which has roots in St. Augustine's distinction between two cities, one of man and the other of God. Writing amid the chaos of the disintegrating Roman Empire, Augustine asserted that Christians and the church must remain pilgrims, in but not of the world. Christians' greatest hope and greatest joy would come not on earth but in the heavenly city that awaited them after death. Augustine's dualism between the two realms and his cynicism about what Christians might hope for and expect in the earthly city have influenced a series of important Christian thinkers since his time. Martin Luther, who was an Augustinian monk prior to his excommunication, revised the image of the two cities into a distinction between two kingdoms, a worldly one in which all humans had to abide for a time and a heavenly one to which all true Christians eternally belonged. Luther's two kingdoms, like Augustine's two cities, were governed by permanently incompatible values and ends. Christians should strive to obey the divergent demands of both, without losing sight of where their ultimate loyalty lay.

In the twentieth century, the neo-orthodox Lutheran theologian Reinhold Niebuhr built on this distinction between what we can hope for in the real world and ultimate Christian ideals, which Niebuhr defined as non-self-interested love, charity, and an altruistic willingness to sacrifice for others. Although individuals might adhere to these standards of Christian morality in their private lives, Niebuhr believed, even the best-intentioned persons could not follow them in the larger society. In the public sphere, then, justice—which entails compromise, negotiation, and often coercive force—is the highest possible good that people can expect to attain. Niebuhr discounted any hope of remaking the world according to Christian principles of unselfish love. However, he appreciated the capacity of religious utopianism to inspire activism, even to "generate a sublime madness in the soul" that might encourage people to confront evil and achieve at least incremental changes.[8] In the end, though, Niebuhr relegates utopianism if not to the dustbin of history then at least to an obscure corner, from whence it attracts naïve and ultimately ineffectual dreamers. Realists do not fool themselves that any society can exist without conflict, corruption, and coercion.

Certain elements of Niebuhr's antiutopian Christian realism have been taken up by social ethicist Jean Bethke Elshtain, who advocates a neo-Augustinian, neo-Niebuhrian just war ethic. In May 2003, in the wake of the U.S. invasion of Iraq, Elshtain lamented the frequency with which pastors and priests used the word "peace." Still, she added, "This is, perhaps, unsurprising. Christians are taught that the Kingdom of God is a peaceable one in which the lion lies down with the lamb. But there is a problem. We do not live in that peaceable kingdom. We can discern intimations of it. We can pray for it. We can strive to embody moments of it in the earthly city. But we must take heed. We live in a fallen world, something Christians too often seem to forget. We live in a world that knows sin."[9]

Like Augustine and Luther, Elshtain marks a divide between the heavenly city, in which Christian peaceableness and love prevail, and the earthly city, in which human sinfulness makes true peace impossible. Like Niebuhr, Elshtain believes she is injecting a note of hard-headed realism into a discussion that misapprehends the way the world works. It is all well and good to celebrate ideals such as peace, she claims, but to think that we could live by them is both naïve and irresponsible. This illusion represents escapism and complacency, embodied by peace activists who claim a moral high ground while ignoring the evils of the world around them and leaving the dirty work of nation building to others. Elshtain sees the reign of God as a beautiful but blurry image, to which Christians might nod on occasion but which has no direct relevance for life on earth. As she puts it, "An end-time ethic cannot be an all-determinative guide to the prudential judgments required of us during our earthly sojourn." In fact, "There is *no* normative blanket spread over any and all situations in which Christians find themselves and within which they are called upon to act."[10] No overarching ethic exists to guide Christian practice. Believers must make the best, day by day, of an inevitably flawed world. This means engaging the world as it is, accepting and cooperating with worldly powers, and, in most situations, choosing among evils rather than championing a higher good.

If Christian "realists" like Elshtain and Niebuhr see utopianism as naïve, others see it as repressive and dangerous. Postmodernist antiutopianism has roots in the suspicion of all grand narratives, as Jean-François Lyotard characterized postmodernism.[11] In place of universalizing narratives and efforts to create cities on a hill, many postmodernists offer up diversity, indeterminacy, fluidity, and fragmentation. They reject overarching visions of an ideal society because such visions inevitably ignore cultural diversity and silence dissenting voices. Worse yet, perhaps a slippery slope leads directly from utopianism to the gulag.

An interesting array of political and cultural theorists share this suspicion, including postmodern skeptics, neorealist Christians like Elshtain, and neoconservatives such as Margaret Thatcher and Francis Fukuyama. Despite their political and theoretical arguments, they agree that utopianism is inextricably tied to Stalinism and, therefore, that the end of the Soviet bloc marks the final blow not just to socialism but to utopianism more generally, perhaps even to "the very notion of an overall alternative to the status quo," in the words of Mexican intellectual Jorge Castañeda.[12] Castañeda echoes (one hopes unintentionally) Thatcher's famous declaration that in the wake of the fall of the Berlin Wall, "there is no alternative" to neoliberal capitalism.[13] As Fukuyama explains, "In our grandparents' time, many reasonable people could foresee a radiant socialist future in which private property and capitalism had been abolished. . . . Today, by contrast, we have trouble imagining a world that is radically better than our own, or a future that is not essentially democratic and capitalist. Within that framework, of course, many things could be improved. . . . But we cannot picture to ourselves a world that is *essentially* different from the present one, and at the same time better."[14]

Fukuyama and Thatcher, like Elshtain, paint themselves as true realists, intellectually as well as morally superior to those who believe in the possibility of "a world that is *essentially* different from the present one, and . . . better." But how realistic are these realists? Despite their self-presentation, these antiutopians ultimately cling to a naïve faith that unfettered capitalism will solve all social problems.[15] This conviction flies in the face of capitalism's historical failures, the obvious fact that peace, democracy, and material abundance do not automatically follow "free" markets any more than they do state-controlled economies. To insist, in the face of massive evidence to the contrary, that an unhindered market will make everything right and that a rising tide will lift even the leakiest boats smacks of a faith as ungrounded and illusory as any millenarian dream.[16] Even the language they use—the "invisible hand of the market"—is magical. If the antisocialists are also unrealistic, however, does this only prove that all utopian dreams, even the most covert, are equally impossible? Is there any reason to keep thinking about utopia?

The Utopian Reign of God

> Being asked by the Pharisees when the kingdom of God was coming, he answered them, "The kingdom of God is not coming with signs to be observed; nor will they say, 'Lo, here it is!' or 'There!' for behold, the kingdom of God is in the midst of you."
>
> —Luke 17:20–21

Christianity has a long history of utopian visions, beginning with John the Baptist's and then Jesus' announcement of the coming reign of God. John and Jesus, along with most of the early disciples, seemed to expect the imminent end of the present world and the start of something entirely new and different. The early Christians disagreed among themselves, however, on the details, such as what the reign of God would look like, who would reside in it, where it was located, and how it would arrive. Disputes about the character of the kingdom soon gave way to disagreements about its timetable. Adding to the confusion were Jesus' frequently cryptic, sometimes contradictory statements about the kingdom, such as the passage from Luke cited above, in which Jesus declares that the kingdom is "in the midst of you."

Since the conversion of Constantine and the establishment of Christianity as the official religion of a worldly empire, the imminence of the reign of God and its relevance for social ethics have become less obvious to many Christians. The groups that advocate an end-time ethic or take the promised reign as a model for human society have been in a distinct minority for centuries. Within this minority stream, Anabaptists may be the most important, or at least the most persistent group. Since their origins, Anabaptists have challenged Constantinian Christianity for its complacent acceptance of the world's sins and have insisted that Christians must live as though the reign of God was indeed in their midst. This has led to occasional apocalyptic, even violent movements such as the ill-fated community in Münster.

Overall, though, the Anabaptist tradition has consistently asserted that, as the Mennonite *Confession of Faith* declares, "The church is called to live now according to the model of the future reign of God. Thus, we are given a fore-taste of the kingdom that God will one day establish in full."[17] Living according to this model, what John Howard Yoder calls "the kingdom as social ethic,"[18] defines Anabaptist politics. In this perspective, the reign of God is utopian insofar as it surpasses all human societies in justice, abundance, and peacea-bleness, but it is not a wholly unrealizable dream. God's kingdom can be a real and compelling model for human social relations, the necessary grounding for Christian ethical, social, and political action. Agreement between progres-sive Catholics and Anabaptists on this point distinguishes both from most mainstream Protestants and traditional Roman Catholics.[19]

Radicals within the Catholic and Reformation traditions disagree, however, on the precise nature of the connection between the congregation and the reign of God and on the practical implications of the connection. Anabaptists reject and withdraw from the corrupt secular world to various degrees. This separa-tion ranges from liberal Mennonites' involvement in a host of mainstream political and cultural activities to the Old Orders' avoidance of most public and secular institutions and processes. Even the most antiworldly groups, however, pay taxes, obey laws that do not threaten religious values, and try to avoid direct confrontations with the powers that wield the sword. Of course, cooperation with the world must stop short of participation in the institutional violence of armies and national defense.

Through congregational decision making and volunteer leadership, mu-tual aid and collective correction, Old Order Amish communities embody a different way to live in the here and now, pointing to the promise of another world. It is not clear, however, whether the Amish do more than promise. They point to a possible world but do not actively work to create it beyond the small community of believers. As John Hostetler notes, most Amish people "show little interest in improving the world that is outside their immediate environ-ment."[20] Their direct involvement in politics is limited to local zoning ordi-nances and, in exceptional cases, to challenges to state or federal laws that threaten their religious lives. Amish leaders proved willing, for example, to go to the Supreme Court to defend their right to educate children only until eighth grade, and a number of Amish parents went to prison before this right was won.[21] These legal struggles underline, again, the fact that the Old Orders require certain concessions from the larger society to maintain their internal rules and ways of life. In general, however, the Amish reject activism to change the government, just as they avoid dependency on it.

Their contribution to making the world better lies in being the right kind of church. They neither convert others, as do evangelical Protestants, nor work through political and social channels for change, as do Catholics. In the Amish perspective, both would violate the principle of Gelassenheit. It is preferable to be a small group that really lives out its values than a larger one that espouses values but does not practice them in everyday life. As a contributor to the Amish magazine *Family Life* wrote, "We are to be a witness to the world, but at the same time to be separate from it (2 Cor. 6:17). How could we better be the 'salt of the earth' and 'a light to the world' than by contentedly living a plain life and by giving up the idols that the world holds so dear?"[22] Links to the outside world are tolerated only if they are necessary for economic survival (e.g., participation in markets), for political obedience (e.g., paying taxes and following regulations), or for the survival of the community (e.g., legal defense of Amish schools and of the right to withhold social security taxes). Beyond that, proactive work in the world is neither desired nor accepted.

Given this insistence on separation, what might the Old Order Amish and the larger Anabaptist tradition contribute to building a better society? Yoder argues that by living gospel values of solidarity, peaceableness, and equality, nonconformist Christians, including Anabaptists, pose "an unavoidable challenge to the powers that be and the beginning of a new set of social alternatives." The new order embodied by the Christian community "condemns and displaces the old order" without using "the arms of the old."[23] Through their very refusal to participate in this world, they show the possibility of a different one and thus offer "a foretaste of the peace for which the world was made." Christian nonconformity does not neglect or reject social change, Yoder contends, but rather contributes to social change in a form that differs radically from that of conventional politics and organizations.

> It is the function of minority communities to remember and to cre-
> ate utopian visions. There is no hope for society without an aware-
> ness of transcendence. Transcendence is kept alive not on the
> grounds of logical proof to the effect that there is a cosmos with a
> hereafter, but by the vitality of communities in which a different way
> of being keeps breaking in here and now. That we can really be led
> on a different way is the real proof of the transcendent power which
> offers hope of peace to the world as well. Nonconformity is the war-
> rant for the promise of another world. Although immersed in this
> world, the church by her way of being represents the promise of an-
> other world, which is not somewhere else but which is to come
> here.[24]

The redemptive community can create a real alternative for the world only apart from it, for the world is ruled by violence, coercion, and division. The church can defeat these evils not by using force but only by demonstrating in concrete practice that another way is possible. This possibility at the same time testifies to the divine power that enables this other way of living, despite the obstacles and persecution imposed by worldly powers. This other way—the reign of God—has necessarily political dimensions. A kingdom is a political form, even if its monarch is divine. Thus, the effort to embody the reign of God, however partially, stands in tension with Amish communities' efforts to withdraw from the political world. The power of their utopian vision may come precisely from this tension, which destabilizes any notion that a holy kingdom can be created on earth while forcing believers to live, nonetheless, as though they could create such a kingdom.

Anabaptist efforts to make their communities into microcosms of the world they wish to create echoes a characteristic of some contemporary social movements. In these cases, the organizations themselves and the members' participation are not merely means to achieve political goals. Rather, the very forms of the movements are "messages" themselves, signs for the rest of society.[25] Many feminist organizations, for example, insist on democratic structures of decision making, shared leadership, and adherence to principles of mutual respect and collaboration. These internal features of the movement are as important as their effects on larger social structures, insofar as they, like Anabaptist communities, embody rather than just announce the values they espouse.

In contrast to the Anabaptist vision, most Catholics have been content with a more distant relationship to the reign of God. Catholic thought has long insisted that both human society and the natural world should, and largely do, reflect God's ultimate aims. However, the actual realization of the reign of God is postponed indefinitely, until either the individual believer's death or some far-off collective realization. Progressive Catholics differ notably from their tradition's mainstream in their adoption of the reign of God as a more immediate ethical and political model for the kind of society they want to build. They share the Anabaptist commitment to the kingdom as social ethic, the notion that Jesus' teachings and his vision of the reign of God constitute a model for human society that Christians should try to live out here and now.

Unlike Anabaptists, however, progressive Catholics do not assert that practicing these values requires separation from the world. Rather, they believe they are called to help create the reign of God in history. They do this through the construction and maintenance of small Christian communities that serve as seeds of the future reign of God, embodying the values of nonviolence, justice, and mutual interdependence, and also through active work in more explicitly political spheres. In the Catholic "both/and" vision, small communities constitute both the living embodiment of alternative values and a practical tool to implement these values in secular culture and political institutions. They work for change by establishing links with other groups; participating at various levels beyond the local, including regional, national, and international; "working the system" through political allies and networks; demonstrating and protesting; and even, in some cases, taking up arms.

These practices are legitimized by a larger Catholic conviction that all aspects of human life, indeed of the entire creation, are related and harmonious. Underlying this perspective is natural law theory, as defined by the medieval theologian Thomas Aquinas, still Catholicism's most important theologian. In his masterwork, the *Summa Theologica*, Thomas proclaimed, "The whole community of the universe is governed by the divine reason." God's will and God's law shape every aspect of creation, such that "everything that in any way is, is from God." According to this cosmology, all aspects of creation are linked together, because "all things partake in some way in the eternal law." Rational creatures participate in natural law, or have it imprinted on them, in their mind and conscience. This rationality, the imprint of eternal law in the soul, places humans literally just below the angels in the hierarchical order of the universe. All aspects of the creation are linked to God and each other, but they are not equal in value or in nearness to the divine. As Thomas explains, "In natural things, species seem to be arranged in a hierarchy: as the mixed things are more perfect than the elements, and plants than minerals, and animals than plants, and men more than other animals."[26]

Natural law assumptions about the hierarchy, order, and essential harmony of the universe, as well as its conviction that humans stand at the top of the hierarchy, continue to shape Roman Catholic theology and ethics. This approach can be problematic, insofar as natural law sometimes glosses over conflicts, simplifies the relationship between scales, and universalizes values that are not really universal. Despite its failings, however, natural law can contribute to an awareness of the connections among events at different scales and among values that can be translated from one situation or scale to another. Natural law denies that the individual conscience or small religious communities are finally separate from what happens in the larger society. Although the differences between Anabaptists and Roman Catholics are real, they agree on this crucial point: there are not two kingdoms, just one, in which Christians can and must live out their faith. They agree also that although divine grace is ultimately necessary to achieve genuine social and moral transformation, human effort is invaluable. Humans are responsible for participating in the construction of the kingdom; they cannot just sit by and wait for God to do it all.

A conviction that different social scales are inextricably related also shapes the Roman Catholic value of subsidiarity. According to this principle, Christian values favor local, close-to-home solutions. However, when these are insufficient, government and public institutions at various levels, from local to international, can and should play a positive role. Subsidiarity thus combines a preference for localism with an appreciation of larger scales and the complex relations among them, avoiding (ideally) the shortsightedness of an exclusive focus on either local or national levels. Subsidiarity rests also on faith in people's ability to know what is right and to resolve problems ethically.

These Catholic principles lead to a generally positive evaluation of political activities and institutions, which has sometimes encouraged the church to identify closely with particular political agendas and movements. This has occurred repeatedly in Latin America, in, for example, the sometimes problematic relationship between progressive Catholics and the Sandinista government in Nicaragua, where church activists' close ties to the Sandinistas made even constructive and loyal criticism difficult. (Of course, the relentless and disproportionate U.S. war against the Sandinistas provided a context in which even sympathetic criticism could undermine the revolution's most basic goals.) Archbishop Romero addressed this question in relation to Christian participation in political movements in El Salvador. Romero argued that the church should "accompany" Christians who undertake concrete political action "as the faith demands for the urgent changes needed in society to make it more human and more Christian."[27] This is not, Romero argued, a politicization of pastoral work but a pastoral effort to guide the conscience of Christians in a politicized environment. Romero's notion of accompaniment permitted cooperation and identification of goals while maintaining a certain distinction in identity and ultimate loyalty, precisely to avoid making political organizations of any kind into idols. Accompaniment acknowledges the immersion of Christians in the world and demands that they participate in it. However, it also calls them to maintain a critical distance, based on the permanent tension between worldly organizations and achievements on the one hand, and ultimate Christian aims on the other.

In accord with the principle of accompaniment, Salvadoran Catholics have sought to retain their most important religious values while immersing themselves in movements to transform their society. This connection remains strong even in the repopulations, where activists appreciate that "we are not a separate nation," as Mauricio puts it. In contrast to Amish efforts to remain apart, Catholic activists emphasize that they live in the midst of a larger society shaped by neoliberal economic policies, globalization, and other forces far beyond their control, and that their achievements take place against this backdrop. They also hope to extend their values beyond the village borders. Villages like Guarjila had long been seen as backward and subversive. Now "Guarjila is like a model for other communities," Mauricio explains. "This region is like the future for this area . . . a vision for the rest of the country."[28] The motto of Ciudad Segundo Montes, a repopulation in Morazán province, also reflects the repobladores' sense of their communities as the model and cornerstone of a new national society: "a hope that is born in the east for all of El Salvador [una esperanza que nace en el Oriente para todo El Salvador]."

Necessary Utopias

So who is right: the repopulators, with their hopes for a new world, or those who claim that history has ended? The latter seem to have the weight of evidence on their side. Progressive activists today face an increasingly dystopian world, distinctly short on plausible alternatives. Hunger, economic inequities, lack of social services, political and criminal violence, environmental destruction, and wars reduce the quality of life for people in both First and Third Worlds. Social ethicist Sharon Welch summarizes the challenge: "What does it mean to work for social transformation in the face of seemingly insurmountable suffering and evil? How can we sustain energy, hope, and commitment in the face of an unrelenting succession of social and political crises?"[29] In answer to this question, Welch explicitly rejects utopianism. She calls for "politics without utopia, ethics without virtue, and spirituality without God." Progressives ought to reject utopianism, she explains, because "dreams of unending progress, absolute justice, and beneficent power and creativity" lead to domination and repression. In the United States, for example, convictions about the rightness of a particular vision of progress created "an America without doubts" that sought, often violently, to impose its model far and wide.[30] Utopianism, in short, is bad for people with political, cultural, and economic power. This is a powerful critique, more nuanced than many postmodernist celebrations of fragmentation for its own sake and also more than neoconservative declarations that history has ended. However, Welch does not explore the question of whether utopianism has the same meaning and consequences for people without power. She leaves open the necessity of examining the social and political functions, as well as the ethical dimensions, of utopian dreams in different settings.

Reynaldo Ileto has done precisely this in his study of religiously based peasant movements in the Philippines, whose struggles continued for decades despite numerous failures and harsh repression. Like Anabaptists and progressive Latin American Catholics, the Philippine movements draw on collective identity rooted in the past and on deeply Christian understandings of sacrifice. Ileto concludes that utopian hopes play an irreplaceable role in these efforts for social change. Social movements are unlikely to succeed unless they build on "the masses' conceptions of the future as well as social and economic conditions." This is true because "what determines human behavior must include not only real and present factors but also a certain object, a certain future, that is to be actualized."[31] This describes the Catholic peasant struggle in El Salvador, in which a persistent dream of a qualitatively different world anchored a movement capable of surviving blow after blow. These experiences bear witness to Paul Tillich's characterization of utopias as enabling people "to transform the given," or, as Ileto puts it, "to go beyond their situation, to determine what its meaning would be instead of merely being determined by it."[32]

Utopias not only point to new and desirable possibilities but also provide a vantage point from which people can judge their own society and discover where it needs to change. This is one of the important contributions of utopian fiction, from Thomas More's *Utopia* (1515–1516) to influential recent works such as Ernest Callenbach's *Ecotopia* and Ursula LeGuin's *The Dispossessed*.[33] Without utopian images and hopes, it may become difficult to conceive of even moderate changes to the status quo. Even the wildest fictional accounts may have value in this respect. And even more valuable and powerful, perhaps, are religious narratives, which strike believers as true, if not literally then morally and psychologically. In this regard, biblical portrayals of the reign of God and of the early Christian community have sparked countless utopian movements and experiments among mystics, monastics, millenarians, and socialists. For both Anabaptists and progressive Catholics, these biblical images and narratives have inspired sharp critiques of both the church and the state of their time. Communities that strive to live according to this vision, like the Amish and the repopulations, offer a real alternative to which we can point, living proof that another way is possible.

The Outline of a Better World

What is this alternative? Recognizing the particularity and complexity of every historical circumstance and every community, we can identify some common characteristics of the modest and ambiguous utopias that are being created by progressive Catholics and Anabaptists in the Americas.

First, this vision of the good life is a communal one. Humans are social animals who can find fulfillment only in collective life. Such a life cannot be based only on a voluntaristic contract model or on accidental groupings. Rather, freedom is defined as the possibility of realizing human capacities and abilities amid and in the service of a larger community. This contradicts the dominant definition of freedom in the United States as the pursuit of individual self-interest, usually defined in material terms. In some parts of the world, socialist and labor movements challenge such isolationism, but in many areas its main critics are religious. Although some religious groups, including many varieties of evangelical Protestantism, reinforce individualism with their emphasis on personal salvation, other faiths challenge isolation and selfishness, proposing instead that "individuality and society are not opposites but require each other," as Robert Bellah and his colleagues hope.[34] This vision is shared by progressive Catholics and Anabaptists. Both replace individualism with the values of solidarity and cooperation, resting not on mechanistic collectivism but on a view of human nature in which collaboration and mutual aid are as fundamental

as competition and self-gratification. This understanding of humanness demands the transformation of both political institutions and moral culture, to
replace a "contract of mutual indifference" with "a pervasive culture of mutual
aid."[35] Both Catholic and Anabaptist communities, further, extend this sense
of solidarity beyond their own circles to encompass other parts of the world
and future generations.

Second, people's material needs are met, and no one falls through the
cracks. Progressive Catholic and Anabaptist communities judge themselves by
whether all members can meet their basic needs, not by how much wealth a
small elite accumulates. This is less a dream of plenty than a vision of sufficiency, of the fulfillment of people's basic needs for food, shelter, health care,
and education. Affluent people in the United States, Latin America, and elsewhere may find this dream uninspiring, but for the millions of people around
the world who lack adequate food, shelter, water, education, and health care, it
can be extremely powerful. With its barefoot children, two-room houses, and
dusty cornfields, Guarjila strikes few well-off Salvadorans or North Americans
as utopian. However, the children live beyond infancy and attend school, the
houses are solid and shelter all in the village, and the fields belong to the people
who work them. The lives of Guarjila's residents are demanding, but in contrast to those of many Salvadoran peasants they constitute a model of health
and sufficiency, well worth a struggle. And unless basic material needs are
met, larger goals of social revolution and political democratization cannot succeed. The victories of the Salvadoran peasant movement, from the first cooperatives to the repopulations, stem from activists' ability to balance the twin
goals of feeding people and at the same time pursuing long-term structural
changes.

Third, members together make and enforce collective decisions at various
levels, including households, workplaces, and schools. The Amish and repopulated communities are deeply democratic in this respect, even though they
may not participate in national elections. This everyday democracy often entails
long meetings and discussions, which would be unwieldy for larger groups.
Clearly, these processes do not guarantee complete democracy. Some people
participate less than others or have less power. Amish women cannot hold
many leadership positions, for example. However, a commitment to collective
decision making and popular participation ensures that goals are more likely
to reflect what people really value and that leaders can be held accountable to
the larger community. In the repopulations, democracy has further included
an explicit commitment to economic democracy, especially evident in a wide
distribution of land ownership as well as some degree of collective control over
land and other means of production. This challenges the neoliberal vision
which holds the free market and utilitarian individualism as the foundations
and also the ultimate aims of democratic governance.[36]

Fourth, residents in these communities strive to meet their material needs in environmentally sustainable ways and to address serious ecological problems to ensure both human quality of life and the preservation of natural goods. They constitute neither a technocratic ideal in which humans achieve total control over natural processes nor a radical ecological utopia in which humans leave wild nature alone. Instead, people acknowledge and appreciate their dependence on nature as well as their power over it. They aim to be good stewards both because their own lives depend on it and because God's creation is good in and of itself. Agriculture is central to this vision, because it provides people with what they need to survive and because it is where people live out their attitudes toward the nonhuman world. In all these communities, farmers try to leave some room for nonhuman nature, to use only the resources they need, and to protect land and water for future generations. These aims constitute a modest vision, hardly utopian at all, unless we compare it to what most people in the world now experience.

These communities are far from perfect, but they have managed to create substantially more just, democratic, and environmentally sustainable models of social organization and resource use than those that surround them. Extending their modest utopias would involve a virtual revolution, a radical transformation of existing economic and political structures as well as of the dominant moral culture.

Critical Utopianism

These revolutions will fail if we imagine the Amish, the repopulations, or any other community, past or present, as a one-size-fits-all program for all people and all circumstances. "If we need images of our desire," Terry Eagleton points out, "we also need to prevent these images from mesmerizing us and so standing in the way of it."[37] Marx also saw this danger in movements that simply hearken to past glories (real or, mostly, imagined). In place of rosy visions of a vague future paradise, we need a critical utopianism, able to change in response to events and circumstances along the way. We need the kind of utopianism that E. P. Thompson described as the "education of desire," capable of opening the way "to an uninterrupted interrogation of our values and also to its own self-interrogation."[38] In this light, not realism but complacency is the worst enemy of utopianism.

A critical, self-interrogating utopianism must be grounded in knowledge of the constraints of its particular social situation, the history that has led to this situation, and the plausibility of different alternatives. From such an assessment might emerge realistic utopias that are grounded in the actual conditions as well as the past history and future possibilities of contemporary society.[39] This is not Elshtain's realism, which discounts far too many possibilities in its smug reading of the signs of the times. By allowing so few possible responses to the status quo, Elshtain's approach ultimately sanctifies the present situation as the best of all possible worlds. This danger also lurked in earlier forms of Christian realism, although Niebuhr tempered his skepticism about utopianism with an even greater skepticism regarding ruling elites and class politics. In the end, however, Niebuhr too quickly dismissed the possibility of substantive change and the extent to which both what is realistic and what is utopian are defined by those in power.

While rejecting conservative cynicism about the possibilities of change, we must also acknowledge that no ideal society will emerge simply from "the movement of history." This illusion made the utopianism of the socialist left sometimes counterproductive and even dangerous. Utopianism becomes counterproductive if the realization that a perfect society is impossible dampens all hopes, and thus all efforts, for social change. It becomes dangerous when people develop a fanatical confidence in the correctness of their own vision and a corresponding intolerance for other perspectives and goals, ignoring the fact that even the most elevated visions of a good society have roots in particular cultures.

All these critiques are valid, yet blanket condemnations of utopianism forget that dreams of a splendid city have inspired not only failed revolutions and totalitarian reactions but also a host of movements, many nonviolent, which have achieved real victories. These victories, never total and never gained without sacrifice, have made concrete improvements in people's lives. Only the arrogance of power can, for example, dismiss the vast reduction in infant and maternal mortality rates in Chalatenango as irrelevant to historical assessments of the revolutionary movement that led to such changes.[40]

The challenge is to see utopia neither as a blueprint that must be followed precisely nor as the result of mechanistic cause-and-effect processes but rather as a resource that enables both critiques of the status quo and efforts to conceive and work toward alternatives. This entails believing that there are always alternatives, that better worlds are always possible. It means conceiving of that better world in substantive terms that leave history open and, especially, acknowledging that any historical embodiment of utopian hopes will fall short of the finality and purity for which the movement aimed. Utopian movements must strive to embody their aspirations in time and space, knowing all the while that such embodiments will always fall short of their ultimate goals.

The tension between history and transcendence creates ambiguity. Tillich notes the tension inherent in the political and social meanings of the most potent Western religious utopia, the reign of God. This vision "fulfils the utopian expectation of a realm of peace and justice" but also acknowledges the impossibility of its complete earthly fulfillment, insofar as there is always a transcendent horizon. Here self-consciously utopian ethics may have a surprising advantage over others. A social ethic centered on the reign of God cannot avoid tensions and ambiguities. The same is true, however, of virtually every ethic that holds out the promise of anything better than the status quo. An explicitly utopian ethic, which acknowledges the impossibility of achieving its own ultimate goals, at least in human time and space, might be more constructive and honest than an ethic whose aims are impossible but nonetheless touted as realistic, as in just war theory or "humane capitalism." Self-conscious utopianism may be better equipped to address, if not resolve, the tensions between goals and achievements, insofar as it incorporates ambiguity into its very definition. An ethic based on the reign of God, as Tillich writes, includes a recognition of permanent incompleteness, an incapacity to reach the "of God" that keeps the kingdom from being fully of this world.⁴¹

At its best, a kingdom-based ethic helps its advocates push toward a better future while remaining open to the unpredictable consequences of both human and divine agency. Self-consciously utopian movements assert that history can move in a positive direction while remaining open to the unpredictable consequences of both human and divine agency. The classic Christian description of the reign of God as "already not yet" neatly encapsulates this tension. The kingdom is within and among us at the same time that it remains forever beyond us, a horizon that always draws us near but is never surmounted. The worst sin of utopianism is not to hope that something better is possible but to believe that we have achieved the best of all possible worlds, that there is nothing new under the sun—that history has ended and there is no alternative. Thus, Tillich proposes, "It is the spirit of utopia that conquers utopia."⁴²

The Road Forward

Progressive Catholic activists construct their theological ethics with frequent reference to the life of Jesus and especially the parables. One favorite in El Salvador is the grain of wheat that dies in order to bear fruit (John 12:24), which a lay leader used to explain the massacre in Corral de Piedra, Chalatenango, described in the introduction. Another frequently cited passage is the story of the mustard seed in Matthew 13:31–32, in which Jesus tells the disciples, "The kingdom of heaven is like a grain of mustard seed which a man took and sowed in his field; it is the smallest of all seeds, but when it has grown it is the greatest of shrubs and becomes a tree, so that the birds of the air come and make nests in its branches." In the mid-1970s, a member of a base community in Solentiname, Nicaragua, reflected on the power and ambiguity of this passage, finding in it a message of hope that resonates with Salvadoran Catholic activists:

> I don't know about the mustard seed, but I do know about the guás-
> ima seed, which is tiny. I'm looking at that guásima tree over there.

It's very large, and the birds come to it too. I say to myself: that's what we are, this little community, a guásima seed. It doesn't seem there's any connection between a thing that round and tiny, like a pebble, and that great big tree. It doesn't seem either that there's any connection between some poor campesinos and a just and well-developed society, where there is abundance and everything is shared. And we are the seed of that society. When the tree will develop we don't know. But we know that we are a seed and not a pebble.[43]

There is a connection, but what it is and how it will play out we don't know. There is no preordained path to a better world; progress toward the reign of God is partial, fallible, and far from inevitable. Leaving the final realization of the kingdom to divine will, Christian utopians accept the unavoidable ambiguity of their vision, which carries with it a message of humility about human power and knowledge. This humility emerges from a worldview in which human agency is not all that moves history and only God is absolute, what James Gustafson calls a theocentric approach to ethics.[44] Progressive Catholics, like Anabaptists, view their work in this theocentric light, and more specifically in terms of a larger salvific history in which individual lives and actions gain meaning from divine power. This leads to a very different view of means and ends from that common in most ideas of utopian social change. Deeply etched in both Anabaptist and progressive Catholic sensibilities is a conviction that worldly failure indicates neither abandonment by God nor the impossibility of progress. "The church," explains John Howard Yoder, "cultivates an alternative consciousness. Another view of what the world is like is kept alive by narration and celebration which fly in the face of some of the 'apparent' lessons of 'realism.' "[45]

These lessons are strong in Anabaptist history, but Yoder might also have been writing about Salvadoran activists who interpreted violent repression of their movement and the deaths of their companions as signs that they are following Jesus' path of redemptive suffering. The deaths of loved ones, a Salvadoran woman explains, are "precisely what has giving meaning to my task [quéhacer] as a Christian and in popular organizations. . . . The example of the closest people is encouragement. To stop would mean that their blood had been shed in vain. We have to continue as long as God lets us live." Echoing Yoder's antiteleological logic, she argues that the deaths of activists, apparently a mark of failure, actually signify that they are on the right track and must continue. "Martyrs leave a commitment for the CEBs. The community meets around their memory. . . . Seeing how valuable people have fallen gives us motivation to continue our faith and our hope . . . to be an authentic Christian follower of Jesus, there's no option. You must go as far as possible."[46] "As far as possible" means, for this activist and many of her companions, not resignation to limited options but a commitment to continue pushing, in the belief that ultimate limits are set not by human knowledge but by God.

This commitment is nurtured by narratives of previous martyrdoms and defeats, signs of hope to those who know how to read them, who are immersed in the past and present that they bridge. By rejecting cause-and-effect calculation, their readings guard "against giving up the battle or 'burning out,'" as Yoder writes, "standard temptations to those whose reason for doing good is too closely correlated to manageable projections of effect." This insight is confirmed in the histories of Anabaptists and progressive Catholics who have endured many more defeats than victories. How might other movements cultivate this disregard for historical outcome, if it is indeed required for endurance over the long haul of an unequal struggle? Perhaps what is necessary is in some sense religious, as Yoder suggests: a "conviction that one's morality and social style are expressive of a transcendent commitment and not just of consequential calculation."[47] Socialist critic Terry Eagleton suggests a secularized version of this faith: activists might focus less on achieving aims than on the powers that a struggle or event incarnates. Spurning the instrumental in this way is "a utopian gesture which might . . . bear fruit for the living."[48] Eagleton echoes a Filipino activist quoted by Ileto: "No uprising fails. Each one is a step in the right direction."[49] This means not just that every movement learns from its predecessors but also that knowledge, commitments, relationships, capacities, and "powers" all build slowly and can lead to unexpected results. There is no unilinear accumulation of forces, because every movement is subject to countless frustrations and losses. However, the mere fact of historical failure, according to instrumental criteria, should not condemn a group or its goals.

If no uprising fails, then every movement for social change, every attempt to steer history in a different direction, demonstrates the possibility of a different world. That knowledge, often saved and transmitted by small groups at the margins of societies, can be redemptive when dystopian agendas dominate and when political repression prevents the open expression of alternatives. Memories of slave rebellions in the southern United States, of indigenous struggles in Latin America, and of other "failed" uprisings resurface generations later, having kept both anger and hope alive until a time when they could be expressed in a politically efficacious way. Such narratives provide emotional, moral, and material support that enable members to continue living out their values and, therefore, to keep alternative values alive. The communal context is crucial, for, as John Howard Yoder points out, dissenters have a "combined power of resistance [that] is far more than the sum of the resistance potential of each member taken separately." No single individual can carry collective memories and aspirations alone, but "when the powers of evil are for a time so successful that all resistance seems to be crushed, it is from the ranks of that community, just now bludgeoned into quiescence, that will come another generation's prophets, in their time."[50]

Both communal and long-term perspectives have been crucial to the success of Christianity and especially to the tradition's capacity to nourish utopian dreams in even the most daunting circumstances. The ability to survive martyrdoms and defeats comes in large part from faith in a transcendent promise, in God's assurance, as Martin Luther King Jr. put it, that "we as a people will get to the promised land," regardless of the fate of individuals.[51] Even those who do not share a theocentric faith find powerful lessons in early Christians' struggles with the Roman Empire, as evidenced by the appeal of this history for a number of secular leftists. In the wake of the November 2004 U.S. elections, for example, Barbara Ehrenreich read the history of the original Christians as "the story of how a steadfast and heroic moral minority undermined the world's greatest empire and eventually came to power. Faced with relentless and spectacular forms of repression, they kept on meeting over their potluck dinners (the origins of later communion rituals), proselytizing and bearing witness wherever they could. For the next four years and well beyond, liberals and progressives will need to emulate these original Christians, who stood against imperial Rome with their bodies, their hearts and their souls."[52]

In a similar vein, the influential book *Empire* by Michael Hardt and Antonio Negri likens anticapitalist and antiglobalization activists to early Christians.[53] Responding to Hardt and Negri, cultural critic John Beverley poses the question "Who are the Christians today? That is, who in the world today, within Empire but not *of* it, carries the possibility of a logic that is opposed to Empire and that will bring about its eventual downfall or transformation?"[54] And environmental philosopher Arran Garé compares alternative communities today to the Roman Christians that St. Augustine described: "strangers in the societies in which they must live their everyday lives." Such groups cannot simply withdraw into monasteries to wait for a new world, but must "begin to build this new civilization while the old civilization, despite its nihilism and the fragmentation of its culture, is still vigorous and powerful; more powerful than any civilization which has ever existed."[55]

This is what the communities I have described, each in its own way, strive to do. They criticize the status quo and point to a more desirable ideal. They straddle the boundaries between the real and the utopian, embodying the productive tension between the already and the not yet of the reign of God. Although the longed-for utopia will always be not yet on earth, it is already among us in these small and vulnerable communities, seeds and promissory notes for the future.

These communities do not lack problems and strains, but neither are they castles in the air. They represent the hope of learning, first, *that* it is possible not only to conceive of a different world but also to create one, to live and make a living by different rules. Second, these small communities help us see *how* they are possible: what they might require of us, what they might promise. Their very existence holds out hope, even while this hope staggers under the combined weight of the empire to which the communities refuse allegiance and of their own human frailties. They are far from perfect, their survival is far from assured, and their visions may never be realized beyond their own borders. Still, their lesson could not be more important: human beings can live better; injustice, destruction, and cruelty are not inevitable; another world is possible.

Notes

INTRODUCTION: RESIDENCE ON EARTH

1. From the Web site of Oregon Action, the successor organization to Fair Share, which closed in 1997: http://www.oregonaction.org/oais.html.

2. I use the terms "reign" and "kingdom" of God interchangeably throughout this book, although I favor the former and generally use "kingdom" only in quotations or in circumstances when that term seems clearly preferable. Like many scholars of religion, I prefer "reign" for its gender inclusiveness; "kingdom" implies that God is male. However, English-speaking Anabaptists almost always use the term kingdom. Salvadorans use the term *reino*, most accurately translated as "reign," which, like its Spanish counterpart, can refer to a realm ruled by a queen or a king. The title of this book comes from a quotation found in the final chapter, a translation from Spanish of comments by a Nicaraguan Catholic recorded by Ernesto Cardenal in *The Gospel in Solentiname*, vol. 2 (Maryknoll, N.Y.: Orbis Books, 1976). The English translators used the then standard translation "kingdom" for the speaker's reino. I follow their usage, largely because "seeds of the reign of God" seemed both obscure and awkward. I apologize for the lack of gender inclusiveness in this case.

3. John Howard Yoder, *The Priestly Kingdom: Social Ethics as Gospel* (Notre Dame, Ind.: University of Notre Dame Press, 1984), 92.

4. Thanks to Les Thiele for the term "embedded practices."

5. Brian Ilbery, Quentin Chiotti, and Timothy Rickard, eds., *Agricultural Restructuring and Sustainability: A Geographical Perspective*, Sustainable Rural Development Series, no. 3 (Oxford: CAB International, 1997).

6. Timothy C. Weiskel, "In Dust and Ashes: The Environmental Crisis in Religious Perspective," *Harvard Divinity Bulletin* 21, no. 3 (1992), quoted in Theodore Hiebert, "The Human Tradition: Origins and Transformations in Christian Tradition," in *Christianity and Ecology: Seeking the Well-Being of*

Earth and Humans, ed. D. Hessel and R. R. Ruether (Cambridge, Mass.: Harvard University Center for the Study of World Religions, 2000), 151.

7. Thieleman J. van Bracht,*The Martyrs' Mirror* (Scottdale, Pa.: Herald Press, 1938), 437.

8. Ibid., 980–981. A letter written by Maeyken is the only "martyr letter" remaining in the hands of Dutch Mennonites today; her tongue screws also survive. John S. Oyer and Robert S. Kreider, *Mirror of the Martyrs* (Intercourse, Pa.: Good Books, 1990), 52–53.

9. van Bracht, *The Martyrs' Mirror*, 613.

10. Ibid., 548.

11. Elmo Stoll, writing in *Family Life* magazine (August/September 1987), quoted in Brad Igou, *The Amish in Their Own Words: Amish Writings from 25 Years of* Family Life *Magazine* (Scottdale, Pa.: Herald Press, 1999), 28.

12. The native Pipil culture in El Salvador declined after the matanza, including a drop in usage of native dress and of the Nahuatl language. Recent scholarship debates the extent to which distinctive indigenous cultures and communities persist in El Salvador today, and many scholars contend that postmatanza accounts underestimated the survival of indigenous culture (especially in western El Salvador) and presented a false picture of a uniformly *mestizo* nation. Although the debate about distinctive indigenous communities is not central to this book, it is relevant to point out that native values and traditions have influenced the country's generalized mestizo culture. They have also helped shape popular Catholicism, even in parts of El Salvador such as Chalatenango, which lost its identifiable indigenous communities long ago. For example, Kay Read, professor of religion at De Paul University, believes that the progressive Catholic emphasis on individual sacrifice for the common good and the importance of martyrdom probably stem in part from native understandings of sacrifice. Kay Read, personal communication, 2004.

13. David Browning, *El Salvador: La Tierra y el hombre* (San Salvador: UCA Editores, 1973), 273.

14. Human Rights Watch, 1990 report on El Salvador, http://www.hrw.org/reports/1990/WR90/AMER.BOU–07.htm.

15. Julio [pseud.], pastoral team, Corral de Piedra/Guancora, Chalatenango, interview by author, March 25, 1990.

16. Beth Cagan and Steve Cagan, *This Promised Land, El Salvador* (New Brunswick, N.J.: Rutgers University Press, 1991); Jenny Pearce, *Promised Land: Peasant Rebellion in Chalatenango, El Salvador* (London: Latin American Bureau, 1986); Scott Wright, *Promised Land: Death and Life in El Salvador* (Maryknoll, N.Y.: Orbis Books, 1994).

CHAPTER I. FARM, LAND, CHURCH

1. Martin Luther, "Secular Authority: To what extent it should be obeyed" (1523), in *Martin Luther: Selections from His Writings*, ed. John Dillenberger (New York: Anchor Books, 1971), 374–375.

2. Paul Tillich, *Systematic Theology*, vol. 3: *Life and the Spirit; History and the Kingdom of God* (Chicago: University of Chicago Press, 1963), 355.

3. Thomas Münzer, *The Letters of Thomas Münzer*, ed. P. Matheson (Edinburgh:

T. and T. Clark, 1988), 140, quoted in Catherine Keller, *Apocalypse Now and Then: A Feminist Guide to the End of the World* (Boston: Beacon Press, 1996), 188.

4. From 1530 on, Luther also supported, albeit reluctantly, the death penalty for Anabaptists. Oyer and Kreider, *Mirror of the Martyrs*, 73.

5. A 1524 letter from Conrad Grebel and the Zurich Anabaptists to Münzer (also spelled Müntzter) points out both areas of agreement, including the rejection of infant baptism, and disagreement, notably on whether Christians could use violence. In Hans Hillerbrand, ed., *The Protestant Reformation* (New York: Harper and Row, 1968), 122–128.

6. John A. Hostetler, *Amish Society*, 4th ed. (Baltimore: Johns Hopkins University Press, 1993), 25.

7. Igou, *The Amish in Their Own Words*, 209.

8. Ibid., 211.

9. Joseph Donnermeyer, George Kreps, and Marty Kreps, *Lessons for Living: A Practical Approach to Daily Life from the Amish Community* (Sugarcreek, Ohio: Carlisle Press, 1999), 26–27.

10. Ibid., 29–30.

11. "The Schleitheim Confession," in Hillerbrand, *The Protestant Reformation*, 132–133.

12. David Kline, interview by author, Fredericksburg, Ohio, May 30, 2001.

13. David Weaver-Zercher, *The Amish in the American Imagination* (Baltimore: Johns Hopkins University Press, 2001), 153.

14. "The Schleitheim Confession," in Hillerbrand, *The Protestant Reformation*, 132.

15. Ibid.

16. The national Mennonite Church USA was created when the two largest Mennonite groups, the General Conference Mennonites and the Mennonite Church, united in 2001.

17. *Confession of Faith in a Mennonite Perspective* (Scottdale, Pa.: Herald Press, 1995), 39.

18. Donald B. Kraybill and Carl F. Bowman, *On the Backroad to Heaven: Old Order Hutterites, Mennonites, Amish and Brethren* (Baltimore: Johns Hopkins University Press, 2001), 267.

19. David Kline, *Scratching the Woodchuck: Nature on an Amish Farm* (Athens: University of Georgia Press, 1997), 195–196.

20. David Kline, *Great Possessions: An Amish Farmer's Journal* (San Francisco: North Point Press, 1990), xxi.

21. Jean Séguy, "Religion and Agricultural Success: The Vocational Life of the French Mennonites from the Seventeenth to the Nineteenth Centuries," trans. Michael Shank, *Mennonite Quarterly Review* 47 (1973): 187.

22. Ibid., 188.

23. Rhonda Lou Yoder, "Amish Agriculture in Iowa: Indigenous Knowledge for Sustainable Small-Farm Systems," *Studies in Technology and Social Change*, no. 15, Iowa State University, 1990, 1.

24. Steven Stoll, "Postmodern Farming, Quietly Flourishing," *Chronicle of Higher Education* 9 (June 21, 2002): B9.

25. R. Yoder, "Amish Agriculture in Iowa," 43.

26. Ibid., 46.

27. See Stoll, "Postmodern Farming," and Gene Logsdon, "Amish Economy," *Orion Nature Quarterly* 7, no. 2 (1988): 22–33.

28. Gene Logsdon, *Living at Nature's Pace: Farming and the American Dream* (White River Junction, Vt.: Chelsea Green, 2000), 140.

29. R. Yoder, "Amish Agriculture in Iowa," 46.

30. Michael Yoder, "The Very Best of Lives," *Christian Living* (Mar. 2002): 7.

31. Warren Johnson, Victor Stoltzfus, and Peter Craumer, "Energy Conservation in Amish Agriculture," *Science* 198, no. 4315 (Oct. 28, 1977): 373–378.

32. Peter Craumer, "Farm Productivity and Energy Efficiency in Amish and Modern Dairy Farming," *Agriculture and Environment* 4 (1979): 292.

33. David Kline, interview by author, May 30, 2001.

34. Deborah H. Stinner, M. G. Paoletti, and B. R. Stinner, "In Search of Traditional Farm Wisdom for a More Sustainable Agriculture: A Study of Amish Farming and Society," *Agriculture, Ecosystems, and Environment* 27 (1989): 83.

35. Mary Jackson, "Amish Agriculture and No-Till: The Hazards of Applying the USLE to Unusual Farms," *Journal of Soil and Water Conservation* 43 (November–December 1988): 483.

36. Ibid., 483–484.

37. Ibid.

38. Stinner et al., "In Search of Traditional Farm Wisdom," 86.

39. Ibid., 86–87.

40. R. Yoder, "Amish Agriculture in Iowa," 46.

41. Katharine V. Blake et al., "Modern Amish Farming as Ecological Agriculture." *Society & Natural Resources* 10, no. 2 (March/April 1997): 144–145.

42. Craumer, "Farm Productivity and Energy Efficiency," 295.

43. Kline, *Scratching the Woodchuck*, 204.

44. Stoll, "Postmodern Farming," B9.

45. Victor Stoltzfus, "Reward and Sanction: The Adaptive Continuity of Amish Life," *Mennonite Quarterly Review* 51, no. 4 (October 1977): 312.

46. Eugene Ericksen, Julia Ericksen, and John Hostetler, "The Cultivation of the Soil as a Moral Directive: Population Growth, Family Ties, and the Maintenance of Community among the Old Order Amish," *Rural Sociology* 45, no. 1 (spring 1980): 64.

47. Stoltzfus, "Reward and Sanction," 311–312.

48. Stoll, "Postmodern Farming," B8.

49. Stoltzfus, "Reward and Sanction," 312.

50. Ibid., 313.

51. http://www.tufts.edu/~eco/tfap/tfap.html. For more on the ecological costs of conventional food production, distribution, and consumption, see www.truecostof food.org.

52. Igou, *The Amish in Their Own Words*, 70–71.

53. Ericksen et al., "The Cultivation of the Soil," 59.

54. M. Yoder, "The Very Best of Lives," 8.

55. David Kline, interview by author, May 30, 2001.

56. M. Yoder, "The Very Best of Lives," 9.

57. Ericksen et al., "The Cultivation of the Soil," 66.

CHAPTER 2. PROMISED LAND

1. CELAM (Conference of Latin America Bishops), *The Church in the Present-Day Transformation of Latin America in the Light of the Council: Medellín Conclusions* (Washington, D.C.: National Conference of Catholic Bishops, 1979).

2. Ibid., 185, 41.

3. See Gustavo Gutiérrez, "Notes for a Theology of Liberation," *Theological Studies* 31, no. 2 (1970): 243–261, and *A Theology of Liberation* (Maryknoll, N.Y.: Orbis Books, 1973).

4. CELAM, "Puebla Final Document," in *Puebla and Beyond*, ed. John Eagleson and Philip Scharper, trans. John Drury (Maryknoll, N.Y.: Orbis, 1979) 222, 264–267.

5. Daniel Vega [pseud.], interview by author, San Salvador, Mar. 27, 1990.

6. Plácido Erdozaín, *Archbishop Romero* (Maryknoll, N.Y.: Orbis, 1981), 1.

7. Archdiocese of San Salvador, *Primera semana de pastoral arquidiocesana, 5–10 enero 1976* (San Salvador: Archdiocese of San Salvador, 1976), 5–6, 9–10.

8. Pearce, *Promised Land*, 102.

9. Ricardo Urioste, director of the *equipo itinerante*, recalled that there was also a *centro de formación* in San Vicente (Ricardo Urioste, Archdiocese of San Salvador, interview by author, June 29, 1994). I have found little information about this center, perhaps because the conservative bishop of San Vicente, Pedro Aparicio, limited both its work and publicity about it. The only published mention of the San Vicente center I found is in CEDES (Episcopal Conference of El Salvador), *Actas de CEDES*, no. 100 (January 20–24, 1975): 12, where Aparicio affirms his trust in the centro in his diocese in response to concerns that other centers might not merit the bishops' confidence.

10. CEDES, *Actas de CEDES*, no. 101 (July 7–11, 1975): 7.

11. Mario Ferrer [pseud.], interview by author, San Salvador, Apr. 5, 1990.

12. Juan Fernando Ascoli, *Tiempo de guerra y tiempo de paz: Organización y lucha de las comunidades del nor-oriente de Chalatenango (1974–1994)*, adapted by Miguel Cavada Diez (San Salvador: Equipo Maíz, n.d.), 20.

13. Guadalupe Mejía, interview by author, San Salvador, June 28, 1994.

14. Berkeley Sister City Project, "Life, Death, and Resurrection of a Salvadoran Village: An Oral History of San Antonio Los Ranchos, Chalatenango, El Salvador: 1970–1989," unpublished manuscript, 1989, 17.

15. Ibid., 7–8.

16. Ascoli, *Tiempo de guerra*, 21.

17. Quoted in Berkeley Sister City Project, "Life, Death, and Resurrection," 10.

18. Present at this meeting were also representatives from another UTC, which had been created the same year in the sugar-growing region of San Vicente. In 1975 the two joined. Ascoli, *Tiempo de guerra*, 28.

19. A. Douglas Kincaid, "Peasants into Rebels: Community and Class in Rural El Salvador," *Comparative Studies in Society and History* 29, no. 3 (July 1987): 485–486.

20. In addition to FECCAS and the UTC, two other peasant organizations emerged in El Salvador in the 1960s and 1970s. The first, the Salvadoran Communal Union (UCS), was set up with support from the U.S. government in 1969 as a "noncommunist" rural labor movement. With financial support from the United States, the UCS grew to 50,000 members by 1975, but U.S. influence could not prevent the

group from radicalizing in response to the intensifying rural crisis, and by the mid-1970s the UCS began experiencing conflicts with landowners over demands for better wages and contracts. The other peasant organization, ORDEN, was founded by landowners and security forces to survey and undermine popular organizing efforts, and was closely associated with death squads in rural areas.

21. Ascoli, *Tiempo de guerra*, 29.

22. Guadalupe Mejía, interview by author, San Salvador, Mar. 28, 1990.

23. Berkeley Sister City Project, "Life, Death, and Resurrection," 18.

24. Guadalupe Mejía, interview by author, San Salvador, Mar. 28, 1990.

25. Ibid. The novel *Un día en la vida* (*One Day of Life*) by Salvadoran writer Manlio Argueta includes a fictionalized account of Justo Mejía's death.

26. The largest of the armies was the Popular Liberation Forces (Fuerzas Populares para la Liberación, FPL), founded in 1970 by eight dissident members of the Salvadoran Communist Party. The best-known of the FPL's founders was Salvador Cayetano Carpio, known as Comandante Marcial. The FPL gave more emphasis to popular organizations and political mobilization than did the Communist Party; its main base lay in peasant organizations in Chalatenango and other rural areas in central El Salvador. The next-largest FMLN group was the People's Revolutionary Army (Ejército Revolucionario del Pueblo, ERP), with a stronghold in Morazán province and some urban *barrios* in San Salvador. The ERP did not work as closely with peasant federations and other civilian organizations as did the FPL, and its leaders adopted a more militaristic style. The other FMLN member organizations were the Revolutionary Party of Central American Workers (Partido Revolutionary de Trabajadores Centroamericanos); the Communist Party (Partido Comunista); and the National Resistance (Resistencia Nacional), which had split off from the ERP in the mid-1970s.

27. At a national level, in the early 1980s the FMLN established a formal alliance with a civilian opposition coalition, the Democratic Revolutionary Front (Frente Democrático Revolucionario, FDR), and the groups became known as the FMLN-FDR. As the revolutionary opposition's political wing, the FDR established offices throughout the United States, Western Europe, and Latin America and received formal recognition from the French and Mexican governments, demonstrating the Salvadoran left's desire and ability to build links with a wide range of governments and NGOs.

28. Leigh Binford, *The El Mozote Massacre: Anthropology and Human Rights* (Tucson: University of Arizona Press, 1996), 116.

29. An oral history of the FMLN's Radio Venceremos reports a telling encounter between a peasant and an army patrol in Torola, Morazán. The soldiers asked if guerrillas had passed. "Sure," the *campesino* replied, "they just went by. . . . Only a few. Actually," he continued, describing the members of a guerrilla special force, "they were wearing underwear and little caps and they were carrying funny bags . . . [and they were] all painted up." Hearing that, the soldiers ran in the opposite direction, even refusing the peasant's offer of a drink of water. José Ignacio López Vigil, *Rebel Radio: The Story of El Salvador's Radio Venceremos* (Willimantic, Conn.: Curbstone Press, 1994), 161.

30. Maxwell S. Peltz, *El Salvador 1990: An Issue Brief* (Washington, D.C.: Commission on U.S.-Latin American Relations, 1990), 36.

31. Pearce, *Promised Land*, 127.

32. Berkeley Sister City Project, "Life, Death, and Resurrection," 23.

33. Ibid., 13–15, 27.

34. See Renato Camarda, *Forced to Move: Salvadorean Refugees in Honduras* (San Francisco: Solidarity Publications, 1985), 19, for a heartbreaking photograph of a man staring at the infant son he had to asphyxiate. Many former refugees and residents of the war zones tell similar stories, which crystallize for them the cruelty of a war whose main target was civilians. For every story of tragic individual choice, there are tales (and documentation) of mass killings in which soldiers who found peasants' hiding places murdered every person they encountered, often impaling children on bayonets and slitting open the abdomens of pregnant women. On human rights violations, see Camarda, *Forced to Move*; Binford, *El Mozote*; Americas Watch, *El Salvador's Decade of Terror: Human Rights Since the Assassination of Archbishop Romero* (New Haven: Yale University Press, 1991); Amnesty International, *El Salvador: "Death Squads." A Government Strategy*, AI Index 29/21/88 (London: Amnesty International, 1988); and Philip Russell, *El Salvador in Crisis* (Austin, Tex.: Colorado River Press, 1984).

35. Berkeley Sister City Project, "Life, Death, and Resurrection," 22.

36. Nicolas Doljanin, *Chalatenango: La guerra descalza* (Mexico City: El Dia, 1982), 15. In northern Morazán, anthropologist Leigh Binford estimates that up to 70 percent of El Mozote's population had already left by the time of the November 1981 massacre (*El Mozote*, 108).

37. The first PPL began in the village of Sicahuite, near Las Vueltas, in November 1982, after guerrillas and local residents expelled the army company stationed in El Jícaro and the National Guard in Las Vueltas. Other PPLs were created as the FMLN and local militias expelled other army groups from their permanent bases in villages in northeastern Chalatenango. In mid-1983, residents established a "subregional junta" to coordinate the PPLs in what they termed "Sub-Zone One," which included most of the communities of northeastern Chalatenango: Arcatao, Nueva Trinidad, Las Flores, Los Ranchos, San Isidro, Las Vueltas, San Antonio la Cruz. The total territory of Sub-Zone One encompassed about one-third of the Chalatenango department, with about 7,000 people (Ascoli, *Tiempo de guerra*, 74).

38. Pearce, *Promised Land*, 252, 253.

39. Ascoli, *Tiempo de guerra*, 77.

40. Ibid., 78–80.

41. Pearce, *Promised Land*, 242.

42. Ibid., 243.

43. John L. Hammond, *Fighting to Learn: Popular Education and Guerrilla War in El Salvador* (New Brunswick, N.J.: Rutgers University Press, 1998), 56. It is worth noting here that the PPLs were unique to FPL-controlled territory. In the ERP stronghold in northern Morazán, there were no similar experiences of civilian self-governance. This was partly due to differences between the peasant populations in Morazán and Chalatenango. They were equally impoverished and discontented, but peasants in Chalatenango were less socially and economically marginalized than those in Morazán, because most Chalatenango residents worked several months a year as wage laborers outside the department, and many were tenant farmers for the rest of the year rather than smallholders, as in Morazán. An equally important difference lay in guerrilla strategies. The ERP in Morazán organized peasants more directly in support of military struggle aimed at resurrection rather than the prolonged struggle envisioned by the FPL leadership. This approach enabled the ERP to build an ef-

fective military force but did not allow time "for the politicization that transforms rebellion into revolution" (Pearce, *Promised Land*, 133).

44. Cagan and Cagan, *This Promised Land*, 50, 82.

45. Hammond, *Fighting to Learn*, 8. Hammond points out the irony of the fact that repressed communities in war zones, refugee camps, and political prisons found the time and space to create some of the most important popular education projects.

46. Mandy Macdonald and Mike Gatehouse, *In the Mountains of Morazán: Portrait of a Returned Refugee Community in El Salvador* (London: Latin American Bureau, 1995), 27.

47. Cagan and Cagan, *This Promised Land*, 96.

48. Macdonald and Gatehouse, *In the Mountains of Morazán*, 1.

49. Cagan and Cagan, *This Promised Land*, 1.

50. Beatrice Edwards and Gretta Tovar Siebentritt, *Places of Origin: The Repopulation of Rural El Salvador* (Boulder, Colo.: Lynne Rienner, 1991), 22.

51. Rutilio Sánchez, interview with author, Managua, Nicaragua, Nov. 12, 1988. Sánchez, a Salvadoran diocesan priest, began working with Christian communities in Chalatenango in December 1981. Mexican journalist Nicolás Doljanin also encountered "repobladores" as early as 1982; see Doljanin, *Chalatenango: La guerra descalza*, 15.

52. See Edwards and Siebentritt, *Places of Origin*, 29-46.

53. Although most refugees did return to their region of origin, many did not return to their particular home village, at least not initially. Because the repatriations took place in stages, people wishing to return to El Salvador at a given time could not choose their exact destination. Some villages, in fact, were never resettled, and some new ones were created. Further, many new family groups had formed in the refugee camps, uniting people from different villages and different departments.

54. Berkeley Sister City Project, "Life, Death, and Resurrection," 28-29.

55. The repopulation of Meanguera/Ciudad Segundo Montes in the department of Morazán is especially well-documented; see Cagan and Cagan, *This Promised Land*; Macdonald and Gatehouse, *In the Mountains of Morazán*.

56. In early 1989, FMLN leaders offered to participate in the upcoming March elections if they were postponed for six months. The guerrillas asserted that they would prefer a negotiated end to the war but were prepared to launch a major offensive if the offer was rejected, as indeed it was; the November offensive followed.

57. Elisabeth Wood, *Forging Democracy from Below* (Cambridge, England: Cambridge University Press, 2000), 85.

58. Stated at a meeting with the Junta Directiva, Guarjila, January 5, 2002.

59. Adam Flint, "The Reemergence of Social Movements in an Era of Neoliberal Democracy in El Salvador," paper presented at the annual meeting of the Latin American Studies Association, Miami, Mar. 16-18, 2000, 5.

60. Donna DeCesare, "The Children of War: Street Gangs in El Salvador," *NACLA Report on the Americas* 32, no. 1 (1998): 21-29. See also Ileana Gómez and Manuel Vásquez, "Youth Gangs and Religion among Salvadorans in Washington and El Salvador," in *Christianity, Social Change, and Globalization in the Americas*, ed. Anna Peterson, Manuel Vásquez, and Philip Williams (New Brunswick, N.J.: Rutgers University Press, 2001), 165-187; Joaquín M. Chávez, "An Anatomy of Violence in El Salvador," *NACLA Report on the Americas* 37, no. 6 (May/June 2004): 31-37.

61. Ricardo Navarro, "Presentación del Libro" [Preface], in Ricardo Navarro, Gabriel Pons, and German Amaya, *El pensamiento ecologista* (San Salvador: Centro Salvadoreño de Tecnología Apropiada, n.d. [1990?]), 8.

62. Carlos Quintanilla, president of Junta Directiva, interview by author, Guarjila, Chalatenango, El Salvador, Jan. 5, 2002.

63. Navarro, "Presentación," 7–8.

64. Berkeley Sister City Project, "Life, Death, and Resurrection," 29.

65. Before the war, the villages had elected mayors, usually local landowners. Virtually all these mayors left the villages by the early 1980s.

66. Peter O'Driscoll, "Peace, Thanks, and God's Blessing: Letters from San Antonio Los Ranchos," unpublished manuscript, Berkeley Sister City Project with El Salvador, 1990, letter of May 3, 1989, 2.

67. David E. Leaman, "Oppositional Outsiders and the Reach of Representation in Post-War El Salvador: A Small Rural Community in Changing Political Contexts," Illinois Political Science Review, http://www.apsanet.org/~illinois/ipsr/salvador.htm, 15.

68. Since the war's end, there have been some assassinations of opposition political leaders, particularly leading up to the 1994 elections, but these have been relatively isolated incidents.

69. Félix Orellana and Oscar Martínez, FMLN National Office, interview by author, San Salvador, June 29, 1994.

70. Eleven parties competed in the 2003 legislative elections, reflecting a wide range of political ideologies and constituencies. Although ARENA is no longer the largest party, its coalition with small conservative parties ensures a conservative majority in most votes.

71. Joe Rubin, "El Salvador: Payback," *Frontline*, PBS, http://www.pbs.org/frontlineworld/elections/elsalvador/.

72. Sarah Garland, "El Salvador: ARENA Wins Elections." *NACLA Report on the Americas* 37, no. 6 (May/June 2004): 1.

73. In addition to Brazil, progressive parties have won national elections recently in several other South American countries, including a November 2004 presidential victory in Uruguay hailed by Venezuela's President Hugo Chávez as "one more step on the road to building a new South America, a new Latin America, a new world that is being born" (http://news.bbc.co.uk/2/hi/americas/3968755.stm).

74. Jack Spence, "Left Gains and Competitive Balance Following El Salvador's March Elections," paper presented at the Latin American Studies Association International Congress, Sept. 2001, 1. The "orthodox" leftist wing has managed to set the party's agenda, although its policies remain influenced by the party's "renovating" faction, which seeks a more reformist or moderate stance on economic issues. See also Rubin, "El Salvador: Payback."

75. Garland, "El Salvador: ARENA Wins Elections," 1.

76. Félix Orellana, interview by author, June 29, 1994.

77. Flint, "The Reemergence of Social Movements," 10.

78. Soyapa, interview by author, Guarjila, Chalatenango, El Salvador, Jan. 5, 2002. Mauricio, interview by author, Guarjila, Jan. 5, 2002.

79. Interviews with author, Guarjila, Jan. 5, 2002.

80. Wood, *Forging Democracy*, 209.

81 And Kelly Rivera et al., *Valió la pena?* (San Salvador: Editorial Sombrero Azul, 1995), 39, quoted in Adam Flint, "Social Movements, NGOs and the State: Contesting Political Space in the Transition to Democracy in El Salvador," paper presented at the Latin American Studies Association meeting, Sept. 1998, Chicago, 12.

CHAPTER 3. NATURE

1. Sir Robert May, addressing a gathering of biodiversity experts in Washington, D.C. in Oct. 1997, http://www.zerowasteamerica.org/MSNBC.htm.

2. Gary Strieker, "Scientists Agree World Faces Mass Extinction." CNN, Aug. 23, 2002, http://www.cnn.com/2002/TECH/science/08/23/green.century.mass.extinction/index.html.

3. United Nations, World Atlas of Biodiversity, http://www.commondreams.org/headlines02/0802-06.htm.

4. Data from Redefining Progress, "Ecological Footprint of Nations," Nov. 2002, available at www.redefiningprogress.org/publications/ef1999.pdf.

5. James Sterngold, "California's New Problem: Sudden Surplus of Energy," *New York Times*, July 19, 2001, 1A.

6. According to 1997 data produced by the Earth Council (http://www.ecouncil .ac.cr/). The organization Redefining Progress reports that 73 percent of the world's people live with less than the world average of 2.3 hectares per person, and 80 percent of the world's footprint is produced by the 97.5 percent of the global population who use less than 12.7 hectares per person. The other 2.5 percent of the world population use 20 percent of the globe's resources; without them, capacity and consumption would roughly balance.

7. Ari Fleischer spoke of the "American way of life" at a White House Press Conference on May 7, 2001; see http://www.whitehouse.gov/news/briefings/20010507.html. Vice President Dick Cheney also described conservation as a "personal virtue" chosen by some, rather than anything that should be mandated by policy. See Joseph Kahn, "Cheney Promotes Increasing Supply as Energy Policy," *New York Times*, May 1, 2001, A1.

8. Thomas Princen, Michael Maniates, and Ken Conca, "Confronting Consumption," in *Confronting Consumption*, ed. T. Princen, M. Maniates, and K. Conca (Cambridge, Mass.: MIT Press, 2002), 5.

9. Of course, the choice need not be either/or; the most effective movement would argue for changes at all stages of production and consumption, rather than targeting one element in isolation. As Princen et al. write, we "need to see consumption not just as an individual's choice among goods but as a stream of choices and decisions winding its way through the various stages of extraction, manufacture, and final use, embedded at every step in social relations of power and authority" (ibid., 12).

10. Historian Lynn White Jr., proposed Francis as the "patron saint of ecology" in his influential article, "The Historical Roots of Our Ecologic Crisis," *Science* 155 (1967): 1203–1207. White's proposal was designed to provoke reflection on Christianity's mixed historical record regarding the environment and probably was not intended as a formal nomination. In November 1979, however, Pope John Paul II officially gave St. Francis the title of "patron saint of ecology" in his Bull *Inter Sanctos*, *AAS* 71[1979], 1509f.

11. See, for example, Francis of Assisi, *The Little Flowers of St. Francis of Assisi*, ed. Louise Bachelder, trans. Abby Langdon Alger (Mount Vernon, N.Y.: Peter Pauper Press, 1964); Roger Sorrell, *St. Francis of Assisi and Nature: Tradition and Innovation in Western Christian Attitudes toward the Environment* (New York: Oxford University Press, 1988).

12. National Conference of Catholic Bishops, *Economic Justice for All* (Washington, D.C.: U.S. Catholic Conference, 1986).

13. John Paul II, *Laborem Exercens* [1981], in *Proclaiming Justice and Peace: Papal Documents from* Rerum Novarum *through* Centesimus Annus, ed. Michael Walsh and Brian Davies (Mystic, Conn.: Twenty-Third Publications, 1991), nos. 6.5, 7.

14. National Conference of Catholic Bishops, *Renewing the Earth: An Invitation to Reflection and Action on Environment in Light of Catholic Social Teaching* (Washington, D.C.: U.S. Catholic Conference, 1991).

15. Vicariato Apostólico de Petén, *El Grito de la Selva en el Año Jubilar: Entre la Agonía y Esperanza* (Petén, Guatemala: Vicariato Apostólico de Petén, 2000), 9. Echoing this theme, Brazilian theologian Leonardo Boff argues, "The very same logic of the prevailing system of accumulation and social organization that leads to the exploitation of workers also leads to the pillaging of whole nations and ultimately the plundering of nature." *Cry of the Earth, Cry of the Poor* (Maryknoll, N.Y.: Orbis Books, 1997), 110–111.

16. John Paul II, *Redemptor Hominis*, in *Proclaiming Justice and Peace: Papal Documents from* Rerum Novarum *through* Centesimus Annus, ed. Michael Walsh and Brian Davies (Mystic, Conn.: Twenty-Third Publications, 1991), no. 15.2.

17. Oscar Romero, homily of Jan. 13, 1980, cited in James Brockman, *Romero: A Life* (Maryknoll, N.Y.: Orbis Books, 1989), 219.

18. For example, the massive (720-page) collection *Christianity and Ecology: Seeking the Well-Being of Earth and Humans*, ed. Dieter Hessel and Rosemary Radford Ruether (Cambridge, Mass.: Harvard University Press, 2000), includes in its index one mention of Mennonites ("environmental evangelicals and") and none under Anabaptists or Amish. Robert Booth Fowler's *The Greening of Protestant Thought* (Chapel Hill: University of North Carolina Press, 1995) includes no mentions under any of these topics, nor does Paul Santmire's influential *The Travail of Nature: The Ambiguous Ecological Promise of Christian Theology* (Minneapolis: Fortress Press, 1985). The same holds for most other works on Christian and Protestant environmental thinking and activism: even liberal Mennonites, much less Old Order groups, are not acknowledged as an important segment of Protestantism. There is one book devoted to Anabaptist and Mennonite thinking about the environment, Calvin Redekop's 2000 edited volume *Creation and the Environment: An Anabaptist Perspective on a Sustainable World* (Baltimore: Johns Hopkins University Press, 2000).

19. David Kline, "God's Spirit and a Theology for Living," in *Creation and the Environment: An Anabaptist Perspective on a Sustainable World*, ed. Calvin Redekop (Baltimore: Johns Hopkins University Press, 2000), 63.

20. Ibid., 61–62.

21. Kline, *Great Possessions*, 219.

22. John Frechione, introduction to *Traditional and Modern Natural Resource Management in Latin America*, ed. Francisco Pichón, Jorge E. Uquillas, and John Frechione (Pittsburgh: University of Pittsburgh Press, 1999), 3.

23. Frank Fischer and Maarten A. Hajer, "Introduction: Beyond Global Discourse: The Rediscovery of Culture in Environmental Politics," in *Living with Nature: Environmental Politics as Cultural Discourse*, ed. Frank Fischer and Maarten A. Hajer (Oxford: Oxford University Press, 1999), 2.

24. Paul Shepard, *Coming Home to the Pleistocene* (San Francisco: Island Press, 1998), 103.

25. Brian Donahue, "The Resettling of America," in *The Essential Agrarian Reader: The Future of Culture, Community, and the Land*, ed. Norman Wirzba (Lexington, Ky.: Shoemaker and Hoard, 2004), 38, 39.

26. Wendell Berry, *The Gift of Good Land: Further Essays Cultural and Agricultural* (San Francisco: North Point Press, 1981), xi. Wes Jackson advocates shrinking the scale of both production and distribution, while at the same time he seeks to address scientifically and pragmatically the destructive consequences of large-scale, fossil fuel–dependent monocrop agriculture.

27. Jack Manno, "Commoditization: Consumption Efficiency and an Economy of Care and Connection," in *Confronting Consumption*, ed. Thomas Princen, Michael Maniates, and Ken Conca (Cambridge, Mass.: MIT Press, 2002), 84–85.

28. Wes Jackson, *New Roots for Agriculture* (Lincoln: University of Nebraska Press, 1980), 96, 93.

29. David Kline, "An Amish Perspective," in *Rooted in the Land: Essays on Community and Place*, ed. William Vitek and Wes Jackson (New Haven: Yale University Press, 1996), 39.

30. Kline notes that not all Amish farmers observe these practices, especially in communities with high land prices, where the temptation is to "farm to the road" to maximize tillable acreage (*Great Possessions*, xx).

31. These goals drive Via Campesina, an international alliance of farmers' groups seeking "food sovereignty" as the cornerstone of an alternative development vision.

32. Benjamin E. Northrup and Benjamin Lipscomb, "Country and City: The Common Vision of Agrarians and New Urbanists," in *The Essential Agrarian Reader: The Future of Culture, Community, and the Land*, ed. Norman Wirzba (Lexington, Ky.: Shoemaker and Hoard, 2004), 192.

33. Wendell Berry, "Out of Your Car, Off Your Horse," in *Sex, Economy, Freedom and Community* (New York: Pantheon, 1993), 25.

34. Northrup and Lipscomb, "Country and City," 201.

35. Lourdes, CORDES (Fundación para la Cooperación y el Desarrollo Comunal de El Salvador), interview by author, San Salvador, Jan. 4, 2002.

36. Timothy Egan, "Growers and Shoppers Crowd Farmers' Markets," *New York Times*, Sept. 29, 2002, 18.

37. See Joan Thirsk, *Alternative Agriculture: A History* (Oxford: Oxford University Press, 1997).

38. Robyn Van En, "Community Supported Agriculture (CSA) in Perspective," in *For All Generations: Making World Agriculture More Sustainable*, ed. J. Patrick Madden and Scott G. Chaplowe (Glendale, Calif.: World Sustainable Agriculture Association, 1997), 115.

39. Ibid., 116, 119.

40. Russell Janzen, interview by author, Elbing, Kansas, July 6, 2000.

41. Russell Janzen, interview by author, Elbing, Kansas, July 5, 2000. Other Mennonites believe that in recent years mutual aid has declined and competitiveness has increased, including competition to purchase available farmland, even from neighbors and church members. When a friend went bankrupt, one farmer recalls, some neighbors seemed more interested in buying his land than in helping him (Darrell Regier, interview by author, Elbing, Kansas, July 8, 2000).

42. Kline, *Great Possessions*, xxiii, xxi.

43. Ariane de Bremond, "Post-War Reconstruction Using Sustainable Agriculture in Chalatenango, El Salvador," http://www.agroecology.org/cases/montaona.htm.

44. Carlos Quintanilla, interview by author, Guarjila, Jan. 5, 2002.

CHAPTER 4. COMMUNITY

1. David L. Kirp, *Almost Home: America's Love-Hate Relationship with Community* (Princeton, N.J.: Princeton University Press, 2000), 6.

2. Mitchell Thomashow, *Bringing the Biosphere Home: Learning to Perceive Global Environmental Change* (Cambridge, Mass.: MIT Press, 2002), 171. Thomashow points out that these debates over the meaning of community occur not only in social sciences and humanities but also among ecologists.

3. Anthony Cohen, *The Symbolic Construction of Community* (New York: Routledge, 1995), 16.

4. Richard Huggett, *Environmental Change: The Evolving Ecosphere* (New York: Routledge, 1997), 269. Huggett is defining community for ecological science, and finishes the term with "belonging to different species."

5. Marc Olshan, "Modernity, the Folk Society, and the Old Order Amish: An Alternative Interpretation," *Rural Sociology* 46 (1981): 297, 300.

6. *Confession of Faith in a Mennonite Perspective*, 28.

7. Second Vatican Council, *Gaudium et spes*, no. 32, in *Documents of Vatican II*, ed. Walter Abbott (New York: American Press, 1966).

8. David Kline, interview by author, May 30, 2001.

9. Robert Bellah, R. Madsen, W. Sullivan, A. Swidler, and S. Tipton, *Habits of the Heart: Individualism and Commitment in American Life* (Berkeley: University of California Press, 1985), 153.

10. Arlyn Entz, interview by author, Elbing, Kansas, July 9, 2000.

11. *Confession of Faith in a Mennonite Perspective*, 65.

12. "Elizabeth, A Dutch Anabaptist martyr: A letter (1573)," in Hillerbrand, *The Protestant Reformation*, 150.

13. Anna Peterson, *Martyrdom and the Politics of Religion: Progressive Catholicism in El Salvador's Civil War* (Albany: State University of New York Press, 1997).

14. Wendell Berry, "The Agrarian Standard," in *The Essential Agrarian Reader: The Future of Culture, Community, and the Land*, ed. Norman Wirzba (Lexington, Ky.: Shoemaker and Hoard, 2004), 28–29.

15. Holmes Rolston III, *Environmental Ethics: Duties to and Values in the Natural World* (Philadelphia: Temple University Press, 1988), 39.

16. Bellah et al., *Habits of the Heart*, 153.

17. Tomás, a peasant in Chalatenango, interviewed in the early 1980s by Pearce, *Promised Land*, 305.

18. John Howard Yoder, *The Politics of Jesus*, 2nd ed. (Grand Rapids, Mich.: William B. Eerdmans, 1994), 150–151.

19. Hostetler, *Amish Society*, 74.

20. Fene Rivera, FUNDE (Fundacion Nacional para el Desarrollo; National Foundation for Development), interview by author, San Salvador, January 8, 2002.

21. José Inocencio Alas, interview by author, San Salvador, July 4, 1994.

22. Some scholars cite the relatively lower requirements for ministry in Protestant Pentecostal churches as a major reason for their recent growth, especially in Latin America.

23. Raymond Williams, *The Country and the City* (New York: Oxford University Press, 1973), 84.

24. David Kline, presentation at "The Good in Nature and Humanity" conference, Yale University, May 2000.

25. Williams, *The Country and the City*, 84, 85.

26. Quoted in Van Andruss, C. Plant, J. Plant, and E. Wright, eds., *Home! A Bioregional Reader* (Philadelphia: New Society Publishers, 1990), 24.

27. Mitchell Thomashow, "Toward a Cosmopolitan Bioregionalism," in *Bioregionalism*, ed. Michael Vincent McGinnis (London: Routledge, 1999), 121–122. In this regard, it is worth noting that some prominent bioregionalists, notably Wendell Berry of Kentucky and Wes Jackson of Kansas, have returned to their place of origin after traveling and living elsewhere. Even David Kline spent two years working in a hospital in Cleveland as his alternative service during the Vietnam War.

28. John Foran, "How Might the Revolutions of the Future Have Better End(ing)s? Lessons from Latin America's Past and Present," paper presented at the Latin American Studies Association annual meeting, Washington, D.C., Sept. 6–8, 2001, 12; Alberto Melucci, *Nomads of the Present: Social Movements and Individual Needs in Contemporary Society*, ed. John Keane and Paul Mier (Philadelphia: Temple University Press, 1989), 227–228; Daniel Levine and Scott Mainwaring, "Religion and Popular Protest in Latin America: Contrasting Experiences," in *Power and Popular Protest in Latin America*, ed. Susan Eckstein (Berkeley: University of California Press, 1989), 341.

29. Daniel Levine, *Popular Voices in Latin American Catholicism* (Princeton, N.J.: Princeton University Press, 1992), 12; Robert Bellah, Richard Madsen, William Sullivan, Ann Swidler, and Steven Tipton, *The Good Society* (New York: Vintage Books, 1991), 14.

30. Raymond Williams, *Resources of Hope: Culture, Democracy, Socialism*, ed. Robin Gable, with an introduction by Robin Blackburn (London: Verso: 1989), 242, 249. David Harvey discusses Williams's notion of "militant particularism" at length in *Spaces of Hope* (Berkeley: University of California Press, 2000).

31. David A. Matthew, personal communication, Aug. 19, 2003. Matthew is commenting on Ursula LeGuin's novel *The Dispossessed: An Ambivalent Utopia* (New York: HarperCollins, 1974) and its failure to "problematize the matter of localization enough. Mobility is taken for granted, and seen as good. The idealists never wonder if they have bodies that evolved for life on Urras, rather than for Anarres."

32. Robert Bellah and coauthors write, "To imagine [large-scale institutions] as autonomous systems operating according to their own mysterious internal logic, to be fine-tuned only by experts, is to opt for some kind of modern gnosticism that sees the

world as controlled by the powers of darkness and encourages us to look only to our private survival. We believe that the modern ideal of a democracy governed by intelligent public opinion not only is worth redeeming in our own society but requires, as far as possible, extension to the human community as a whole" (*The Good Society*, 15).

CHAPTER 5. UTOPIA

1. Anna Peterson, Manuel Vásquez, and Philip Williams, preface to *Christianity, Social Change, and Globalization in the Americas* (New Brunswick, N.J.: Rutgers University Press, 2001), viii–ix.

2. Carlos Zarcos Mera, Leonor Tellería, and Carlos Manuel Sánchez, "The Ministry of Coordinators in the Popular Christian Community," in *La Iglesia Popular: Between Fear and Hope*, ed. L. Boff and V. Elizondo, special issue of *Concilium* 176 (1984): 70.

3. Pablo Neruda, *Toward the Splendid City/Hacia la ciudad esplendida* (New York: Farrar, Strauss, and Giroux, 1973). Neruda takes the phrase "the splendid city" from Rimbaud.

4. Marcha de la Unidad, words and letters by Sergio Ortega; available on "Quilapayún: El Pueblo Unido Jamás Sera Vencido" [recording] (1974).

5. Woody Guthrie, "Better World A'Comin'." Guthrie wrote this song during World War II, and the lyrics express the connection that he, like many other radicals of his time, made between the fight against fascism and working-class movements. The song continues: "I'm a union man in a union war; it's a union world I'm fighting for." Available on *Woody Guthrie: The Asch Recordings*, vol. 3, Smithsonian Folkways 40112, compiled by Jeff Place and Guy Logsdon.

6. Karl Marx, *Critique of the Gotha Program*, in *The Marx/Engels Reader*, ed. Robert Tucker (New York: Norton, 1978), 531.

7. Karl Marx and Friedrich Engels, *The Manifesto of the Communist Party*, in *The Marx/Engels Reader*, ed. Robert Tucker (New York: Norton, 1978), 491.

8. Reinhold Niebuhr, *Moral Man and Immoral Society: A Study in Ethics and Politics* (New York: Charles Scribner's Sons, 1932), 277.

9. Jean Bethke Elshtain, "Thinking about War and Justice," Religion and Culture Web forum, Martin Marty Center, University of Chicago Divinity School, May 2003, p. 1, http:/http://marty-center.uchicago.edu/webforum/052003/index.shtml.

10. Ibid.

11. Jean-François Lyotard, *The Postmodern Condition* (Minneapolis: University of Minnesota Press, 1984), xxiv.

12. Jorge G. Castañeda, *Utopia Unarmed: The Latin American Left after the Cold War* (New York: Vintage, 1993), 240–241. Castañeda has in mind, among other events, the defeat of the Sandinista Front for National Liberation (FSLN) in Nicaragua's 1990 elections. Roger Lancaster's reflections on the Sandinistas' electoral loss (and the trials and tribulations that preceded it) are helpful. Nicaragua, he argues, should not be lumped together with Eastern Europe. Nor should the end of FSLN rule be seen as a refutation of Marxism, revolution, or radical politics in general. Instead, "what events really demonstrate is that even the class consciousness, political commitment, and national will of a revolution can be undercut by a long enough cri-

sis." Roger Lancaster, *Life Is Hard: Machismo, Danger, and the Intimacy of Power in Nicaragua* (Berkeley: University of California Press, 1992), 287.

13. Daniel Singer, *Whose Millennium? Theirs or Ours?* (New York: Monthly Review Press, 1999), 1.

14. Francis Fukuyama, *The End of History and the Last Man* (New York: Avon, 1993), 46, quoted in Russell Jacoby, *The End of Utopia: Politics and Culture in an Age of Apathy* (New York: Basic Books, 1999), 10.

15. Of course, many postmodernists do not embrace capitalism. However, critics from the left, including David Harvey and Nancy Fraser, contend that some versions of postmodernism provide no resources, and perhaps even close off possibilities, for critiquing global processes such as the spread of neoliberal capitalism. See, for example, Harvey, *The Condition of Postmodernity: An Enquiry into the Origins of Cultural Change* (Oxford: Basil Blackwell, 1990).

16. Along similar lines, John Howard Yoder has pointed out that just war theories are often less realistic than pacifist approaches to war and violence. Even apparently utopian forms of pacifism, Yoder argues, trust less to irrational leaps of faith than to militarism—and boast a much less damaging historical record. Yoder, *Nevertheless: The Varieties and Shortcomings of Religious Pacifism* (Scottdale, Pa.: Herald Press, 1992), 76.

17. *Confession of Faith in Mennonite Perspective*, 89.

18. J. Yoder, *The Priestly Kingdom*; chapter 4 is titled "The Kingdom as Social Ethic."

19. Many Protestants from both "historic" and evangelical denominations are committed to social justice and peacemaking and work hard, often at significant risk, for these goals. My point is not to exclude or stereotype any denomination but rather to highlight long-standing and clear-cut differences in theological ethics, which influence individual and institutional practice, although hardly in uniform ways.

20. Hostetler, *Amish Society*, 76.

21. See Donald B. Kraybill, ed., *The Amish and the State* (Baltimore: Johns Hopkins University Press, 1993), especially chapter 5, "Education and Schooling," by Thomas J. Meyers, pp. 87–108.

22. Igou, *The Amish in Their Own Words*, 64.

23. J. Yoder, *The Politics of Jesus*, 39, 43. Yoder's phrase echoes the title of an essay by feminist poet Audre Lorde: "The master's tools will never dismantle the master's house."

24. J. Yoder, *The Priestly Kingdom*, 94.

25. Melucci, *Nomads of the Present*, 2.

26. Aquinas, *Introduction to St. Thomas Aquinas: The Summa Theologica, The Summa Contra Gentiles*, ed. Anton C. Pegis (New York: Modern Library, 1948), 616, 234, 618, 263.

27. Oscar Romero, *The Voice of the Voiceless: Four Pastoral Letters and Other Statements* (Maryknoll, N.Y.: Orbis Books, 1985), 152.

28. Interview with Junta Directiva, Guarjila, Jan. 5, 2002.

29. Sharon Welch, *A Feminist Ethic of Risk* (Fortress Press, 1990), 1.

30. Sharon Welch, *Sweet Dreams in America: Making Ethics and Spirituality Work* (New York: Routledge, 1999), xix, 61, xvii–xviii.

31. Reynaldo Clemeña Ileto, *Pasyon and Revolution: Popular Movements in the Philippines, 1840–1910* (Manila: Ateneo de Manila University Press, 1979), 256.

32. Paul Tillich, "The Political Meaning of Utopia," in *Political Expectation*, ed. James Luther Adams (New York: Harper and Row, 1971), 169; Ileto, *Pasyon and Revolution*, 256.

33. See Ursula LeGuin, *The Dispossessed: An Ambivalent Utopia* (New York: HarperCollins, 1974); Ernest Callenbach, *Ecotopia* (New York: Bantam, 1990).

34. Bellah et al., *Habits of the Heart*, 247.

35. Norman Geras, "Minimum Utopia: Ten Theses," in *Necessary and Unnecessary Utopias: Socialist Register 2000*, ed. Leo Panitch and Colin Leys (Rendlesham, England: Merlin Press, 1999), 50.

36. For an interesting challenge to the role of private property in ensuring sustainable land use, and even democracy, in the United States, see Donahue, "The Resettling of America," especially 37–38 and 43.

37. Terry Eagleton, "Utopia and Its Opposites," in *Necessary and Unnecessary Utopias: Socialist Register 2000*, ed. Leo Panitch and Colin Leys (Rendlesham, England: Merlin Press, 1999), 34.

38. E. P. Thompson, *William Morris: Romantic to Revolutionary* (New York: Pantheon Books, 1977), quoted in Phillip E. Wegner, *Imaginary Communities: Utopia, the Nation, and the Spatial Histories of Modernity* (Berkeley: University of California Press, 2002), 180.

39. On the rationality of alternatives, see Immanuel Wallerstein, *Utopistics; Or, Historical Choices of the Twenty-first Century* (New York: New Press, 1998), 1. On "realistic utopia," see Singer, *Whose Millennium?*, 6–7.

40. With regard to the continuing relevance of utopianism for the Latin American left, it is interesting to note how often the notion of utopia is used in relation to the Zapatista movement in the southern Mexican state of Chiapas. This association echoes the notion of a promised land in connection with El Salvador's peasant movement. See Antonio García de Leon, *Resistencia y utopía: Memoria de agravios y crónica de revueltas y profecías en la provincia de Chiapas durante los últimos quinientos años de su historia*, 2 vols. (Mexico City: Ediciones Era, 1985); Marcelo Quezada G. and Maya Lorena Pérez Ruiz, eds., *EZLN: La utopía armada. Una visión plural del movimiento zapatista* (La Paz, Bolivia: Plural Editores, 1998).

41. Tillich, *Systematic Theology*, 358.

42. Tillich, "The Political Meaning of Utopia," 180.

43. Cardenal, *The Gospel in Solentiname*, 2: 54.

44. Gustafson elaborates his approach in two systematic works: *Ethics from a Theocentric Perspective*, vol. 1: *Theology and Ethics* (Chicago: University of Chicago Press, 1981) and vol. 2: *Ethics and Theology* (Chicago: University of Chicago Press, 1984).

45. J. Yoder, *The Priestly Kingdom*, 94.

46. Amelia [pseud.], interview by author, San Salvador, Apr. 9, 1990.

47. J. Yoder, *The Priestly Kingdom*, 97.

48. Eagleton, "Utopia and Its Opposites," 40.

49. Ileto, *Pasyon and Revolution*, 5.

50. J. Yoder, *The Priestly Kingdom*, 91–92.

51. Martin Luther King Jr., speech in Memphis, Apr. 3, 1968 (one day before his assassination). Full text of the speech available at http://www.afscme.org/about/kings pch.htm.

52. Barbara Ehrenreich, "The Faith Factor," *The Nation* (Nov. 29, 2004), 7. Following the elections, progressives also found consolation in another faith-based narrative, Martin Luther King's conviction that "The arc of history is long, but it bends toward justice." Among numerous mentions of the quote in November 2004, see the message from MoveOn.org at http://www.moveon.org/pac/news/hope.html.

53. Michael Hardt and Antonio Negri, *Empire* (Cambridge, Mass.: Harvard University Press, 2000). They also compare their utopian vision to that of Augustine: "The divine city is a universal city of aliens, coming together, cooperating, communicating. Our pilgrimage on earth, however, in contrast to Augustine's, has no transcendent telos beyond; it is and remains absolutely immanent" (206–207).

54. John Beverley, *Testimonio: On the Politics of Truth* (Minneapolis: University of Minnesota Press, 2004), 4.

55. Arran Garé, *Postmodernism and the Environmental Crisis* (London: Routledge, 1995), 144.

Bibliography

Agrawal, Arun, and Clark C. Gibson. "The Role of Community in Natural Resource Conservation." In *Communities and the Environment: Ethnicity, Gender, and the State in Community-Based Conservation,* ed. Arun Agrawal and Clark C. Gibson. New Brunswick, N.J.: Rutgers University Press, 2001.

Americas Watch. *El Salvador's Decade of Terror: Human Rights Since the Assassination of Archbishop Romero.* New Haven: Yale University Press, 1991.

Amnesty International. *El Salvador: "Death Squads." A Government Strategy.* AI Index 29/21/88. London: Amnesty International, 1988.

Andruss, Van, C. Plant, J. Plant, and E. Wright, eds. *Home! A Bioregional Reader.* Philadelphia: New Society Publishers, 1990.

Aquinas. *Introduction to St. Thomas Aquinas: The Summa Theologica, The Summa Contra Gentiles.* Ed. Anton C. Pegis. New York: Modern Library, 1948.

Archdiocese of San Salvador. *Plan Pastoral Arquidiocesano 1998–2003.* San Salvador: Archdiocese of San Salvador, 1998.

———. *Primera semana de pastoral arquidiocesana, 5–10 enero 1976.* San Salvador: Archdiocese of San Salvador, 1976.

Ardón, Patricia. *Post-war Reconstruction in Central America: Lessons from El Salvador, Guatemala, and Nicaragua.* Trans. Deborah Eade. Oxford: Oxfam, 1999.

Ascoli, Juan Fernando. *Tiempo de guerra y tiempo de paz: Organización y lucha de las comunidades del nor-oriente de Chalatenango (1974–1994).* Adapted by Miguel Cavada Diez. San Salvador: Equipo Maíz, n.d.

Bean, Heather Ann Ackley. "Toward an Anabaptist/Mennonite Environmental Ethic." In *Creation and the Environment: An Anabaptist Perspective on a Sustainable World,* ed. Calvin Redekop. Baltimore: Johns Hopkins University Press, 2000.

Bellah, Robert, Richard Madsen, William Sullivan, Ann Swidler, and Steven Tipton. *The Good Society.* New York: Vintage Books, 1991.

———. *Habits of the Heart: Individualism and Commitment in American Life.* Berkeley: University of California Press, 1985.

———. *Habits of the Heart: Individualism and Commitment in American Life.* 2nd ed., with a new introduction. Berkeley: University of California Press, 1996.

Berkeley Sister City Project. "Diary of a Lay Missionary Who Traveled in Chalatenango, June–July 1983." Unpublished manuscript, n.d.

———. "Life, Death, and Resurrection of a Salvadoran Village: An Oral History of San Antonio Los Ranchos, Chalatenango, El Salvador: 1970–1989." Unpublished manuscript, 1989.

Bernard, Ted, and Jora Young. *The Ecology of Hope: Communities Collaborate for Sustainability.* Gabriola Island, Canada: New Society Publishers, 1997.

Berry, Wendell. "The Agrarian Standard." In *The Essential Agrarian Reader: The Future of Culture, Community, and the Land,* ed. Norman Wirzba. Lexington, Ky.: Shoemaker and Hoard, 2004.

———. *The Gift of Good Land: Further Essays Cultural and Agricultural.* San Francisco: North Point Press, 1981.

———. *Sex, Economy, Freedom and Community.* New York: Pantheon, 1993.

———. *The Unsettling of America: Culture and Agriculture.* San Francisco: Sierra Club Books, 1977.

Beverley, John. *Testimonio: On the Politics of Truth.* Minneapolis: University of Minnesota Press, 2004.

Binford, Leigh. *The El Mozote Massacre: Anthropology and Human Rights.* Tucson: University of Arizona Press, 1996.

Blake, Katharine V., Enrico A. Cardamone, Steven D. Hall, Glenn R. Harris, and Susan M. Moore. "Modern Amish Farming as Ecological Agriculture." *Society & Natural Resources* 10, no. 2 (March–April 1997): 143–159.

Boff, Leonardo. *Cry of the Earth, Cry of the Poor.* Maryknoll, N.Y.: Orbis Books, 1997.

Brockman, James. *Romero: A Life.* Maryknoll, N.Y.: Orbis Books, 1989.

Browning, David. *El Salvador: La tierra y el hombre.* San Salvador: UCA Editores, 1973. (Orig. *El Salvador: Landscape and Society.* Oxford: Oxford University Press, 1971.)

Cagan, Beth, and Steve Cagan. *This Promised Land, El Salvador: The Refugee Community of Colomoncagua and Their Return to Morazán.* New Brunswick, N.J.: Rutgers University Press, 1991.

Callenbach, Ernest *Ecotopia.* New York: Bantam, 1990.

Callicott, J. Baird. *Earth's Insights: A Multicultural Survey of Environmental Ethics from the Mediterranean Basin to the Australian Outback.* Berkeley: University of California Press, 1994.

Camarda, Renato. *Forced to Move: Salvadorean Refugees in Honduras.* San Francisco: Solidarity Publications, 1985.

Cardenal, Ernesto. *The Gospel in Solentiname.* Vol. 2. Maryknoll, N.Y.: Orbis Books, 1976.

Castañeda, Jorge G. *Utopia Unarmed: The Latin American Left after the Cold War.* New York: Vintage, 1993.

CEDES (Episcopal Conference of El Salvador). *Actas de CEDES*, no. 100 (January 20–24, 1975).

———. *Actas de CEDES*, no. 101 (July 7–11, 1975).

CELAM (Conference of Latin American Bishops). *The Church in the Present-Day Transformation of Latin America in the Light of the Council: Medellín Conclusions.* Washington, D.C.: National Conference of Catholic Bishops, 1979.

———. "Puebla Final Document." In *Puebla and Beyond*, ed. John Eagleson and Philip Scharper. Trans. John Drury. Maryknoll, N.Y.: Orbis Books, 1979.

Chávez, Joaquín M. "An Anatomy of Violence in El Salvador." *NACLA Report on the Americas* 37, no. 6 (May/June 2004): 31–37.

Cohen, Anthony. *The Symbolic Construction of Community.* New York: Routledge, 1995.

Coleman, John, ed. *100 Years of Catholic Social Thought.* Maryknoll, N.Y.: Orbis Books, 1991.

Compher, Vic, and Betsy Morgan. *Going Home: Building Peace in El Salvador. The Story of Repatriation.* New York: Apex Press, 1991.

Confession of Faith in a Mennonite Perspective. Scottdale, Pa.: Herald Press, 1995.

Craumer, Peter. "Farm Productivity and Energy Efficiency in Amish and Modern Dairy Farming." *Agriculture and Environment* 4 (1979): 281–289.

Cronk, Sandra. "*Gelassenheit*: The Rites of the Redemptive Process in Old Order Amish and Old Order Mennonite Communities." *Mennonite Quarterly Review* 55 (January 1981): 5–44.

de Bremond, Ariane. "Post-War Reconstruction Using Sustainable Agriculture in Chalatenango, El Salvador." http://www.agroecology.org/cases/montanona.htm.

DeCesare, Donna. "The Children of War: Street Gangs in El Salvador," *NACLA Report on the Americas* 32, no. 1 (1998): 21–29.

Doljanin, Nicolás. *Chalatenango: La guerra descalza.* Mexico City: El Dia, 1982.

Donahue, Brian. "The Resettling of America." In *The Essential Agrarian Reader: The Future of Culture, Community, and the Land,* ed. Norman Wirzba. Lexington, Ky.: Shoemaker and Hoard, 2004.

Donnermeyer, Joseph, George Kreps, and Marty Kreps. *Lessons for Living: A Practical Approach to Daily Life from the Amish Community.* Sugarcreek, Ohio: Carlisle Press, 1999.

Duncan, Colin. "The Centrality of Agriculture: History, Ecology, and Feasible Socialism." In *Necessary and Unnecessary Utopias: Socialist Register 2000,* ed. Leo Panitch and Colin Leys. Rendlesham, England: Merlin Press, 1999.

Eagleton, Terry. "Defending Utopia." Review of Russell Jacoby, *The End of Utopia. New Left Review,* 2nd ser., 4 (July–August 2000): 173–176.

———. "Utopia and Its Opposites." In *Necessary and Unnecessary Utopias: Socialist Register 2000,* ed. Leo Panitch and Colin Leys. Rendlesham, England: Merlin Press, 1999.

Edwards, Beatrice, and Gretta Tovar Siebentritt. *Places of Origin: The Repopulation of Rural El Salvador.* Boulder, Colo.: Lynne Rienner, 1991.

Ehrenreich, Barbara. "The Faith Factor." *The Nation* (Nov. 29, 2004): 6–7.

El Salvador: Rural Development Study. A World Bank Country Study. Washington, D.C.: World Bank, 1998.

Elshtain, Jean Bethke. *Just War against Terror: The Burden of American Power in a Violent World.* New York: Basic Books, 2003.

———. "Thinking about War and Justice." Religion and Culture Web forum, Martin Marty Center, University of Chicago Divinity School, May 2003. http://marty -center.uchicago.edu/webforum/052003/index.shtml.

Erdozaín, Plácido. *Archbishop Romero.* Maryknoll, N.Y.: Orbis, 1981.

Ericksen, Eugene, Julia Ericksen, and John Hostetler. "The Cultivation of the Soil as a Moral Directive: Population Growth, Family Ties, and the Maintenance of Community among the Old Order Amish." *Rural Sociology* 45, no. 1 (spring 1980): 49–68.

Finger, Thomas. "An Anabaptist/Mennonite Theology of Creation." In *Creation and the Environment: An Anabaptist Perspective on a Sustainable World,* ed. Calvin Redekop. Baltimore: Johns Hopkins University Press, 2000.

Fischer, Frank, and Maarten A. Hajer. "Introduction: Beyond Global Discourse: The Rediscovery of Culture in Environmental Politics." In *Living with Nature: Environmental Politics as Cultural Discourse,* ed. Frank Fischer and Maarten A. Hajer. Oxford: Oxford University Press, 1999.

———, eds. *Living with Nature: Environmental Politics as Cultural Discourse.* Oxford: Oxford University Press, 1999.

Flint, Adam. "The Reemergence of Social Movements in an Era of Neo-liberal Democracy in El Salvador." Paper presented at the Latin American Studies Association meeting. Miami, Mar. 16–18, 2000.

———. "Social Movements, NGOs and the State: Contesting Political Space in the Transition to Democracy in El Salvador." Paper presented at the Latin American Studies Association meeting. Chicago, Sept. 1998.

Flores Cruz, Selmira. "La perspectiva de la autogestión comunitaria para un desarrollo rural alternativo." In *Desarrollo rural alternativo: Compartiendo experiencias,* ed. Lina Pohl. Mexico City: Ediciones Heinrich Böll, 2000.

Foley, Michael W. "Laying the Groundwork: The Struggle for Civil Society in El Salvador." *Journal of Interamerican Studies and World Affairs* 38, no. 1 (spring 1996): 67–105.

Foran, John. "How Might the Revolutions of the Future Have Better End(ing)s? Lessons from Latin America's Past and Present." Paper presented at the Latin American Studies Association annual meeting. Washington, D.C., Sept. 6–8, 2001.

Fowler, Robert Booth. *The Greening of Protestant Thought.* Chapel Hill: University of North Carolina Press, 1995.

Francis of Assisi. *The Little Flowers of St. Francis of Assisi.* Ed. Louise Bachelder. Trans. Abby Langdon Alger. Mount Vernon, N.Y.: Peter Pauper Press, 1964.

Frechione, John. Introduction to *Traditional and Modern Natural Resource Management in Latin America,* ed. Francisco Pichón, Jorge E. Uquillas, and John Frechione. Pittsburgh: University of Pittsburgh Press, 1999.

Friesen, Abraham. "Wilhelm Zimmerman and Friedrich Engels: Two Sources of the Marxist Interpretation of Anabaptism." *Mennonite Quarterly Review* 53 (July 1979): 240–270.

Fukuyama, Francis. *The End of History and the Last Man.* New York: Avon, 1993.

Fundación Cordes. "Memoria de Labores: Enero–Diciembre 2000: Luchas solidarias, sueños comunitarios y opciones de una vida digna para todos." San Salvador: CORDES, March 2001.

García de Leon, Antonio. *Resistencia y utopía: Memoria de agravios y crónica de revueltas y profecías en la provincia de Chiapas durante los últimos quinientos años de su historia.* 2 vols. Mexico City: Ediciones Era, 1985.

Garé, Arran. *Postmodernism and the Environmental Crisis.* London: Routledge, 1995.

Garland, Sarah. "El Salvador: ARENA Wins Elections." *NACLA Report on the Americas* 37, no. 6 (May/June 2004): 1.

Geras, Norman. "Minimum Utopia: Ten Theses." In *Necessary and Unnecessary Utopias: Socialist Register 2000,* ed. Leo Panitch and Colin Leys. Rendlesham, England: Merlin Press, 1999.

Goldman, Michael. "Introduction: The Political Resurgence of the Commons." In *Privatizing Nature: Political Struggles for the Global Commons,* ed. Michael Goldman. New Brunswick, N.J.: Rutgers University Press, 1998.

Gómez, Ileana, and Manuel Vásquez. "Youth Gangs and Religion among Salvadorans in Washington and El Salvador." In *Christianity, Social Change, and Globalization in the Americas,* ed. Anna Peterson, Manuel Vásquez, and Philip Williams. New Brunswick, N.J.: Rutgers University Press, 2001.

Gustafson, James. *Ethics from a Theocentric Perspective.* Vol. 1: *Theology and Ethics.* Chicago: University of Chicago Press, 1981.

———. *Ethics from a Theocentric Perspective.* Vol. 2: *Ethics and Theology.* Chicago: University of Chicago Press, 1984.

Gutiérrez, Gustavo. "Notes for a Theology of Liberation." *Theological Studies* 31, no. 2 (1970): 243–261.

———. *A Theology of Liberation.* Maryknoll, N.Y.: Orbis Books, 1973.

Guzman, José Luis, et al. *Las escuelas populares de Chalatenango: Un aporte para el desarrollo de la educación en las zonas rurales de El Salvador.* San Salvador/Chalatenango: ED-UCA, CCR, and Prodere ELS, 1994.

Hammond, John L. *Fighting to Learn: Popular Education and Guerrilla War in El Salvador.* New Brunswick, N.J.: Rutgers University Press, 1998.

Hardt, Michael, and Antonio Negri. *Empire.* Cambridge, Mass.: Harvard University Press, 2000.

Hart, Lawrence. "The Earth Is a Song Made Visible." In *Creation and the Environment: An Anabaptist Perspective on a Sustainable World,* ed. Calvin Redekop. Baltimore: Johns Hopkins University Press, 2000.

Harvey, David. *The Condition of Postmodernity: An Enquiry into the Origins of Cultural Change.* Oxford: Basil Blackwell, 1990.

———. *Justice, Nature and the Geography of Difference.* Oxford: Blackwell, 1996.

———. *Spaces of Hope.* Berkeley: University of California Press, 2000.

Hassanein, Neva. *Changing the Way America Farms: Knowledge and Community in the Sustainable Agriculture Movement.* Lincoln: University of Nebraska Press, 1999.

Haury, David A. *Prairie People: A History of the Western Conference.* Newton, Kan.: Faith and Life Press, 1981.

Heartland Regional Catholic Bishops Conference. *Strangers and Guests: Toward Community in the Heartland.* Des Moines, Iowa: Heartland Project, 1980.

Hertsgaard, Mark. *Earth Odyssey: Around the World in Search of Our Environmental Future.* New York: Broadway Books, 1999.

Hessel, Dieter, and Rosemary Radford Ruether, eds. *Christianity and Ecology: Seeking the Well-Being of Earth and Humans.* Cambridge, Mass.: Harvard University Press, 2000.

Hiebert, Theodore. "The Human Tradition: Origins and Transformations in Christian Tradition." In *Christianity and Ecology: Seeking the Well-Being of Earth and Humans,* ed. D. Hessel and R. R. Ruether. Cambridge, Mass.: Harvard University Press, 2000.

Hillerbrand, Hans J., ed. *The Protestant Reformation: Documentary History of Western Civilization.* New York: Harper and Row, 1968.

Hostetler, John A. *Amish Society.* 4th ed. Baltimore: Johns Hopkins University Press, 1993.

———. "A New Look at the Old Order." *Rural Sociologist* 7, no. 4 (1987): 278–292.

Huggett, Richard. *Environmental Change: The Evolving Ecosphere.* New York: Routledge, 1997.

Human Rights Watch. Report on El Salvador, 1990. http://www.hrw.org/reports/ 1990/WR90/AMER.BOU-07.htm.

Igou, Brad. *The Amish in Their Own Words: Amish Writings from 25 Years of Family Life Magazine.* Scottdale, Pa.: Herald Press, 1999.

Ilbery, Brian, Quentin Chiotti, and Timothy Rickard, eds. *Agricultural Restructuring and Sustainability: A Geographical Perspective.* Sustainable Rural Development Series, no. 3. Oxford: CAB International, 1997.

Ileto, Reynaldo Clemeña. *Pasyon and Revolution: Popular Movements in the Philippines, 1840–1910.* Manila: Ateneo de Manila University Press, 1979.

Jackson, Mary. "Amish Agriculture and No-Till: The Hazards of Applying the USLE to Unusual Farms." *Journal of Soil and Water Conservation* 43 (November–December 1988): 382–484.

Jackson, Wes. *Becoming Native to This Place.* Lexington: University Press of Kentucky, 1994.

———. *New Roots for Agriculture.* Lincoln: University of Nebraska Press, 1980.

Jackson, Wes, Wendell Berry, and Bruce Colman. *Meeting the Expectations of the Land: Essays in Sustainable Agriculture and Stewardship.* San Francisco: North Point Press, 1984.

Jacoby, Russell. *The End of Utopia: Politics and Culture in an Age of Apathy.* New York: Basic Books, 1999.

Jameson, Fredric. *The Political Unconscious: Narrative as a Socially Symbolic Act.* Ithaca, N.Y.: Cornell University Press, 1981.

John Paul II. *Inter Sanctos: AAS* 71. 1979.

———. *Laborem Exercens* [1981]. In *Proclaiming Justice and Peace: Papal Documents from Rerum Novarum through Centesimus Annus,* ed. Michael Walsh and Brian Davies. Mystic, Conn.: Twenty-Third Publications, 1991.

———. *Redemptor Hominis.* In *Proclaiming Justice and Peace: Papal Documents from Rerum Novarum through Centesimus Annus,* ed. Michael Walsh and Brian Davies. Mystic, Conn.: Twenty-Third Publications, 1991.

Johnson, Warren, Victor Stoltzfus, and Peter Craumer. "Energy Conservation in Amish Agriculture." *Science* 198, no. 4315 (Oct. 28, 1977): 373–378.

Kahn, Joseph. "Cheney Promotes Increasing Supply as Energy Policy." *New York Times*, May 1, 2001, A1.

Keller, Catherine. *Apocalypse Now and Then: A Feminist Guide to the End of the World.* Boston: Beacon Press, 1996.

Kincaid, A. Douglas. "Peasants into Rebels: Community and Class in Rural El Salvador." *Comparative Studies in Society and History* 29, no. 3 (July 1987): 466–494.

Kirkpatrick, Frank G. *The Ethics of Community.* Oxford: Blackwell, 2001.

Kirp, David L. *Almost Home: America's Love-Hate Relationship with Community.* Princeton, N.J.: Princeton University Press, 2000.

Klaasen, Walter. "The Anabaptist Critique of Constantinian Christendom." *Mennonite Quarterly Review* 53 (July 1979): 218–230.

———. "Pacificism, Nonviolence, and the Peaceful Reign of God." In *Creation and the Environment: An Anabaptist Perspective on a Sustainable World,* ed. Calvin Redekop. Baltimore: Johns Hopkins University Press, 2000.

Kline, David. "An Amish Perspective." In *Rooted in the Land: Essays on Community and Place,* ed. William Vitek and Wes Jackson. New Haven: Yale University Press, 1996.

———. "God's Spirit and a Theology for Living." In *Creation and the Environment: An Anabaptist Perspective on a Sustainable World,* ed. Calvin Redekop. Baltimore: Johns Hopkins University Press, 2000.

———. *Great Possessions: An Amish Farmer's Journal.* Foreword by Wendell Berry. San Francisco: North Point Press, 1990.

———. "No-Till Farming and Its Threat to the Amish Community." *Festival Quarterly* 13, no. 3 (1986): 7–10.

———. Presentation at "The Good in Nature and Humanity" conference. Yale University, New Haven, May 2000.

———. *Scratching the Woodchuck: Nature on an Amish Farm.* Athens: University of Georgia Press, 1997.

Kniss, Fred. *Disquiet in the Land: Cultural Conflict in American Mennonite Communities.* Newark, N.J.: Rutgers University Press, 1997.

Kollmorgan, Walter. "The Agricultural Stability of the Old Order Amish Mennonites of Lancaster County, Pennsylvania." *American Journal of Sociology* 49, no. 3 (1943): 233–241.

Kraybill, Donald B. *Old Order Amish: Their Enduring Way of Life.* Photos by Lucien Niemeyer. Baltimore: Johns Hopkins University Press, 1993.

———, ed. *The Amish and the State.* Baltimore: Johns Hopkins University Press, 1993.

Kraybill, Donald B., and Carl F. Bowman. *On the Backroad to Heaven: Old Order Hutterites, Mennonites, Amish and Brethren.* Baltimore: Johns Hopkins University Press, 2001.

Lancaster, Roger. *Life Is Hard: Machismo, Danger, and the Intimacy of Power in Nicaragua.* Berkeley: University of California Press, 1992.

Larson, Gerald James. " 'Conceptual Resources' in South Asia for 'Environmental Ethics.' " In *Nature in Asian Traditions of Thought,* ed. J. Baird Callicott and Roger Ames. Albany: State University of New York Press, 1989.

Leaman, David E. "Oppositional Outsiders and the Reach of Representation in Post-War El Salvador: A Small Rural Community in Changing Political Contexts." *Illinois Political Science Review.* http://www.apsanet.org/~illinois/ipsr/salvador.htm.

LeGuin, Ursula. *The Dispossessed: An Ambivalent Utopia*. New York: HarperCollins, 1974.

Levine, Daniel. *Popular Voices in Latin American Catholicism*. Princeton, N.J.: Princeton University Press, 1992.

Levine, Daniel, and Scott Mainwaring. "Religion and Popular Protest in Latin America: Contrasting Experiences." In *Power and Popular Protest in Latin America*, ed. Susan Eckstein. Berkeley: University of California Press, 1989.

Li, Tania Murray. "Boundary Work: Community, Market, and State Reconsidered." In *Communities and the Environment: Ethnicity, Gender, and the State in Community-Based Conservation*, ed. Arun Agrawal and Clark C. Gibson. New Brunswick, N.J.: Rutgers University Press, 2001.

Logsdon, Gene. "Amish Economy." *Orion Nature Quarterly* 7, no. 2 (1988): 22–33.

———. *Living at Nature's Pace: Farming and the American Dream*. White River Junction, Vt.: Chelsea Green, 2000.

Longhofer, Jeffrey. "Specifying the Commons: Mennonites, Intensive Agriculture, and Landlessness in Nineteenth-Century Russia." *Ethnohistory* 40, no. 3 (summer 1993): 384–409.

Loomis, Charles P. "A Farmhand's Diary." *Mennonite Quarterly Review* 53 (July 1979): 235–256.

Lopez, Barry. *The Rediscovery of North America*. New York: Vintage Books, 1990.

López Vigil, José Ignacio. *Rebel Radio: The Story of El Salvador's Radio Venceremos*. Willimantic, Conn.: Curbstone Press, 1994.

Lungo, Mario, Juan Serarols, and Ana Silvia de Sintigo. *Economía y sostenibilidad en las zonas ex-conflictivas en El Salvador*. San Salvador: FUNDASAL, 1997.

Luther, Martin. *Martin Luther: Selections from His Writings*. Ed. John Dillenberger. New York: Anchor Books, 1971.

Lyotard, Jean-François. *The Postmodern Condition*. Minneapolis: University of Minnesota Press, 1984.

Macdonald, Mandy, and Mike Gatehouse. *In the Mountains of Morazán: Portrait of a Returned Refugee Community in El Salvador*. London: Latin American Bureau, 1995.

Manno, Jack. "Commoditization: Consumption Efficiency and an Economy of Care and Connection." In *Confronting Consumption*, ed. Thomas Princen, Michael Maniates, and Ken Conca. Cambridge, Mass.: MIT Press, 2002.

Marx, Karl. *Critique of the Gotha Program*. In *The Marx-Engels Reader*, ed. Robert Tucker. New York: Norton, 1978.

———. "The Eighteenth Brumaire of Louis Bonaparte." In *The Marx-Engels Reader*, ed. Robert Tucker. New York: Norton, 1978.

Marx, Karl, and Friedrich Engels. *The Manifesto of the Communist Party*. In *The Marx-Engels Reader*, ed. Robert Tucker. New York: Norton, 1978.

May, Sir Robert. Address to biodiversity experts, Washington, D.C., Oct. 1997. http://www.zerowasteamerica.org/MSNBC.htm.

Melucci, Alberto. *Nomads of the Present: Social Movements and Individual Needs in Contemporary Society*. Ed. John Keane and Paul Mier. Philadelphia: Temple University Press, 1989.

Metzi, Francisco. *Por los caminos de Chalatenango: La salud en la mochila*. San Salvador: UCA Editores, 1988.

Meyer, Art, and Jocele Meyer. *Earth-Keepers: Environmental Perspectives on Hunger, Poverty, and Injustice.* Scottdale, Pa.: Herald Press, 1991.

Miller, Levi. *Our People: The Amish and Mennonites of Ohio.* 1983. Rev. ed., Scottdale, Pa.: Herald Press, 1992.

Münzer, Thomas. *The Letters of Thomas Münzer.* Ed. P. Matheson. Edinburgh: T. and T. Clark, 1988.

Nabhan, Gary Paul. *Cultures of Habitat: On Nature, Culture, and Story.* Washington, D.C.: Counterpoint, 1997.

National Conference of Catholic Bishops. *Economic Justice for All.* Washington, D.C.: U.S. Catholic Conference, 1986.

———. *Renewing the Earth: An Invitation to Reflection and Action on Environment in Light of Catholic Social Teaching.* Washington, D.C.: U.S. Catholic Conference, 1991.

Navarro, Ricardo. "Presentación del Libro" [Preface]. In Ricardo Navarro, Gabriel Pons, and German Amaya, *El pensamiento ecologista.* San Salvador: Centro Salvadoreño de Tecnología Apropiada, n.d. [1990?].

Navarro, Ricardo, Gabriel Pons, and Germán Amaya. *El pensamiento ecologista.* San Salvador: Centro Salvadoreño de Tecnología Apropiada, n.d.

Neruda, Pablo. "Canto al Ejército Rojo a su llegada a las puertas de Prusia," *Residence on Earth (Residencia en la tierra).* Trans. Donald D. Walsh. New York: New Directions, 1973.

———. *Toward the Splendid City/Hacia la ciudad esplendida.* New York: Farrar, Strauss, and Giroux, 1973.

Niebuhr, Reinhold. *Moral Man and Immoral Society: A Study in Ethics and Politics.* New York: Charles Scribner's Sons, 1932.

Northrup, Benjamin E., and Benjamin Lipscomb. "Country and City: The Common Vision of Agrarians and New Urbanists." In *The Essential Agrarian Reader: The Future of Culture, Community, and the Land,* ed. Norman Wirzba. Lexington, Ky.: Shoemaker and Hoard, 2004.

Núñez, Carlos, Frei Betto, Fernando Cardenal, Orlando Fals Borda, and Jorge Osorio. *Vigencia de las Utopías en América Latina.* Guadalajara, Mexico: Instituto Mexicano para el Desarrollo Comunitario, 1993.

O'Driscoll, Peter. "Peace, Thanks, and God's Blessing: Letters from San Antonio Los Ranchos." Unpublished manuscript. Berkeley Sister City Project with El Salvador, 1990.

Olshan, Marc. "Modernity, the Folk Society, and the Old Order Amish: An Alternative Interpretation." *Rural Sociology* 46 (1981): 297–309.

Oyer, John S., and Robert S. Kreider. *Mirror of the Martyrs.* Intercourse, Pa.: Good Books, 1990.

Panitch, Leo, and Colin Leys, eds. *Necessary and Unnecessary Utopias: Socialist Register 2000.* Rendlesham, England: Merlin Press, 1999.

———. Preface to *Necessary and Unnecessary Utopias: Socialist Register 2000,* ed. Leo Panitch and Colin Leys. Rendlesham, England: Merlin Press, 1999.

Pearce, Jenny. *Promised Land: Peasant Rebellion in Chalatenango, El Salvador.* London: Latin American Bureau, 1986.

Peltz, Maxwell S. *El Salvador 1990: An Issue Brief.* Washington, D.C.: Commission on U.S.-Latin American Relations, 1990.

Peterson, Anna L. *Being Human: Ethics, Environment, and Our Place in the World.* Berkeley: University of California Press, 2001.

———. *Martyrdom and the Politics of Religion: Progressive Catholicism in El Salvador's Civil War.* Albany: State University of New York Press, 1997.

Peterson, Anna, Manuel Vásquez, and Philip Williams, eds. *Christianity, Social Change, and Globalization in the Americas.* New Brunswick, N.J.: Rutgers University Press, 2001.

———. Preface to *Christianity, Social Change, and Globalization in the Americas,* ed. A. Peterson, M. Vásquez, and P. Williams. New Brunswick, N.J.: Rutgers University Press, 2001.

Peterson, Brandt G. "The Sorrows of the Poor: Revelation and Resistance in the Canyons of the Lacandón Forest." Unpublished master's thesis, University of Texas at Austin, 1999.

Princen, Thomas. "Distancing: Consumption and the Severing of Feedback." In *Confronting Consumption,* ed. T. Princen, M. Maniates, and K. Conca. Cambridge, Mass.: MIT Press, 2002.

Princen, Thomas, Michael Maniates, and Ken Conca, eds. *Confronting Consumption.* Cambridge, Mass.: MIT Press, 2002.

———. "Confronting Consumption." In *Confronting Consumption,* ed. T. Princen, M. Maniates, and K. Conca. Cambridge, Mass.: MIT Press, 2002.

Quezada G., Marcelo, and Maya Lorena Pérez Ruiz, eds. *EZLN: La utopía armada. Una visión plural del movimiento zapatista.* La Paz, Bolivia: Plural Editores, 1998.

Redefining Progress. "Ecological Footprint of Nations." Nov. 2002, www.redefining progress.org/publications/ef1999.pdf.

Redekop, Calvin, ed. *Creation and the Environment: An Anabaptist Perspective on a Sustainable World.* Baltimore: Johns Hopkins University Press, 2000.

———. "The Environmental Challenge before Us." In *Creation and the Environment: An Anabaptist Perspective on a Sustainable World,* ed. Calvin Redekop. Baltimore: Johns Hopkins University Press, 2000.

———. *Mennonite Society.* Baltimore: Johns Hopkins University Press, 1989.

Reschly, Steven D., and Katherine Jellison. "Production Patterns, Consumption Strategies, and Gender Relations in Amish and Non-Amish Farm Households in Lancaster County, Pennsylvania, 1935–36." *Agricultural History* 67, no. 2 (spring 1993): 134–162.

Rivera, Ana Kelly, Edy Arelí Ortiz Cañas, Liza Domínguez Magaña, and María Candelaria Navas. *Valió la pena? Testimonios de salvadoreñas que vivieron la guerra.* San Salvador: Editorial Sombrero Azul, 1995.

Rolston, Holmes, III. *Environmental Ethics: Duties to and Values in the Natural World.* Philadelphia: Temple University Press, 1988.

Romero, Oscar. *The Voice of the Voiceless: Four Pastoral Letters and Other Statements.* Maryknoll, N.Y.: Orbis Books, 1985.

Rubin, Joe. "El Salvador: Payback." *Frontline.* PBS. Transcript available at http://www .pbs.org/frontlineworld/elections/elsalvador/.

Rubio Fabián, Roberto, Anne Germain, and Roberto Góchez. *La situación ecológica de El Salvador en cifras.* San Salvador: UCA Editores, 1996.

Russell, Philip. *El Salvador in Crisis.* Austin, Texas: Colorado River Press, 1984.

Sachs, Wolfgang. "Sustainable Development and the Crisis of Nature: On the Political

Anatomy of an Oxymoron." In *Living with Nature: Environmental Politics as Cultural Discourse*, ed. Frank Fischer and Maarten A. Hajer. Oxford: Oxford University Press, 1999.

Santmire, Paul. *The Travail of Nature: The Ambiguous Ecological Promise of Christian Theology*. Minneapolis: Fortress Press, 1985.

Savells, Jerry. "Economic and Social Acculturation among the Old Order Amish in Select Communities: Surviving in a High-Tech Society." *Journal of Comparative Family Studies* 19, no. 1 (spring 1988): 123–135.

Savells, Jerry, and Thomas Foster. "The Challenges and Limitations of Conducting Research among the Old Order Amish." *Explorations in Ethnic Studies* 10, no 1 (January 1987): 25–36.

Schrading, Roger. *El movimiento de repoblación en El Salvador*. San José, Costa Rica: Instituto Interamericano de Derechos Humanos, 1991.

Second Vatican Council. *Gaudium et spes*. In *Documents of Vatican II*, ed. Walter Abbott. New York: American Press, 1966.

Séguy, Jean. "Religion and Agricultural Success: The Vocational Life of the French Mennonites from the Seventeenth to the Nineteenth Centuries." Trans. Michael Shank. *Mennonite Quarterly Review* 47 (1973): 181–224.

Shadows of Tender Fury: The Letters and Communiqués of Subcomandante Marcos and the Zapatista Army of National Liberation. Trans. Frank Bardacke, Leslie López, and the Watsonville, California, Human Rights Committee. Introduction by John Ross. Afterword by Frank Bardacke. New York: Monthly Review Press, 1995.

Shepard, Paul. *Coming Home to the Pleistocene*. San Francisco: Island Press, 1998.

Shuman, Michael H. *Going Local: Creating Self-Reliant Communities in a Global Age*. New York: Routledge, 2000.

Silber, Irina Carlota. "A Spectral Reconstruction: Rebuilding Post-War El Salvador." Unpublished Ph.D. diss., Department of Anthropology, New York University, 2000.

Singer, Daniel. *Whose Millennium? Theirs or Ours?* New York: Monthly Review Press, 1999.

Snyder, Gary. *A Place in Space: Ethics, Aesthetics, and Watersheds. New and Selected Prose*. Washington, D.C.: Counterpoint, 1995.

———. *The Practice of the Wild*. San Francisco: North Point Press, 1990.

Sommers, David, and Ted Napier. "Comparison of Amish and Non-Amish Farmers: A Diffusion/Farm-Structure Perspective." *Rural Sociology* 58, no. 1 (1993): 130–145.

Sorrell, Roger. *St. Francis of Assisi and Nature: Tradition and Innovation in Western Christian Attitudes toward the Environment*. New York: Oxford University Press, 1988.

Spence, Jack. "Left Gains and Competitive Balance Following El Salvador's March Elections." Paper presented at the Latin American Studies Association meeting. Washington, D.C., Sept. 6–8, 2001.

Sterngold, James. "California's New Problem: Sudden Surplus of Energy." *New York Times*, July 19, 2001, 1A.

Stinner, Deborah H., M. G. Paoletti, and B. R. Stinner. "In Search of Traditional Farm Wisdom for a More Sustainable Agriculture: A Study of Amish Farming and Society." *Agriculture, Ecosystems, and Environment* 27 (1989): 77–90.

Stoll, Steven. "Postmodern Farming, Quietly Flourishing." *Chronicle of Higher Education* 9 (June 21, 2002): B7–B9.

Stoltzfus, Victor. "Amish Agriculture: Adaptive Strategies for Economic Survival of Community Life." *Rural Sociology* 38, no 2 (summer 1973): 196–206.

———. "Reward and Sanction: The Adaptive Continuity of Amish Life." *Mennonite Quarterly Review* 51, no. 4 (Oct. 1977): 308–318.

Strieker, Gary. "Scientists Agree World Faces Mass Extinction." CNN, Aug. 23, 2002. http://www.cnn.com/2002/TECH/science/08/23/green.century.mass.extinction/index.html.

Swartley, William M., and Donald B. Kraybill, eds. *Building Communities of Compassion: Mennonite Mutual Aid in Theory and Practice.* Scottdale, Pa.: Herald Press, 1998.

Testa, Randy-Michael. *After the Fire: The Destruction of the Lancaster County Amish.* Foreword by John Hostetler. Afterword by Robert Coles. Hanover, N.H.: University Press of New England, 1992.

Thiele, Leslie Paul. *Environmentalism for a New Millennium: The Challenge of Coevolution.* Oxford: Oxford University Press, 1999.

Thirsk, Joan. *Alternative Agriculture: A History.* Oxford: Oxford University Press, 1997.

Thomashow, Mitchell. *Bringing the Biosphere Home: Learning to Perceive Global Environmental Change.* Cambridge, Mass.: MIT Press, 2002.

———. "Toward a Cosmopolitan Bioregionalism." In *Bioregionalism,* ed. Michael Vincent McGinnis. London: Routledge, 1999.

Thompson, E. P. *William Morris: Romantic to Revolutionary.* New York: Pantheon Books, 1977.

Thompson, Martha. "Repopulated Communities in El Salvador." In *The New Politics of Survival: Grassroots Movements in Central America,* ed. Minor Sinclair. New York: Monthly Review Press, 1995.

Tillich, Paul. "The Political Meaning of Utopia." In *Political Expectation,* ed. James Luther Adams. New York: Harper and Row, 1971.

———. *Systematic Theology.* Vol. 3: *Life and the Spirit; History and the Kingdom of God.* Chicago: University of Chicago Press, 1963.

United Nations. World Atlas of Biodiversity. http://www.commondreams.org/headlines02/0802-06.htm.

Valmore Pérez, Alejandro, Wilber Alejandro Jiménez, and Raúl Antonio Machado. *Chalatenango, Las Flores, San Antonio Los Ranchos, Nueva Trinidad, y Arcatao: Estudio socioeconómico y ambiental de la microregión.* AVANCES, no. 15. San Salvador: Fundación Nacional para el Desarrollo, June 2000.

van Bracht, Thieleman J. *The Martyrs' Mirror.* Scottdale, Pa.: Herald Press, 1938.

Van En, Robyn. "Community Supported Agriculture (CSA) in Perspective." In *For All Generations: Making World Agriculture More Sustainable,* ed. J. Patrick Madden and Scott G. Chaplowe. Glendale, Calif.: World Sustainable Agriculture Association, 1997.

Vicariato Apostólico de Petén. *El Grito de la Selva en el Año Jubilar: Entre la Agonía y Esperanza.* Petén, Guatemala: Vicariato Apostólico de Petén, 2000.

Vitek, William, and Wes Jackson, eds. *Rooted in the Land: Essays on Community and Place.* New Haven: Yale University Press, 1996.

Wallerstein, Immanuel. *Utopistics; Or, Historical Choices of the Twenty-first Century.* New York: New Press, 1998.

Weaver, J. Denny. *Anabaptist Theology in Face of Postmodernity: A Proposal for the Third Millennium.* Telford, Pa.: Pandora Press, 2000.

Weaver-Zercher, David. *The Amish in the American Imagination.* Baltimore: Johns Hopkins University Press, 2001.

Wegner, Phillip E. *Imaginary Communities: Utopia, the Nation, and the Spatial Histories of Modernity.* Berkeley: University of California Press, 2002.

Welch, Sharon. *A Feminist Ethic of Risk.* New York: Fortress Press, 1990.

———. *Sweet Dreams in America: Making Ethics and Spirituality Work.* New York: Routledge, 1999.

White, Lynn, Jr. "The Historical Roots of Our Ecologic Crisis." *Science* 155 (1967): 1203–1207.

Williams, Raymond. *The Country and the City.* New York: Oxford University Press, 1973.

———. *Problems in Materialism and Culture: Selected Essays.* London: Verso, 1980.

———. *Resources of Hope: Culture, Democracy, Socialism.* Ed. Robin Gable. Introduction by Robin Blackburn. London: Verso: 1989.

Wirzba, Norman, ed. *The Essential Agrarian Reader: The Future of Culture, Community, and the Land.* Lexington, Ky.: Shoemaker and Hoard, 2004.

Wood, Elisabeth J. *Forging Democracy from Below: Contested Transitions in South Africa and El Salvador.* Cambridge, England: Cambridge University Press, 2000.

Wright, Scott. *Promised Land: Death and Life in El Salvador.* Maryknoll, N.Y.: Orbis Books, 1994.

Yoder, John Howard. *Nevertheless: The Varieties and Shortcomings of Religious Pacifism.* Scottdale, Pa.: Herald Press, 1992.

———. *The Politics of Jesus.* 2nd ed. Grand Rapids, Mich.: William B. Eerdmans, 1994.

———. *The Priestly Kingdom: Social Ethics as Gospel.* Notre Dame, Ind.: University of Notre Dame Press, 1984.

Yoder, Michael. "Mennonites, Economics, and the Care of Creation." In *Creation and the Environment: An Anabaptist Perspective on a Sustainable World,* ed. Calvin Redekop. Baltimore: Johns Hopkins University Press, 2000.

———. "The Very Best of Lives" [Interview with David Kline]. *Christian Living* (Mar. 2002): 6–9.

Yoder, Rhonda Lou. "Amish Agriculture in Iowa: Indigenous Knowledge for Sustainable Small-Farm Systems." *Studies in Technology and Social Change,* no. 15. Technology and Social Change Program, Iowa State University, 1990.

Zarcos Mera, Carlos, Leonor Tellería, and Carlos Manuel Sánchez. "The Ministry of Coordinators in the Popular Christian Community." In *La Iglesia Popular: Between Fear and Hope,* ed. L. Boff and V. Elizondo. Special issue of *Concilium* 176 (1984): 65–70.

Zencey, Eric. "A Whole Earth Catalogue." Review of Norman Wirzba, ed., *The Art of the Commonplace: The Agrarian Essays of Wendell Berry. The Nation* (July 1, 2002): 35–39.

Index